YALE ROMANIC STUDIES: *Second Series*

VI

THE POST-SYMBOLIST PERIOD

French Poetic Currents 1900–1920

BY THE SAME AUTHOR

Adolphe Retté, 1863–1930
The Symbolist Movement

French

6 00 210969 8   TELEPEN

30/–

udents and External Readers │ Stan & n

THE
POST-SYMBOLIST
PERIOD

French Poetic Currents, 1900-1920

BY KENNETH CORNELL

New Haven: YALE UNIVERSITY PRESS, 1958

Paris: Presses Universitaires de France

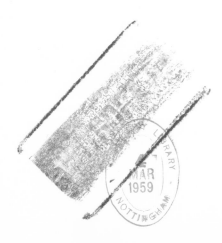

LIBRARY
MAR
1959
NOTTINGHAM

© 1958 by Yale University Press, Inc. Printed in the United States of America by Vail-Ballou Press, Inc., Binghamton, N.Y. and set in Granjon type. All rights reserved. This book may not be reproduced, in whole or in part, in any form (except by reviewers for the public press), without written permission from the publishers. Library of Congress catalog card number: 58-11250

FOREWORD

THIS VOLUME embraces the period between 1900 and the advent of surrealism. Like *The Symbolist Movement,* to which it is in a measure a sequel, it is largely factual; it is principally a book of reference. My purpose has been to give greater precision and more information on an era which histories of poetry, such as those by Dérieux, Clouard, and Fort and Mandin, treat in a summary fashion. The problem of inclusion and exclusion has proved vexing. I have simply tried, by reading as widely as possible, to encompass the authors, the works, the ideas, and the theories which chiefly represent these complicated and confused years. If I have slighted many regionalistic manifestations in poetry, it was because they were so often brief and unproductive of real talent. The greatest distortion probably occurs in relation to writers, such as Claudel and Apollinaire, whose fame came, not at the moment of publication of their work, but after the first World War. The attention given them seemed warranted by present interest; the inclusion of other names now forgotten is explained by the informative purpose of the book.

In a concluding chapter, I abandoned the objectivity which I strove to maintain in the body of the composition. In any selective process, personal bias is a constant hazard, but in the main, I attempted to allow a literary period to speak for itself. At the end of study, the investigator is left with his private, individual opinions. Trusting that such matter is not inapposite to the word "conclusion," under that heading I have ignored certain self-imposed restrictions which I thought proper for a useful purpose in the body of the book.

In writing the story of modern poetry, one can scarcely fail to sense how much sacrifice, how much altruism have gone into the creation and publication of this much-praised but financially unrewarding literary form. The more popular novel and drama offer the investigator a much greater facility of access than verse, which is so often found in little-known magazines or in limited editions paid for by the authors themselves. These very conditions, the lack of ready availability of texts in small libraries and at times even in more important collections, have seemed sufficient reason for undertaking this study. Another motivating principle, this being a personal one, was to inform myself on a period when poetic discussion turned on the acceptance or rejection of symbolist models.

Several kind friends have supplied me with information I needed and which was not available in New Haven. They have again my expression of gratitude. The encouragement and advice of the editor of this series, Professor Henri Peyre, the aid for publication from Yale University, the generous consideration of the Committee on Publications of the Yale University Press all deserve my grateful acknowledgment.

CONTENTS

IN THE CLOSING YEARS of the nineteenth century France had seen death successively claim those of her poets around whom was an aura of greatness. Leconte de Lisle, in 1894, and Mallarmé, in 1898, passed into the realm which represented for them an enigmatic void. In 1896 Verlaine left the earth, possibly envisaging pardon and paradise, although his final word, "François," gives us little information concerning his last sentiments. Whatever may have been their fate in the beyond, their active influence was uninterrupted on earth. Each had been the focus of admiration of a considerable number of writers, and each had represented an attitude toward poetry, which had won adherents. The Parnassian outlook, predicated on craftmanship, traditional versification, and clarity (objectivity is no longer valid in the prolongations of Parnassianism); the Verlainian manner with its tone of intimate confession, its absence of eloquence, and its dependence on the suggested rather than the expressed; the subtle hermeticism of Mallarmé, with its constant search for magic evocation—all three styles had won staunch advocates, all three poets had imitators but not peers.

Of the tenets, the Parnassian seemed most secure in 1900. Symbolism, split apart by the romanism of Moréas, weakened by discussions of naturism, separated into groups by questions of free verse, and made incoherent by the very desire for originality among its members, had not the stability of its more conservative adversary. Heredia did not die until 1905, Sully-Prudhomme until 1907, and Coppée until 1908. Thus many of Leconte de Lisle's precepts were voiced after his death, and voiced by writers who enjoyed prestige. True, their poetic work was largely completed before the turn of the century; true, their ideas turned within the inflexible circle of tradition. Even if the most alert and original poets of 1900 did not openly enroll in their ranks, Heredia's salon, Sully-Prudhomme's Nobel prize in 1900, Coppée's undiminished journalistic importance are not to be discounted. Time has been unkind to a number of poets who clung to Parnassian tradition, and who in the early years of the century had a very respectable following. One of these, Sébastien-Charles Leconte, the author of *La Tentation de l'homme* (1903), *Le Sang de Méduse* (1905), and *Le Masque de fer* (1911), is a good example of this transitory renown. Born in 1860, he had been only passingly affected by the symbolist currents of his generation. He accepted Heredia as guide and mentor, devoting his energies to perfection in form, and often choosing his themes from Greek or Hebrew antiquity. He came to be known as the poet of impeccable diction; his imagery, for the most part bloody and violent, was couched in sonorous language. Each of his volumes was constructed on a central idea; the guiding themes were not strikingly original. *Le Sang de Méduse,* for example, restated the fascination and torment of man's search for beauty. The descriptive and didactic tone of the Parnassians was also his. His nearest approach to a philosophical concept was his notion of history, which he saw as a present phenomenon in man's collective mind. To a degree, this explains the quality of vividness which won him praise.

S.-C. Leconte was one of many conservative poets who are forgotten today. The reader of their verse cannot fail to sense in the cadence, in the impressive descriptions, and in the dignified, often tragic tone, the presence of Leconte de Lisle or Heredia. This form of imitation received both praise and blame from critics, but those who followed in the wake of Parnassianism regularly carried away the prizes of the Academy, and seemingly were the cornerstones of lyric art. Posterity has denied them its approval. The sonnets and orderly series of alexandrines composed by Maurice Olivaint (1860–1929), inspired by his sojourns, as colonial magistrate and traveler, in Indo-China, Algeria, and the Ile Bourbon, have passed into oblivion. His work is occasionally mentioned by specialists in exoticism in French literature. Even the liberal Parnassian Pierre de Bouchaud (liberal because he admitted displacement of the caesura, rhyme for the ear rather than the eye, and certain kinds of hiatus) is scarcely remembered save for his evocations of the landscapes and art of Italy. Born in 1866, he carefully avoided Parisian groups. His published verse (1895–1925) appeared from the presses of Lemerre or Sansot. In the early years of the century his *Heures de la muse* (1902) was a successful volume for which rural landscape, classical mythology, and Italy furnished the thematic material.

Léonce Depont (1862–1913), Georges Druilhet (1868–1928), and Alfred Droin (1878–19—) are others of the conservative group who at the beginning of the century clung to eloquence, precise description, and clarity in expression. Tradition and good workmanship were their watchwords; these were the qualities that the French Academy recognized and rewarded. That *L'Absolution, Fleurs de corail, Les Lauriers d'Olympe, Pèlerinages, Les Haltes sereines, Amours divines et terrestres,* and *La Jonque victorieuse,* all composed by the poets we have been discussing, received official awards and prizes during the early years of the century has little meaning for us now, except that these were writers who carefully followed rules of versification and respected syntax, and whose sentiments and ideals were above reproach. Epithet and image, for them, had a reasonable and visual quality which called for little effort from the reader. No surprise in transitions, no ellipsis in thought interrupted the metrical flow. In their dignified work an echo of Leconte de Lisle was often heard: "Devant les mondes morts et les cieux à venir," "Le soir qui les grandit tombe sur leur destin," "Et les nids s'étaient tus dans la frondaison neuve," "La ténébreuse horreur des vieux temps se déroule." [1]

The tinge of fantasy, the feigned carelessness, the light musical touch of Verlaine are almost entirely absent from the works of Leconte, Olivaint, Depont, Druilhet, Droin, and others of their lyric persuasion. But Verlaine's passage had left profound marks on the poetry of 1900. Short poems that resemble little songs, depending for their effect on alliteration and repetition, melodies which offer only a few sensory impressions as points of reality and which fuse mood and landscape are abundant in the period. The poets who best show this heritage of Verlaine had begun writing while "le pauvre Lélian" was still alive. When one reads in Robert de Souza's *Les Graines d'un jour* (1901), a poem which begins "De plaines en plaines lointaines," and when one observes the casual expression, the conversational simplicity, and the repetitive effects in Francis Jammes' *Le Deuil des primevères* (1901), he feels the undeniable presence of Verlaine in the background. Nor are flagrant imitations lacking. A poem entitled "Lunaire," in Edmond Blanguernon's *L'Ombre amoureuse* (1900), begins:

> Aux grises allées
> Du parc endormi,
> Douces ont frémi
> Les brises ailées.

and manages to include in its fourteen lines a device all too patently derivative:

> Lentes vaguement,
> Vagues lentement, . . .

Verlaine's sentimental landscapes had created a pattern. In André-Ferdinand Herold's *Au hasard des chemins* (1900), lines such as these:

> La flûte amère de l'automne
> Pleure dans le soir anxieux,
> Et les arbres mouillés frissonnent
> Tandis que sanglotent les cieux.

1. These few examples are to be found in G. Walch, *Anthologie des poètes contemporains* (Delagrave, 1937), Vol. 3. One could collect hundreds of such lines. Those quoted are from S.-C. Leconte's "Au Dieu qui s'éloigne," Depont's "Les Glaneuses," Druilhet's "La Brève Journée," and Droin's "La Forteresse."

are more paraphrase than creation. Such emulation, when compared with the models to which it owes its inspiration, appears clumsy and even forced. Verlaine's deftness was not often transmitted, but many were the poets who were so fascinated by *Fêtes galantes* or *Romances sans paroles* that they could not resist making their "counterfeit presentment." A twentieth-century anthology, bearing Verlaine's titles but far larger than his volumes, could be easily assembled. Contributors would include Léon Deubel, most of the "poètes fantaisistes," the Belgian Victor Kinon, as well as Fernand Gregh and Charles Guérin. Verlaine was the source of much modern sentimental verse, the poems of confession which lack the ample and logical progression of the romanticists, and in which what is left unsaid is as important as the written line.

The Parnassian and Verlainian influences in the early years of the twentieth century are thus easy to discern. Mallarmé's case is much more complicated. An initial distinction must be made between prestige and influence, and indeed between works and ideas. Gide, just after Mallarmé's death, had sagely observed that imitation of that particular master was utter folly. Charles Morice, replying in 1905 to the Le Cardonnel and Vellay inquiry, contrasted the overt imitation of Verlaine with the absence of direct disciples of Mallarmé. It is true that until 1906, when Jean Royère created *La Phalange* and collected in his group such young Mallarmé enthusiasts as Guy Lavaud and Louis Mandin, as well as some older poets of the symbolist era, Mallarmé's style was rarely visible in poetry. An unusual turn of expression or odd connotative sense of a word may suggest his name, but only fleetingly. Of all the admirers of Mallarmé, the Belgian poet André Fontainas revealed most clearly the cadence of the master, both in prose and verse. The literary allegiances and sources of inspiration were, it is true, multiple in the work of Fontainas; his use of free meters often created a total effect quite different from that of Mallarmé's poems. Yet his verses are filled with themes and vocabulary usages which recall Mallarmean creations, from the "Brise marine," through the "Après-midi d'un faune," to the sonnets of the *Revue indépendante*. A series of lines from "Déclamation" in *Le Jardin des îles claires* (1901) will illustrate this parallelism:

> Et je veux fuir! Fuir où fermente l'ivresse,
> Où tressaille la mer d'un triomphe inconnu,
> Où d'étranges clartés en frissonnant paraissent
> Dans la nuit d'arbres l'éclair naissant des membres nus,
> Où luit riante la fureur des dents du faune,
> Où ses yeux fauves étincellent
> Tandis que dansent, et la rosée à l'herbe y ruisselle,
> Les nymphes dont il guette anxieux la beauté.

In a later volume, *La Nef désemparée* (1908), Fontainas presented four little sonnets which are all too like parodies of the Mallarmé of 1885. A quatrain from one of them reads:

> De toi seul fils et aïeul
> Naît aux portiques du rêve
> Le guerrier de qui le glaive
> Soit le simple et clair glaïeul.

This same collection contained an "Hommage" to Mallarmé, a sonnet on Valvins, and two other poems commemorating Mallarmé's death. In these Fontainas openly imitated, just as he did in poems addressed to other writers, dead or living, whom he admired. By 1908 there were other strong imprints of Mallarmé's style in French poetry, but in the first years of the century Fontainas was an isolated case.[2]

This does not mean that Mallarmé was less a directive force for the poets than was Verlaine. His message of artistic independence and of consecrated devotion to art was not lost. The symbolist generation that had known him continued to keep his name before the public. Remy de Gourmont in *La Culture des idées* (1900), Henri de Régnier in *Figures et Caractères* (1901), Camille Mauclair in *L'Art en silence* (1901), and André Gide in *Prétextes* (1903) were among the commentators who upheld the continuity of Mallarmé's reputation until 1906.

This is the moment of ebb tide in the literary heritage of Rimbaud. Berrichon's 1898 edition of the *Œuvres* and 1899 edition of the *Lettres de Jean-Arthur Rimbaud* had increased the number of the poet's readers, but the new century showed no immediate disciples of his art. Even the impact of Rimbaud on Paul Claudel was not so clearly discernible that critics often mentioned them in the same context until Claudel gave them reason for so doing in his preface for the 1912 edition of Rimbaud's work. Certainly during the early years of the century there seemed little inclination among poets to by-pass literature in the creation of the visionary. Rather was there a desire to come to terms with reality; separation of the poetic and the real was what the critics of symbolism had denounced as its greatest failure. By 1900 the erstwhile members of that group who had effected a compromise between dream and physical existence were the leaders. Albert Samain and Henri de Régnier, Francis Jammes and Charles Guérin all showed this tendency toward lucidity, although none of them rejected the symbolist credo of suggestion. These poets had, as they matured, cast aside

2. Mallarmé retained an important place in Fontainas' work throughout his life. The reader of Fontainas' critical reviews in the *Mercure de France* between 1919 and 1938, and especially of the *Confession d'un poète* (1936), will appreciate this lasting influence of Mallarmé's prose style.

interest in literary schools, but their mingling of artistic tenets helped to stimulate revived interest in poetic theory: Gregh's humanism, neoromanticism, unanimism, neoclassicism, and many later groupings. Accepting some ideas of preceding poetic schools, rejecting others, adding new emphasis here and there, the poet could obtain multiple combinations. This appears to be what actually happened in the manifestoes which were formulated.

The recent past dominated the so-called new ideas. The new century was not unaware of the important place poetry had held between 1885 and 1895. Many of the secondary lyricists of that period were still writing; they, and even the professional critics, often looked backward as though fascinated by a heroic period that was irretrievably past.

A survey of poetry published in books and periodicals during 1900 and 1901, as well as of the critical comments made on it, does indeed reveal that no great change had occurred in form or theme since 1895. The principal books of poetry continued a lyric mode already definitely established. Each poet had attained a particular manner. Merrill (*Les Quatre Saisons,* 1900), Retté (*Lumières tranquilles,* 1901), and André Fontainas (*Le Jardin des îles claires,* 1901) followed the pattern of reverie in the setting of nature that they had adopted some five years before. Signoret's and Samain's last volumes, given much publicity because of their authors' deaths in 1900, showed no great change from previous work. Moréas was the author of four more sections of *Les Stances* and Paul Fort of divisions IV and V of the *Ballades françaises.* Henri de Régnier's *Les Médailles d'argile* (1900) was a continuation of *Les Jeux rustiques et divins* (1897). Vielé-Griffin, still one of the chief exponents of free verse, retained his love of narrative poems in *La Légende ailée de Wieland le forgeron* and *Sainte Agnès.* Francis Jammes, in *Le Deuil des primevères,* offered many of the poems which have since been chosen for anthologies as among his best writing (notably from the section "Quatorze Prières"), but the diction and syntax retained the artless and simple expression of *De l'Angélus de l'aube à l'angélus du soir.*

The absence of new directions in poetic expression resulted in singularly uninspired criticism. The reviewer could often quote passages which revealed the technical sureness born of long practice; he could return to the poet's earliest work and demonstrate the evolution toward clarity and order, love of nature, and kinship with humanity which had taken place; but he could make few discoveries of great import or state much that had not already been said.

In the first years of the century the best magazines for poetic expression were the four periodicals which had been founded during the symbolist period and had managed to endure. They were the *Mercure de France* of Alfred Vallette, *La Revue blanche* of the Natansons, *L'Ermitage* of Edouard

Ducoté, and *La Plume* of Karl Boès. While all four publications remained loyal to their old contributors, publishing verse by André Fontainas, Paul Fort, Charles Guérin, Francis Jammes, Stuart Merrill, Jean Moréas, Henri de Régnier, Adolphe Retté, Emile Verhaeren, and Francis Vielé-Griffin, they also welcomed young poets in their early twenties: Lucie Delarue-Mardrus, Emile Despax, Guillaume Apollinaire, and the slightly older Anna de Noailles. Even though discussion of poetry in these periodicals so often centered on the past, and memories of symbolism rather than new perspectives were the chief matter of comment, these four magazines offered the best commentary on poetry. A brief survey of what they printed in 1901 will show their faults and virtues.

Although the *Mercure de France* published little poetry during 1901, its pages were filled with interesting and important essays treating of poets and their work. André Beaunier wrote on Stuart Merrill and on F. Vielé-Griffin as well as on free verse and on the more general subject of Parnassians and symbolists.[3] Pierre Quillard, the regular editor of the *Mercure*'s poetry department, in addition to his short reviews, composed essays on Jean Moréas, on Francis Jammes and Charles Guérin, and on Adolphe Retté.[4] Emile Magne, in an article entitled "Les Poètes des pauvres," studied A. Bruant, Jehan Rictus, and Jean Richepin. Francis de Miomandre presented a study of Remy de Gourmont,[5] while Marius-Ary Leblond, in a series of three chapters, gave a succinct résumé of Leconte de Lisle's life and work.[6]

Several of these essays were inspired by recently published volumes of the poets who had been prominent during the symbolist movement. Since their current work presented divergences from their early manner, the critics passed in review the successive volumes of poetry they had written. Stuart Merrill's *Les Quatre Saisons,* Adolphe Retté's *Lumières tranquilles,* and Moréas' *Stances* bore little resemblance to *Les Gammes* or *Cloches en la nuit* or *Les Syrtes.* Even if Vielé-Griffin showed less patent change, his long experimentation in free verse, and the two clear divisions of his work (the personal lyric and the dramatic poem) offered ample material for extended discussion. This is what gave Beaunier's and Quillard's essays their special quality. The articles were both timely and retrospective; they showed the writers as they had been in the tumult of the symbolist era and as they now appeared. The evolution toward greater regularity in prosody, the return of interest in nature and life, the gradual incursion of the antique myths were all studied, as well as the individual writers' changes in outlook on life.

3. *Mercure de France, 37,* 5–23; 375–88; 613–33; *40,* 577–610.
4. *37,* 289–98; *39,* 5–19, 648–55.   5. *40,* 289–300.
6. *39,* 653–99; *40,* 54–97, 400–35.

Francis Jammes and Charles Guérin, both of whom had become known to the poetic world toward the close of the nineteenth century (*De l'Angélus de l'aube à l'angélus du soir* was published in 1898 and *Le Sang des crépuscules* in 1895), did not reflect the direct impact of symbolism but rather a return to simplicity and to religious sentiment. Jammes, as Henri de Régnier had written in 1897, seemed to belong to no school. Guérin, abandoning any daring innovations in prosody after his first volume, was generally thought of as a neoromantic, extremely deft in describing the delights and tortures of sentiment.

Leconte de Lisle, who had been the target of unkind remarks from the symbolists, was now receiving more just treatment. By the publication of some "Romances" composed by the Parnassian during his youth,[7] M.-A. Leblond demonstrated how unfair was the accusation of impassivity that became a synonym for Leconte de Lisle's personality and art. Leblond's three articles in the *Mercure de France* revealed a sensitive and humanitarian poet rather than a haughty and selfish egoist.

In addition to the essays on poets and poetry that occupied such an important place in the *Mercure* during 1901, there were critical notes by Quillard on current volumes of verse. He commented with understanding and admiration on the rhythm and images of Paul Fort's *L'Amour marin,* the background of Greek legends in Louis Payen's *A l'ombre du portique,* the eloquence of Joachim Gasquet's *L'Arbre et les Vents,* the music of Samain's *Le Chariot d'or.* But Quillard could be severe at times. He deplored the preciosity and occasional cacophony in Robert de Souza's *Les Graines d'un jour;* he underlined the cheap facility and triteness which he discerned in Maurice Magre's *Le Poème de la jeunesse.* As one reads Quillard's abundant criticism of verse composed over the span of two decades, two definite dislikes become apparent. Quillard was suspicious of poetry which tried to reach the common people at the expense of dignity and art. At the other extreme, he deplored affected mannerisms and unusual vocabulary. His love of Greek letters, evidenced in part by able translations of Sophocles, Herondas, Jamblichus, his three-year stay in Constantinople during the 1890's, his own poems in which classical references and themes were numerous, allied Quillard with neoclassicism. Yet his school-day friendships with Ghil, Roux, and Fontainas and his frequentation of early symbolist groups also left their imprint on his taste and ideas. The *Mercure de France,* in entrusting the criticism of poetry between 1898 and 1912 to a man who thus represented a classical inclination and a tolerance toward modern innovators, had made a reasonable choice.[8] While fanatical claims for new poetic theories were

7. *L'Ermitage,* 24 (Oct. 1901), 289–309.

8. But Remy de Gourmont, according to Paul Léautaud, felt that Quillard's column was one of the worst in the magazine.

being voiced, Quillard remained moderate and yet not unjustly hostile.

A critical literature on poetry equal to that in the *Mercure* is not to be found in other magazines of 1901. In *L'Ermitage,* Henri Ghéon wrote brief comments on current volumes of poetry. He favored complete liberty in poetic form, and he believed that each poet possessed an individual talent which naturally sought its own kind of expression.[9] Yet Ghéon seldom wrote noteworthy criticism in the field of poetry, his articles on dramatic works being much more stimulating and original. A single poet received extended study in *L'Ermitage* in 1901. This was Emmanuel Signoret who had died on December 20, 1900. André Gide composed an obituary article and Vielé-Griffin a threnody. Ghéon, departing from his usual caution, called Signoret the last and only great Parnassian.[10]

Signoret was also honored by *La Plume,* which had published much of his poetry. Stuart Merrill wrote a column which both commemorated Signoret's death and discussed the *Premier Livre des élégies. La Plume* also published "Elégies sur la mort d'Emmanuel Signoret" by Paul Souchon. Souchon had been one of Signoret's closest friends and was a fellow countryman from Provence. His threnody was composed in exalted diction reminiscent of Signoret's, and he was quite bitter in his condemnation of those who did not realize Signoret's greatness:

> Pendant que tu vivais, ils ne t'ont pas connu
> Et, s'ils te connaissaient, c'était pour te maudire! [11]

The criticism of poetry is disappointing in *La Plume* in that it centered around problems and quarrels that had already received much fruitless discussion. The director of the magazine, Karl Boès, asked Stuart Merrill to review volumes of verse during 1901. Merrill acceded, but made it clear in his initial article that he had little admiration for the naturalists and was definitely a champion of the erstwhile symbolists. During the year Merrill contributed only seven review columns on poetry, giving favorable reports to works by Moréas, Verhaeren, Jammes, Retté, Samain, and Guérin. His adverse remarks were directed against naturism and against manifestations of neoromanticism. He spent some time demonstrating that Edmond Rostand was a mediocre poet and that Joachim Gasquet was too close an imitator of Victor Hugo. Two young poets, both about twenty-five years of age, in whom he saw promise were Jean Vignaud (*L'Accueil,* 1901) and Louis Payen (*A l'ombre du portique,* 1900). Both were provincial poets, Vignaud coming from the Charente region and Payen from the Gard. Merrill's prediction of their future was overly optimistic.

In *La Revue blanche* Gustave Kahn's reviews of poetry were brief and

---

9. See *L'Ermitage,* 21 (April 1901), 245–60, "La Poésie et l'Empirisme."
10. 21, 159, 160–4, 241.   11. *La Plume,* No. 298 (Sept. 15, 1901), p. 728.

uninformative. His bias in favor of free verse still dominated his opinions and he was hostile toward the Parnassians and their emulators. Kahn was occupied at this time with the composition of his volume *Symbolistes et Décadents,* and his ideas, like those of Merrill, often concerned the immediate past.

Those who had been the prime poetic forces during the youth of Merrill and Kahn continued to receive posthumous attention. Thus Verlaine's complete works, in five volumes, had been published by Vanier and this publication occasioned an article by René Doumic in the *Revue des Deux Mondes.*[12] In Doumic's judgment, not very much that Verlaine had written was worth preserving for posterity. Gustave Kahn was so sorely irritated by this belittling that he wrote a stinging rebuttal[13] in which he indicated his low opinion of professors as critics. In 1901 Verlaine's name appeared often in reviews of volumes by young poets. He apparently exercised great and sometimes unfortunate influence over them. (Serge Raffalovich's *Poèmes* offered perhaps the closest imitation of Verlaine in 1901, but Suarès' *Airs* were equally clear examples of Verlainian inspiration.)

Mallarmé, currently the subject of Camille Mauclair's *L'Art en silence* and of an essay in Henri de Régnier's *Figures et Caractères,* was far from forgotten in 1901. Vielé-Griffin published that year some fragments of his "Thrène pour Stéphane Mallarmé,"[14] the title suggesting quite well what stage criticism of Mallarmé had reached during the early years of the twentieth century. Henri de Régnier's chapter in *Figures et Caractères* was the reprint of an essay he had written for the *Revue de Paris* in 1898 a few days after Mallarmé's death, supplemented by a column published in *Le Gaulois* in 1899 which described his visits to Mallarmé at Valvins. Mauclair's article also dates back to 1898 when he published "L'Esthétique de Stéphane Mallarmé" in *La Grande Revue.* Those who had heard the meditations enunciated in the rue de Rome or had held conversations with Mallarmé in his rural retreat were eager to relay a part of his unpublished message, but their elucidation was enclosed in an atmosphere of personal loss. The period of mourning for Mallarmé had to be terminated before a less biographical and more objective and penetrating study of his work could be accomplished.

Rimbaud's name, at least, appeared in the newspapers in 1901. On July 21 of that year a bust, wrought by Paterne Berrichon, was unveiled in the public square of Charleville. A subscription begun in January by the *Revue blanche* and the *Mercure de France,* and soon joined by *La Plume, L'Ermitage,* and *La Vogue,* had collected in six months nearly 1900 francs. The Ministry of Fine Arts had supplemented this sum with 500 francs for the purchase of

---

12. Vᵉ série, *1* (Jan. 15, 1901), 445–56.   13. *Revue blanche, 24* (March 1901), 256–9.
14. *L'Ermitage, 22* (Oct. 1901), 241–3, 256–9.

Berrichon's bronze. A commemorative plaque was also placed on the house where Rimbaud had been born. According to lines in a sonnet composed by Ernest Raynaud for the occasion:

> Aujourd'hui que s'expie un tragique abandon,
> La Foule et le Poète échangent leur pardon
> Et la Meuse honorée en coule plus fertile.

It is to be feared that the "tragique abandon" continued in Charleville and indeed elsewhere, except for Berrichon's activities, until the period of surrealism; it is dubious whether any reconciliation between the author of *Les Illuminations* and the general public had taken place or could ever occur. The list of subscribers for Rimbaud's monument does reveal however a general esteem for him among poets. Among the contributors were Paul Fort, Fagus, Pierre Louÿs, Henri de Régnier, Maeterlinck, Klingsor, Gide, Moréas, Dierx, Retté, Merrill, Ghil, and Robert de Souza. These loyalties to a literary memory were opposed by the strongholds of tradition. It was in this year of the unveiling of Rimbaud's bust that Gaston Deschamps, on a lecture tour in the United States, expressed his disgust, in an open letter to *Le Temps*, at finding in the Yale University library *Les Illuminations*, as well as "beaucoup de cantilènes mallarmistes."

Deschamps' discovery of these objectionable items in faraway New Haven, in 1901 suggests the status of symbolism beyond French borders. During the symbolist period French poetry had become a matter of international interest, even though its manifestations outside France, except in Belgium, were confined to small circles. At the opening of the twentieth century there were not many close bonds between current French verse and foreign lands, but the literature on the recent past of French poetry began to assume proportions. In Denmark Georg Brandes' chapter "Fransk Lyrik" (*Samlede Skrifter, 7*, 1901); in Italy D. de Roberto's *Poeti francesi contemporanei*, 1901; in Sweden Emil Zilliacus' *Den Nyare franska Poesin och antiken*, 1905; in England Edmond Gosse's *French Profiles*, 1905; in Holland A. van Hamel's essays in *De Gids*, collected in *Fransche Symbolisten*, 1902; and in the United States Albert Schinz' essay of 1903 in *PMLA*, "Literary Symbolism in France," were among the works which maintained the interest in Verlaine and Mallarmé, and to a lesser degree in Henri de Régnier and Albert Samain.

It was in 1901 that Paris began to hear about a Nicaraguan poet who, as he became famous in his own land, also revealed symbolism to South America. He was Rubén Darío, hailed as an apostle of modernism, as a literary disciple of Paul Verlaine, as a liberator of Spanish verse from declamation and rigorous rules. He had visited Paris briefly in 1893, had gone to see

Moréas and Verlaine, and returned to South America with a collection of symbolist poetry and magazines. His essays on French authors, published in 1893 under the title *Los Raros,* attracted little notice in France. Nor did his volume of poetry, *Prosas profanas* (1896), receive great attention in the French press. But in 1901, when Darío was traveling about in Europe as a foreign correspondent for *La Nación* of Buenos Aires, interest was shown in his work. The *Mercure de France* created a new column, "Lettres hispano-américaines," with Eugenio Diaz Romero as critic. Here the reader could learn not only how much Darío had accomplished in acquainting Argentina with modern French literature but also how profoundly he had been affected by nineteenth-century French poetry.[15] In a letter of March 18, 1901, published in the *Mercure de France,* Darío gave credit to *La Nación* for disseminating knowledge of French culture in South America.

For a time it had seemed that French symbolism was becoming influential in Portugal. Eugenio de Castro and Manuel da Silva-Gayo, in writing their free verse, had acknowledged their indebtedness to Vielé-Griffin and Henri de Régnier and had voiced especial admiration for Verlaine. But the young Portuguese writers of the twentieth century appeared to be returning to more regular and traditional forms. De Castro had, indeed, been the originator of a new conception of versification and whenever a poet broke the traditional rules of Portuguese prosody the name of the author of *Oaristos* and *Horas* was invoked. But with the publication of *Saüdades do céu* (1899) and *Constança* (1900), Castro's abandonment of French influence became apparent. Both his thought and its expression were authentically in the Portuguese tradition. The era of the *Nefelibatos* was ended.

The bonds between French and Belgian poetry, although not broken, were much more tenuous than in the symbolist period. Certain Belgian poets who spent much of their time in Paris (Verhaeren and Fontainas, for example) had been for years incorporated into French literature, but in Belgium itself there were only a few magazines seeking the close Franco-Belgian poetic ties which had been the policy of *La Wallonie, Le Réveil, Le Coq rouge,* and *L'Art jeune.* In March 1900 Christian Beck founded *La Vie nouvelle* in Brussels. The first number included poems by Vielé-Griffin and Verhaeren, and to the second issue Charles Guérin and André Gide were contributors. In January 1901 another little literary review, *L'Idée libre,* appeared in the same city. Among its contributors were Verhaeren, Fontainas, Mockel, and Retté. *L'Art moderne* continued to give some space to reviews of volumes of poetry and spoke of French writers in these columns. In 1901 Jammes' *Le Deuil des primevères,* Moréas' *Les Stances,* and

15. The great diversity of Rubén Darío's admirations is discussed in E. K. Mapes' *L'Influence française dans l'œuvre de Rubén Darío.*

Mme. de Noailles' *Le Cœur innombrable* were among the volumes examined. In general Belgian periodicals kept within national frontiers for their list of contributors, their fears of pan-germanism making them exalt the French language but also increasing their nationalistic outlook.

From this rapid survey of French poetry in the opening years of the century, the general picture emerges of a literary genre so preoccupied with the past that innovation and individual liberty were negligible. Poets occupied with following a Parnassian, a symbolist, or an eclectic pattern of former groupings, and critics constantly reverting to the past decade for their points of discussion do not offer an exciting or promising perspective. Yet such a negative picture is false for many reasons. The critic, in studying the past, is providing new outlooks: the serious poet is never fully an imitator, since he draws his inspiration and creates his images from his own experience and knowledge. That experience and knowledge will never be identical to those of a precursor he admires, for in following the patterns of literary schools the poet has a wide choice of models and themes. Resemblance occurs in the general rather than the specific. The opening of the twentieth century was certainly not brilliant for lyric styles so individual that they could belong to only one writer. On the other hand, the accumulated possibilities offered by the romanticists, the Parnassians, and the symbolists, both in theme and technique, enlarged the variety of poetic expression. Nor is literature ever static. There are always names emerging from obscurity, new writers giving a fresh vision, independent spirits eager to protest. Against the past must be set the forces of novelty, the outlook of the future.

THE SYMBOLIST PERIOD had been a propitious one for poets who longed, as most naturally did, to see their poems in print and their names in critical columns. The presses of the *Mercure de France* and of *La Plume* had published not only a great many poems in individual issues but also in book form. The portion of pages allotted to verse in *L'Ermitage, La Revue blanche,* and in the numerous little magazines of the period was great enough for almost all poets of talent to find a means of reaching a public, small though it was.

Rare indeed then were the poets who between 1885 and 1900 had wished for some form of public recognition and not received it. There existed, however, the exceptional case, the poet who did not come into the public eye, partly because of his own reticence and partly because of factors of career and even place of residence. The striking example of delayed emergence in 1900 was Paul Claudel.

The anonymous publication of *Tête d'or* in 1890 and of *La Ville* in 1893 had gone almost unnoticed. Now, in 1900 and 1901, Paul Claudel came forth from obscurity. In three issues of *L'Ermitage* during 1900 appeared the text of his drama *L'Echange,* written in 1893 and 1894 while he was consul in America. The same year saw the publication of a volume of prose-poems, *Connaissance de l'Est,* set against the Chinese landscape and the ocean, and filled with curious meditations on time and space as well as personal feeling. During 1901 the *Mercure* offered its readers a new version of *La Ville,* quite different from the anonymous edition of two hundred copies which had appeared in 1893. *L'Arbre* appeared the same year, a volume comprising *Tête d'or, La Ville, L'Echange, La Jeune Fille Violaine,* and *Le Repos du septième jour.* The text of *Tête d'or* was quite different from that of 1890. The text of *La Jeune Fille Violaine* represented a recent revision, Claudel having composed the first form of the play in 1892 and left it in manuscript form. The years 1900–01 mark Claudel's return to France from his post in China; he profited from this sojourn in his native land to get into print the fruit of ten years of patient literary labor, accumulated, as he has explained, through a daily hour set apart from diplomatic duties.

From the date of these publications Claudel became a factor in the poetic scene. Not that his texts created a great stir in the press. But the Claudelian prose-poem and the Claudelian dramatic "verset" were common knowledge in the literary world after 1901. A new cadence and an original sort of imagery were suddenly in print; these attracted a few critics. Among the first was Camille Mauclair, the author of an essay in two parts in *La Revue* (September 15 and October 1, 1901). In this essay, entitled "Quelques beaux poètes français mal connus," Mauclair chose to speak of Claudel and Saint-Pol-Roux. He sought all the influences which could explain the strange beauty of the dramas in *L'Arbre*. What he wrote in 1901 was perhaps the first extensive critical article on Claudel, for Mauclair stressed the inspirational factors of the Bible and of Rimbaud, the intense love of nature which was at the heart of Claudel's imagery, and the stylistic excellence and originality of the plays and of *Connaissance de l'Est*. Apart from the work itself, Mauclair showed interest in what he called the intense but disciplined poetic spirit which had created *La Ville* and *L'Echange*. In *L'Ermitage,* Gide wrote a review of *L'Arbre,* but cautious as he was in matters of influences, he insisted that the five plays were like nothing else in literature. Claudel's name was even carried to Italy where Luciano Zuccoli reviewed the dramas in *Il Marzocco*.

Adrien Mithouard was another innovator. He had begun publishing verse as early as 1893 but it was not until after he founded *L'Occident* in December 1901 that he began to have a wide reputation. Meanwhile the first suggestions of his artistic credo were published in two essays in *L'Ermitage*. In "L'Art gothique et l'Art impressionniste," Mithouard announced the symbol which was to dominate all his writing: the Gothic cathedral with its dual personality, its sense of order, and its imaginative fantasy. These were later fused in Mithouard's mind into a concept of French literature, combining the symmetry of classicism and the disorder of romanticism, both necessary and both contributing to the artistic nature of the French. Other essays of Mithouard's ("Vers la simplicité," [1] "Dualisme," [2] and "Esthétique de la vibration" [3]) also conveyed the message that beauty is not to be found within the limits of a literary or artistic school but rather in their fusion and synthesis.

After these initial demonstrations of his artistic beliefs, Mithouard gathered a number of writers, artists, and musicians in order to found a periodical. Vincent d'Indy and René de Castéra were his chief music critics; Maurice Denis, Jean Baffier, Louis Rouart, and Henry Bidou were among those who judged the current productions in fine arts. Robert de Souza, Vielé-Griffin, André Lebey, Louis le Cardonnel, Tristan Klingsor, and Mithouard himself were among the poets. A collective declaration of principles in the third issue of the magazine [4] defended the notions of art and beauty, defining

1. *L'Ermitage,* 22 (July 1901), 26–39.   2. *La Vogue, 10* (May 15, 1901), 79–88.
3. *10* (June 15, 1901), 162–70.   4. *L'Occident, 1* (Feb. 1902), 115–24.

them as of equal importance with science and truth. The groups protested against literary propaganda, social or political goals in art, the tyranny of literary formulas, and in particular against the nature of Hugo's coming centenary celebration. The complaint of *L'Occident* was that it was not Hugo the poet and artist who was receiving acclaim but rather the orator, the man of the people, the actor. Mithouard himself wrote most of the declarations of belief for *L'Occident*. His periodical, partly because he was a staunch defender of Catholicism, often had a religious note. In the early issues contributions by Claudel, Louis le Cardonnel, and the poems by Vielé-Griffin celebrating women saints created this atmosphere. Mithouard's vision of France, his symbol of the Gothic cathedral, his opposition to literary schools dominated the magazine but did not prevent its becoming an important organ for the poetry and the prose-poems of the period.

The opening years of the twentieth century witnessed the return of women poets to literature. They had been few and relatively unimportant during the symbolist period.[5] *Occident,* by Lucie Delarue-Mardrus in 1900, *Le Cœur innombrable,* by the Countess de Noailles, and the *Etudes et Préludes* by Renée Vivien in 1901 inaugurated a period when "la poésie féminine" received much critical attention and often favorable comment. These poets were not audacious in their versification. Their lyric expression almost always sprang from their own emotional experience. The striking element in their poetry is the absence of Christian themes. In place of religious fervor one finds the pantheism of the Countess de Noailles, the "cœur païen" of Lucie Delarue-Mardrus, or the Sapphism of Renée Vivien. The artistic tonality, although less vague, appears not far removed from that of Samain or Charles Guérin, both of whom had been taxed with writing poems which lacked virility. Aspiration toward idealized love, the passionate claims of the flesh, the obsession with death, and the earnest search for solution of enigmas in their own natures were their favorite themes. The Countess de Noailles, less completely subjective than Renée Vivien or Lucie Delarue-Mardrus, filled many pages with ardent tenderness for nature: "Je vous tiens toute vive entre mes bras, Nature."

This line might well serve as a text for much of the criticism, both favorable and adverse, which was written on "la poésie féminine." During the early years of the twentieth century, since the volumes of poetry by women were numerous and since all the literary magazines offered examples of

5. Marie Krysinska, the author of *Rythmes pittoresques,* who claimed for herself an important role in the evolution of free verse, was the most prominent woman poet of symbolist circles. There were some poetesses in the Parnassian tradition who were published by Lemerre during the 1880–1900 period. One might name among these Hélène Vacaresco, the Baronne de Baye, Mme. Alphonse Daudet, and Tola Dorian. Rosemond Gérard (Mme. Edmond Rostand), with *Les Pipeaux* (1889), and Amélie Mesureur, with *Rimes roses* (1895), were recipients of the Archon-Despérouses poetry prize.

their work, many writers tried to discover the spirit underlying this poetry. Admirers and disparagers found the same word, "sensuality." Those who were favorably disposed turned the word into a symbol of sincerity; the hostile critics gave it the sense of bacchanalian excess. The Countess de Noailles, who wrote of herself "J'ai vécu, exaltée et mourante de flammes," Lucie Delarue-Mardrus, whose favorite words were "ferveur" and "tendresse," and Renée Vivien, who sometimes abused the word "extase," were vulnerable to accusations of intemperate sensuality. The total work of these poetesses, however, is so varied in theme and inspiration that much injustice has been done it by critics, overzealous in discoursing on feminine emotions rather than the poetry itself.

Among the earliest of the hostile critics was Charles Maurras, who treated the question of women poets in a series of essays (1903) for the magazine *Minerva*.[6] Renée Vivien, Mme. de Régnier, Lucie Delarue-Mardrus, and the Countess de Noailles became the targets of his politely sarcastic judgments. Maurras entitled his essays "Le Romantisme féminin—Allégorie du sentiment désordonné." This heading and the artistic principles which Maurras discerned in the works of the poetesses led to entirely negative reactions to their work. The taste for the foreign or exotic, for independence to the point of anarchy, and unrestrained self-expression must end, said Maurras, in crudity and artificiality. Maurras did not censure his four poetesses in equal degree, but women of letters were in his eyes ridiculous yet dangerous creatures trying to be masculine. Little by little he took from them any claim to originality: Renée Vivien's verse derived from the poetry of Verlaine and Baudelaire, Lucie Delarue-Mardrus recalled the whole range of great and secondary symbolist poets, the inspiration of the Countess de Noailles was directly romantic. In lamenting the tendencies of feminine poets, Charles Maurras was of course attacking the whole nineteenth century movement which he felt had made poetry effeminate. Just as he had held that Verlaine was a natural product of the poetry of 1830, so he contended that frenetic need for exaltation and confession among women poets was a logical outgrowth of the symbolist period. Even though they emerged from the later movement, for Maurras the French poetesses represented merely a form of romanticism. Their literary and emotional outlooks were outgrowths of Rousseau, Chateaubriand, and Victor Hugo; they were guilty of bringing into French culture part of the barbarism of the Germanic races, a taste for the strange and perverse, a cult of the importance of self, and, in their style, a cult of the word. Their desire to be individualists led to literary anarchy; their wild emotional cry, to aridity. In a word, they sacrificed intelligence.

Whatever may have been their faults, the women poets of 1900 were

6. Reprinted in 1905 in *L'Avenir de l'intelligence.*

rather more interesting than most of their male contemporaries who were publishing first volumes. Twenty-two-year-old Léon Deubel, painfully enduring his term of military service in Nancy, was almost unknown in Paris but was the author of two volumes of verse entitled *La Chanson balbutiante* (1899) and *Le Chant des routes et des déroutes* (1901), the latter of which has furnished modern anthologies with some noteworthy poems. In this second volume Deubel's originality in expression was patently the result of mingling two inspirations. An enthusiastic admirer of Laforgue and Verlaine, he often interwove the music of the latter with the irony of the former and from this double imitation arrived at something new. But Deubel's volume, published at his own expense in Poligny, did not reach a wide public. His verse, published in some fifty different periodicals between 1900 and 1913, kept him from complete obscurity, but it was not until after his suicide, at the age of thirty-four, that extensive critical evaluation was made of his work. At this time, in 1901, the young soldier in Nancy was occupied in founding, with Hector Fleischmann, the *Revue verlainienne, d'art, d'esthétisme et de piété.* This periodical, which lasted only a few months, contributed little to the critical literature on Verlaine save for Vielé-Griffin's "Notes inédites" published in the November 1901 issue. Deubel and Fleishmann organized a commemorative ceremony in January marking the sixth anniversary of Verlaine's death.

A second newcomer in the French poetic world was Marcel Marchandeau, known in literature as Touny-Lérys. His volume of 1901, *Dans l'idéal et dans la vie,* appeared in his home town, Gaillac, where he had founded a little magazine called *Gallia.* Just as Deubel's early verse evoked the names of Laforgue and Verlaine, so Touny-Lérys' writing suggested a combination of Francis Jammes and Charles Guérin. *Dans l'idéal et dans la vie* showed voluntary artlessness in expression and the unpretentious, confidential tone which the author was later to define as "primitivisme."

These men and women who were just emerging in French poetry had at least in their favor a note of sincerity and a clear message. In *Le Cœur innombrable* the author appeared as a priestess offering libations to nature with which she wished to identify herself. In *Occident,* twenty-year-old Lucie Delarue-Mardrus expressed a much more youthful enthusiasm and, what is more important, unusual comprehension of the torments of the adolescent girl. Renée Vivien's *Etudes et Préludes,* with their constant recall of the Greek antiquity she adored, showed her a master of the regular French meters, and moreover a creator of musical and beautiful images. Her eternal theme, love for and reproaches against her women friends, was her obstacle in gaining literary recognition. Periodicals preferred the less talented, but normal, inspiration of Marie Dauguet, the loving wife, the singer of rural life in the Franche-Comté region. Deubel, from the very beginning identifying himself with the poets of unhappy destiny, with Laforgue, Verlaine, and Rimbaud, voiced his distress in the problems of existence, interpolating some happier notes when he considered his gift of poetry. Touny-Lérys, the exuberant southerner, transferred his inner life and his visual impressions of the Tarn region into poetic avowals.

The authentic voice of poets is reassuring when contrasted with those poetic manifestations of the period which revolved about problems of poetry rather than its creation. Mithouard's *L'Occident* was created in part as a protest against the vanity of official meetings and discussions which sought to solve technical problems of verse and define its aims. Certain of these events apparently merited the derision of those who formed the group of *L'Occident*. Yet they received much current publicity and deserve reporting as part of the spirit of the age.

On May 27, 1901, Paris was the scene of a "Congrès des poètes," with Léon Dierx and Catulle Mendès presiding. The meeting was described in the newspapers as a noisy affair where it was impossible to hear the speakers, yet the organizers, M.-C. Poinsot, Georges Normandy, and Fernand Halley, issued a dignified report on the proceedings, giving the texts of many speeches. Three main problems were presented: (1) Paris and the provinces, or literary decentralization, (2) the social role of poetry, and (3) questions of prosody. *La Revue picarde* had sponsored the meeting and the first part of the program was spent in extolling the provincial magazines. In the discussion of the poet's importance in society, Han Ryner's impassioned oration stood out. Ryner maintained that only the poet who had no thought of leading society could be really effective. René Ghil, in denouncing other poetic credos, gave his reasons for finding "la poésie scientifique" the only salvation for verse.

The metrical question brought back into the picture an obscure poet and musician who had received some attention in 1897 when his pamphlet "La Crise poétique" had been published. Adolphe Boschot, neither a Parnassian nor a symbolist, had insisted that verse should be written for the ear alone. Since, at the same time, he was not an advocate of free verse, he had encountered few admirers or adherents. Sully-Prudhomme had answered Boschot's booklet in two articles which appeared in the *Revue de Paris*. For the next three years Boschot devoted himself principally to his musical studies, then in 1900 gained warm praise from conservative critics for his *Poèmes dialogués*.[7] After his allocution at the Congrès des Poètes, Boschot composed an open letter to Gaston Boissier, the perpetual secretary to the French

7. Emile Faguet in *La Revue bleue, 38* (May 18, 1901), 619–21, and Gustave Lanson in *La Revue universitaire, 9*, No. 10 (1900), 502–3.

Academy. This was printed in the *Revue de Paris* on August 15, 1901, and bore the title "La Réforme de la prosodie."

In this letter the proposals outlined by Boschot did not differ greatly from those he had enunciated in 1897 and were certainly not new or daring. The abolition of the caesura (for the eye) when the rhythm of the alexandrine is ternary, rhyme for the ear alone, and freedom to use hiatus when it does not create a disagreeable sound were his principal ideas.

Reactions to Boschot's letter were of two kinds. In the magazines which had long ago accepted free verse, the tone was that of scornful hilarity, but in newspapers and conservative periodicals Boschot's proposals were treated with grave solemnity. The strict regulations of the Parnassians still had many adherents, the principal organ of reactionary forces being the *Revue des poètes,* founded in 1897 by Ernest Prévost. Prévost's cautious attitude toward liberty in prosody is well exemplified by a note he appended to a review of *Le Cœur innombrable:* "Madame de Noailles fait rimer, aussi souvent que l'occasion s'en présente, le singulier et le pluriel. Nous ne nous insurgeons pas personnellement contre cette licence; mais nous déplorons l'usage immodéré et le plus souvent fantaisiste qu'en font les poètes des nouvelles écoles." [8]

In *La Revue des poètes,* the erstwhile Parnassians and the so-called neo-classicists had an organ for their lyric expression. Achille Paysant, Auguste Dorchain, Albert Mérat, Gustave Zidler, Henri Chantavoine, André Lemoyne, Charles Dornier, and a host of other conservative poets contributed to the monthly issues of the periodical short pieces of lofty idealism, praise of nature, expression of family piety, sonnets and narrative verse on historical subjects which endlessly restated romantic and Parnassian themes. Occasionally one of the reactionary poets took it upon himself to chide those who had defied the established rules of syntax or versification, as in the "Stances à Verlaine," by Berthe de Puybesque, a poem which won third prize in a contest held in 1902 by the *Revue des poètes:*

> Frère, êtes-vous bien sûr que la complicité
> D'un siècle décadent et ses métamorphoses
> Demandent tant de mots, d'études et de gloses,
> Et que, trop sculptural dans sa simplicité,
> Racine ait à jamais perdu sa vérité? [9]

When Sully-Prudhomme was announced as the first recipient of the Nobel Prize in literature in the final months of 1901, the *Revue des poètes* applauded. Irony and satiric comment greeted the choice in many of the magazines however. Remy de Gourmont's acidulous comments in his "Epi-

8. *Revue des poètes,* 5 (Nov. 1902), 168.   9. 5 (Oct. 1902), 156.

logues" of the *Mercure de France,* and Mithouard's more overt sarcasms in
L'Occident were among the manifestations of hostility.

Thus the rift between Parnassians and symbolists, in spite of the latters'
evolution toward nature and reality, and despite their gradual eradication
of strange diction and imagery, was never quite healed. Poetry, for most
of those who had passed through the symbolist movement, meant more freedom and liberty, more spontaneity and search for beauty, more mystery and
subtlety than Sully-Prudhomme's moralizing permitted. *La Revue des poètes,* on the one hand, and the tetrad of magazines born under the sign of
symbolism, on the other, illustrate this cleavage.

Decentralization, a popular theme during the last years of the nineteenth
century, continued in full vigor. In January 1901 Roger Frène founded *La
Revue provinciale* in Toulouse. The poets from the south were its chief
contributors: Marc Lafargue, Emmanuel Delbousquet, Joachim Gasquet,
and Pierre Camo; but a few northerners appeared in its pages. The magazine's attitude, a familiar one since the publication of *Les Déracinés,* was
based on a belief in the pernicious influence of Paris and its writers' loss of
contact with native soil. French culture should not be confined to Paris, but
should spread over the whole of France.

Another center of regional activity was Lille. Here, in May of 1900, A.-M.
Gossez and Léon Bocquet formed a periodical that was long identified with
"La Poésie septentrionale." Its name was *Le Beffroi,* and while few of its
contributors gained fame as great writers, it performed an important service
as a publishing house for a number of minor poets. Volumes by Philéas
Lebesgue, Charles Vildrac, Paul Castiaux, Théo Varlet, Roger Allard, Léon
Deubel, Louis Pergaud, Amédée Prouvost, Jacques Noir, and Gaston Syffert
appeared from its presses between 1903 and 1909.[10] Léon Bocquet, who remained as director of *Le Beffroi* when his colleague Gossez became in 1904
managing editor of La Villehervé's *La Province,* another regional magazine
published in Le Havre, heroically kept it in existence, publishing six issues
year after year. His poetry (*Les Sensations,* 1897; *Flandre,* 1901; *Les Cygnes
noirs,* 1906) never received a good press, but the particular devotion he had
for the memory of Albert Samain was responsible for the first complete
study of that poet's life and work, his *Albert Samain* of 1905.

Le Beffroi had the longest existence of any of the regional magazines, but
it aroused little interest outside the Nord department. Other regional maga-

10. Some of the principal poetic publications of *Le Beffroi* were Lebesgue, *Les Folles Verveines*
(1903); Castiaux, *Au long des terrasses* (1905); Varlet, *Notes et Poèmes,* (1905) and *Notations* (1906); Deubel, *Vers la vie* (1904), *La Lumière natale* (1905), *Poésies* (1906), and
Poèmes choisis (1909); Pergaud, *L'Aube* (1904) and *L'Herbe d'avril* (1908); Prouvost, *Le
Poème du travail et du rêve* (1905); Syffert, *Les Brumes de la vie* (1907); Vildrac, *Poèmes*
(1906); Allard, *La Divine Aventure* (1905).

zines mentioned it, but in Paris its numbers were seldom spoken of, save perhaps the November-December issue of 1904 which gave the results of a referendum creating a mythical Academy of Poets. This idea had been inspired by the Goncourt Academy, which had at last begun sitting in 1903. *Le Beffroi* proposed to name ten poets, in imitation of the Goncourt Academy. The proposal was treated in Paris as a kind of joke, but Bocquet's intentions were quite serious. He collected 102 answers, the majority from regional poets. Whatever the faults of such an inquiry might be, the results are probably not an inaccurate indication of the esteem in which the winning poets were held in 1904. Verhaeren, with sixty votes, and Régnier, with fifty-six, were in first place. Then in descending order came Moréas, Guérin, Jammes, Noailles, Vielé-Griffin, Merrill, and Van Lerberghe. Dierx and Maeterlinck tied for tenth place with fifteen votes each.

Lille was the meeting place for the "Deuxième Congrès des poètes" in July 1902. The group of *Le Beffroi* had small part in that assembly, for one of their fellow townsmen and rivals, the poet Emile Lante, was a leading figure in it. The second "congrès" was dominated by a group of nineteen writers who had taken the name "L'Ecole française" after Adolphe Boschot had come to an understanding with two indefatigable organizers and partisans of decentralization, Georges Normandy and M.-C. Poinsot. These three created the new grouping soon after the first "Congrès des poètes" in Paris. Their program was founded on two principles: the return of clarity and human feelings to French poetry, and the liberation of verse from classic and romantic rules. Such a program would seem to have been accomplished by a considerable group of poets before the "Ecole française" came into being, but Boschot, Normandy, and Poinsot were eager to establish a difference between free verse, which they felt had insufficient discipline, and "vers libéré" which would obey a number of rules. They found enough writers to form with them a collective volume of poetry. This anthology appeared in July 1902, simultaneously with the second Congress, under the inspiring title *La Foi nouvelle*.

The "Ecole française," unlike many later attempts at forming poetic schools, at least had some temporary followers. None of the contributors to *La Foi nouvelle* gained great renown in poetry, although names like those of the Algerian Robert Randau or the southerner, Marcel Roland, had some place in the history of the novel, and others, like Han Ryner and Charles Méré, are in the theatrical currents of the twentieth century. Still others, like Adolphe Lacuzon and Paul Loewengard, later issued manifestoes of their own. The story of "L'Ecole française" is similar to that of most poetic associations of the early twentieth century, at least those which tried to build on doctrine. Much pretentiousness in aims, scornful antagonism from almost everyone outside their narrow orbits, little real influence on the course of lyricism, quick dissolution are the standard phenomena in the life of twentieth-century poetic schools. The exasperating result of these doctrinal pronouncements, which persisted uninterruptedly until the first World War, was that they begot many articles of protest almost as empty as the theories they were attacking. This was much the case with the "Ecole française": partisans of free verse saw little occasion for creation of "vers libéré"; defenders of tradition were even more hostile. Fortunately Adolphe Boschot soon turned to musical history, gathering materials for his monumental life of Hector Berlioz; Poinsot and Normandy expended their energies in many directions, writing plays, novels, biographies, essays, and anthologies, working in behalf of the "Fédération régionaliste française." The not brilliant career of the "Ecole française" should have acted as a deterrent to future would-be leaders. Apparently, however, hope of a new poetic formula was a perennial dream, and in most cases not a happy one.

THE CENTENARY OF Victor Hugo's birth made 1902 a year of commemoration. A new century "avait deux ans"; a vast poetic upheaval had taken place since the day of apotheosis in 1885 when Hugo had received the most pompous third-class funeral that Paris had seen. In December 1901 Remy de Gourmont, foreseeing the excess of praise that the centenary would inevitably provoke, offered some words of cautionary advice to young journalists.[1] Noting that Hugo had already been called "toute la poésie et toute la pensée du dix-neuvième siècle," Gourmont asked whether one could represent the totality of the century's poetry without evoking the names of Vigny, Lamartine, Musset, Baudelaire, and Verlaine.

Gourmont's remarks inspired the editors of *L'Ermitage* with the idea of a questionnaire. Letters asking the question "Quel est votre poète?" were sent to two hundred poets. In the responses no living writers were to be named. Over 120 answers were received, and though many correspondents refused to limit themselves to a single name, Victor Hugo emerged easily the winner. Second in the admiration of the poets was Alfred de Vigny; Verlaine was third. The others thereafter in order of descending popularity were: Baudelaire, Lamartine, Musset, Leconte de Lisle, Mallarmé, and Albert Samain.[2] Such a list does not strike us as odd today, save for the absence of Rimbaud's name and the inclusion of Samain's. Several circumstances, not the least of which was Samain's recent death, contributed to the importance accorded the author of *Aux flancs du vase*. Among those who voiced special admiration for Samain were three fellow citizens of Lille: Léon Bocquet, R.-M. Clerfeyt, and Jules Mouquet. *Le Beffroi* had been founded in Lille in 1900, and one of its early issues had been a special number celebrating Samain.[3]

Remy de Gourmont, who had inspired the questionnaire, pronounced himself well satisfied with the results. The high esteem in which poets held Verlaine, Baudelaire, and Mallarmé seemed to him a victory over Hugolian idolatry. These three names placed among the four great romanticists and the chief Parnassian proved, according to Gourmont, the living quality and the logic of French literary history.[4]

1. *Mercure de France, 40,* 769.

2. Results of the questionnaire were given in *L'Ermitage, 23* (Feb. 1901), 81–146.

3. *Le Beffroi* (July–Aug. 1900). Articles by A. Ségard, L. Bocquet, Paul Castiaux, Edmond Blanguernon, A.-M. Gossez.

4. *Mercure de France, 41* (March 1902), 763–8.

The periodical items on Victor Hugo during 1902 would constitute an extensive bibliography. In the month of March alone appeared magazine articles by Brunetière, Gustave Kahn, Stuart Merrill, Fernand Gregh, and Charles Méré, and this represents but a fragment of the total. The significance of this literature on Hugo is not great, save in its revelation of two attitudes toward the poet. On the one hand, the writers who had been in the symbolist groups were often restrained in their admiration of the poet, while those who had not accepted the movement of the 1880's were usually unreservedly adulatory.

La Plume devoted its entire March 1 number [5] to the commemoration of Hugo. This magazine prided itself on the fact that it had organized a banquet to celebrate the posthumous publication of the final part of *Toute la Lyre* in 1893. Writers associated with *La Plume* repeatedly protested against the idea that the symbolists were hostile to Hugo, and indeed many poems printed in the commemorative issue were by men who had begun writing shortly after Hugo's death and who had been figures in poetic change.

Discussion concerning Victor Hugo's greatness was prolonged by Catulle Mendès' *Rapport sur le mouvement poétique français de 1867 à 1900*. This 200-page document, in the two editions of 1902 and 1903, was particularly offensive to the poets who had accepted as guides Baudelaire, Verlaine, Rimbaud, and Mallarmé. Mendès had probably tried to be more equitable in his judgments than in *La Légende du Parnasse contemporain,* but in truth his report was a panegyric of Victor Hugo. His concluding remarks, celebrating Rostand as the herald of the new century even as Hugo had been the leader of the old; his image of Hugo's last years as a twilight followed by night, and Rostand's appearance as the dawn "née d'une dernière étincelle du couchant"; his implication that the symbolists had invented little except incorrect diction and syntax; and his attack against free versé aroused a number of writers. Mendès was accused of confusing success and talent. Ernest Raynaud reminded him that Voiture and Delille were accounted great in their periods.[6] Merrill suggested that Claudel (and Elémir Bourges!) would offer better examples than Rostand of the dawn of the new century.[7] Mendès' remark that free verse seemed to be a lost cause, except for a Belgian (Verhaeren) and two writers born in the United States (Vielé-Griffin and Merrill), brought rebuttal on all sides.

The attention given to Victor Hugo, and later in the year the large number of articles devoted to Emile Zola (who died on September 28, 1902) explain to some extent the small amount of space accorded poetic criticism in periodicals. Publication of André Beaunier's *La Poésie nouvelle* elicited some

5. No. 309 (March 1, 1902), 257-319.   6. *La Plume,* No. 351 (Dec. 1, 1903), p. 584.
7. No. 342 (July 15, 1903), p. 50.

comment, inspiring Gustave Kahn to write an article on "Le Vers libre," [8] and Remy de Gourmont to discuss the role of mute "e" in poetry.[9] Eugène Montfort, in the August issue of *La Revue des revues,* was the author of an essay on "La Nouvelle Génération littéraire française." Though less outspoken than in his earlier writings, he was still under the spell of Bouhélier and naturism. In the return to descriptive rural setting in poetry, he saw an evolution which the naturists had not only foretold but for which they were also responsible.

One of the important texts for the history of the symbolist movement was published in 1902. The author was Gustave Kahn, the title *Symbolistes et Décadents.* Kahn was writing about a period in which he had been active, and, despite inevitable personal bias, he was well informed. A more objective viewpoint was presented in two long essays by a Dutch professor, A. G. van Hamel in *De Gids*[10] of Amsterdam. Van Hamel, under the title "Fransche Symbolisten," gave a concise but well-documented history of the poetic movement between 1880 and 1900. Unlike Kahn, he did not overemphasize the importance of free verse; his was a scholarly approach lacking the anecdotal quality of *Symbolistes et Décadents.*

The year witnessed an attempt to channel poetry according to a system of belief. At the end of 1902, in the December 12 issue of *Le Figaro,* Fernand Gregh published his manifesto of humanism. This document won for its author more enemies than friends, since many writers thought that Gregh was trying to arrogate the title of leader of a poetic school. Gregh said that after the Parnassian cult of beauty for beauty's sake and the symbolist credo of beauty for dreams' sake, it was time to establish a literary school for life's sake. Artistry and obscurity should give way to the presentation of the human being in his totality, not alone his sensations and his fantasy but his ideas and his sentiments as well. Gregh's ideas were certainly not contrary to the beliefs of many of his contemporaries, but he found no disciples, unless the later group which contributed to *Les Essais* in 1906 may be loosely considered as such. Gaston Deschamps became Gregh's champion in newspaper articles, but others, among them Paul Fort, considered Gregh an opportunist.

Gregh was concerned with the present and future of poetry; in this regard he stood apart from most of his contemporaries. Not only the volumes by Kahn and Beaunier but almost all articles on poetry were concerned with problems and figures of the late nineteenth century rather than the twentieth.

8. *La Nouvelle Revue, 16,* 2ᵉ série (May 15, 1902), 171–9.
9. *Mercure de France, 42* (May 1902), 289–303.
10. *De Gids, 1902 1* (March 1902), 407–42; *1902 2* (June 1902), 448–89. This periodical had not hitherto offered much of importance on symbolist literature, a noteworthy exception being W. G. C. Byvanck's two essays on Claudel's *Tête d'or* and *La Ville* in 1894.

Verlaine's name was still prominent. Léon Deubel composed his poem "A la gloire de Paul Verlaine" which was read at the sixth anniversary of the poet's death; Lepelletier contributed some memories of Verlaine's youth to the *Echo de Paris*,[11] André Mary wrote a "Méditation sur Verlaine" for *L'Ermitage*,[12] and the presses of the *Mercure de France* were printing the first volume of Verlaine's *Œuvres Posthumes*. Jules Laforgue was another of the poets who still had contemporary interest. Between 1901 and 1903 appeared the four volumes of his *Œuvres complètes*, an edition prepared by Camille Mauclair which was to be the standard text for the next twenty years. The great part of Laforgue's posthumous works had been printed in the *Entretiens politiques et littéraires* and in the *Revue blanche*, but in 1903 Mithouard's magazine *L'Occident* published three series of Laforgue's letters to his sister, edited by Vielé-Griffin. An essay by Francis de Miomandre in the *Mercure de France* [13] and James Huneker's article in the *New York Sun*, "A Masterpiece of Irony, the Hamlet of Jules Laforgue," [14] were two of the items inspired by publication of Laforgue's works.

During 1902 and 1903 the magazine which best represented a balanced sampling of poetry by the poets of the symbolist generation and the younger writers was *L'Ermitage* under the direction of Edouard Ducoté. Several of Paul Fort's "Ballades," some sylvan verses by Adolphe Retté, fragments of Vielé-Griffin's "Pindare," love poems by Charles Guérin, pieces taken from Léo Larguier's *La Maison du poète,* and contributions by Francis Jammes established a definite link with the magazine's past. Two mature Belgians, Van Lerberghe and Fernand Séverin, also were represented. André Gide's dramatic poem "Bethsabé" was printed in the January and February issues of 1903. But *L'Ermitage* was not immured in the past. Two young women poets, Lucie Delarue-Mardrus and Nicolette Hennique, and many of the young male lyricists, among them Touny-Lérys, Hector Fleishmann, Emile Despax, Ernest Gaubert, Pierre Fons, and Charles Derennes (all in their early twenties), were among the contributors. Albert Erlande and François Porché, just a few years older than the preceding group, were also recent arrivals in the poetic world.

Henri Ghéon's brief reviews of books constituted the principal comments in *L'Ermitage* on volumes of poetry. Succinct and equitable on most questions of prosody but the enemy of didactic qualities in verse (which he deplored in the work of Ducoté, the director of *L'Ermitage*), Ghéon constantly defined poetic tonality by comparisons. Thus, Jean Dominique's

11. December 17, 1901.   12. *1902* 2 (July 1902), 27–41.

13. *45* (Feb. 1903), 289–314.

14. January 11, 1903. For bibliographical information on Laforgue, consult Warren Ramsey's *Jules Laforgue and the Ironic Inheritance,* Oxford Univ. Press, 1953.

L'Ombre des roses had the charm of Verlaine, Laforgue, and Jammes, Mockel's *Clartés* combined the inspiration of Mallarmé and the free verse form of Vielé-Griffin, Henri Albert imitated Jammes in his *Neuvaine pour la petite au doigt coupé,* Erlande continued Lamartinian romanticism but avoided description, the religious sincerity of Louis le Cardonnel's poems suggested Verlaine's *Sagesse,* and Jean Schlumberger's early poems had a sonority which recalled Leconte de Lisle. Ghéon spoke with admiration of Vielé-Griffin, Verhaeren, Van Lerberghe, Degron, Régnier, and Klingsor, in all of whom he found a note of personal sincerity. His adverse criticism was directed against what was artificial or excessive. He recommended that Marinetti subdue his vehemence, that Hector Fleishmann be less "somptueux," [15] that Georges Casella be less mannered, and that Saint-Pol-Roux use more restraint in his imagery.

Brief though these notations were, Ghéon's coverage of current poetry in *L'Ermitage* was fairly complete. *La Plume* had no such critic during 1902. Karl Boès, probably catering to public taste, chose to give more importance to the novel and the theater, and these two genres were discussed regularly. Part of the difficulty may have been his choice of Stuart Merrill to report from time to time on volumes of verse. During 1902 only one article by Merrill appeared. It contained three parts, two of which were inspired by his hostility toward the naturists. Eugène Montfort's essay on "La Nouvelle génération littéraire française" aroused Merrill's ire through its representation of Saint-Georges de Bouhélier as the inspiring force which had effected evolution in the poetry of Vielé-Griffin, Jammes, Verhaeren, Saint-Pol-Roux, Retté, and Merrill himself. Merrill, calling Montfort the faithful shepherd dog of the flockless herdsman Bouhélier, categorically denied any such influence. Then, reporting on Bouhélier's *Les Chants de la vie ardente,* he quoted the most absurd of the images in the volume in order to demonstrate the fact that much of the verse resembled the fumbling efforts of a high-school boy. In addition to these two indignant portions of denigrating criticism, Merrill did write some paragraphs praising André Beaunier's *La Poésie nouvelle.* This he called the best work that had appeared on the symbolist poets. His one adverse comment on the volume was that Beaunier should have pointed out the faults in the early writings of the poets he was so stoutly defending.

Besides this diatribe against Bouhélier's mediocre volume, only one review of a book of verse appeared in *La Plume* during 1902. Merrill was not the author of this article. He had written a cordial preface for the volume in question: Henri Degron's *Poèmes de Chevreuse.* Another of Degron's

15. Hector Fleishmann, in 1902, the year Ghéon was writing about him, made an abortive attempt to establish a school of writing called "Le Somptuarisme."

friends, Adolphe Retté, composed the review. Inevitably it was favorable, not only by reason of comradeship but also because Retté, celebrating the rural isolation of Fontainebleau, was currently writing poetry very much like that of Degron. Since *La Plume* in 1902 was the publishing house of Georges Périn's *Les Emois blottis,* Jeanne Perdriel-Vaissière's *Le Sourire de Joconde,* and Marinetti's *La Conquête des étoiles,* it is strange that no current article in the magazine discussed these volumes.

During Léon Deschamps' directorship, *La Plume* had given a relatively large amount of space to the publication of poetry. Under Karl Boès, as the magazine increased in size, verse became more and more sparse. In 1901, when the year's pagination totaled over 1400 pages, only some seventy were given to poetry or the prose-poem. Ernest Raynaud, who had made a trip to England and Belgium, twice contributed verses under the general title "Impressions de voyage," Paul Fort on two occasions gave selections from his *Paris sentimental.* Tristan Klingsor, Pierre Louÿs, Paul Souchon, Stuart Merrill, P.-N. Roinard, Georges Périn, Fagus, Pierre Fons, J.-A. Nau, Isi Collin, André Mary, Emile Despax, Saint-Pol-Roux, and Henri de Régnier were among the contributors. Such a list shows the close poetic affinities of *La Plume* with *L'Ermitage,* and, to a lesser degree, with the *Mercure de France* and *L'Occident.*

During 1903 *La Plume* returned to a policy of presenting criticism on poetry. Stuart Merrill was, during the first half of the year, the chief critic, reporting on volumes which he admired, some of which had been published in 1902. The women writers (Dauguet, Delarue-Mardrus, Perdriel-Vaissière, and Renée Vivien), the poets of his own generation (Fontainas, Régnier, and Vielé-Griffin), and a few of the collaborators of *La Plume* (Despax, Périn, and Mary) won his special approbation. During the last half of the year Henri Degron wrote appreciative essays on Tristan Klingsor and Adolphe Retté, while W. Claude-Emile took up the cudgels for Jean Moréas in reply to Ernest Charles' derogatory article on the author of *Les Stances* in *La Revue bleue* of June 6, 1903.

During this year *La Plume* appeared eager to recapture memories of its past by resuming a series of evening gatherings and dinners. Ernest Raynaud, one of the old guard, wrote an article on "Les Soirées de *La Plume*," [16] telling of many picturesque writers and artists who had gathered during the 1890's in the Café du Soleil d'or, with Léon Deschamps as master of ceremonies. At the end of 1903 and in the early months of 1904 *La Plume* published two series, "Souvenirs sur le symbolisme" by Stuart Merrill, [17]

16. *La Plume,* No. 336 (April 15, 1903), pp. 425–40.
17. No. 352 (Dec. 15, 1903), pp. 613–21; No. 353 (Jan. 1, 1904), pp. 2–11; No. 355 (Feb. 1, 1904), pp. 107–15.

and "Les Poètes décadents" by Ernest Raynaud.[18] Both were inspired by the publication of Adolphe Retté's *Le Symbolisme,* a volume of memoirs, which Merrill and Raynaud wished to supplement from their own experience.

Returning to a former practice of the magazine, Boès gave greater prominence to the publication of verse by issuing special supplements. During 1903 poems were largely concentrated in two issues, that of May 1 and the double number of August 1–15. As in the days when Léon Deschamps had been director, *La Plume* made an effort to print the work of young poets. The general results were as in the 1890's: most of the youthful lyricists later disappeared from literature or turned to other forms of writing. But in these special numbers of *La Plume* were several poets who endured: Apollinaire, Salmon, Derennes, Despax, Ernest Gaubert, and Paul Géraldy. Older poets, born in the 1870's, who were represented in the poetic issues of the magazine, were Georges Périn, André Mary, Louis Payen, Blanguernon, Fagus, Paul Souchon, and Daniel Thaly. The oldest of them all, J.-A. Nau, had begun publishing verse only after his thirty-fifth year, and in 1903 was suddenly famous as the first winner of the Goncourt prize for the novel. His first volume of verse, published by Vanier in 1897, had gone almost unnoticed. After the Goncourt award for *Force ennemie,* which had been published by *La Plume,* Nau enjoyed some momentary fame and collected verses he had written during the past decade under the title *Hiers bleus.* His wandering existence and his insouciant attitude concerning publication of his verse might have left him in complete obscurity had not Jean Royère, after 1906, made him one of the principal contributors of *La Phalange,* and, as literary executor, continued publication of the Nau manuscripts after 1918.[19]

Besides the special numbers given to poetry, *La Plume* printed a few poems in other issues of 1903. Here, as in preceding years, there was a fair representation of the older generation, Fontainas, Degron, Merrill, Verhaeren, Raynaud, Moréas, Saint-Pol-Roux, and Morice. The younger group differed little from that of 1902; they represented a greater kinship with symbolism than with the Parnassians.

What would have been the outcome of this renewed interest by *La Plume* in the symbolist period, and especially the renewal of interest in poetry, cannot be known. Financial difficulties—the result of Boès' desire to expand the magazine, to include many illustrations, to issue special supplements (on Finland, on Charles Baudelaire, on the art of Constantin Meunier,

---

18. No. 352 (Dec. 15, 1903), pp. 634–41; No. 353 (Jan. 1, 1904), pp. 65–74.

19. Especially the novels *Thérèse Donati* (1920), *Les Galanteries d'Anthime Budin* (1923), *Les Trois Amours de Benigno Reyes* (1923), and the volume of poetry, *Poèmes triviaux et mystiques* (1924).

and on Boleslas Biegas)—were besetting the periodical. *La Plume* struggled on until July 1904, and, before it ceased publication, it made one last effort in behalf of poetry. To encourage young writers, *La Plume* announced in its October 1903 number a contest for poets under twenty-five years of age. Jean Moréas, Emile Verhaeren, and Henri de Régnier were to judge the manuscripts, and the winning poems were to be published in the magazine. Of the 103 poems entered in the contest, some forty were at first selected as the best. Henri Martineau, who was to found *Le Divan* in 1909, was acclaimed winner with his poem "Les Roses," both by the votes of the judges and those of fellow contestants. Through this contest the magazine professed the hope of discovering something concerning the current trends in verse. The meager answer to this hope, if we are to judge by the winning poem, was absence of admiration for originality. "Les Roses" was composed in alexandrines and arranged in quatrains. While rhymes of singulars with plurals were numerous, the alternation of feminines and masculines was rigorously observed and the poem contained only one outstanding example of *enjambement.* The theme, in part suggested by Verlaine's line from *Sagesse,* "Oh, quand refleuriront les roses de septembre," developed an age-old comparison, the brief life of the rose and the relentless progress of time.

The contest did include the names of other writers who were to be well known in a few years. There was J.-M. Bernard, born in 1881, who had become fervently interested in poetry after meeting Louis le Cardonnel at Valence in 1902. Another contestant was Robert Vallery-Radot, a youth of seventeen, who submitted a group of "Ritournelles." Francis Eon, the future author of *La Promeneuse, Trois Années,* and *La Vie continue,* was still another young writer whose talent received recognition through the competition.

The contest provided material for another poetic supplement for *La Plume.* The forty-four poems, by thirty-eight authors, which had been selected by Verhaeren, Moréas, and Régnier were printed in the March 1, 1904 issue of the magazine.[20] It was from this list that the final choice of Martineau was made, the voters being the authors of the poems. Thus one of the final gestures of *La Plume* was close to the announced intentions of the magazine in 1889, the encouragement of young writers. During its sixteen years of existence, the magazine had published almost fifty volumes of verse. Among the authors were Abadie, Dubus, Merrill, Moréas, Raynaud, Retté, Signoret, Verlaine, F. T. Marinetti, and Mme. Perdriel-Vaissière.

La Plume was to have two later revivals, in 1905 and in 1911. But, because of changes in the editorial staffs of these new series, the magazine did not have the continuity in contributors and outlook which had existed from

20. No. 357, pp. 225–88.

1889 to 1904. The disappearance of *La Plume* left a hiatus in poetic expression which was soon filled by Jean Royère's *Phalange* and by Paul Fort's *Vers et Prose.*

La Revue blanche, another magazine which had been a mouthpiece for poetic expression during the symbolist period, ceased publication a year before *La Plume.* In 1902 and 1903, it is true, its role had not been outstanding in support of verse, for very little was published in the periodical during the last sixteen months of its existence (January 1, 1902–April 15, 1903). Two women, Lucie Delarue-Mardrus and Nicolette Hennique, were clearly favorites of the magazine, the former with her lyrics of personal confession and the latter with her poems on mythological subjects.[21] Other poets who appeared in the pages of *La Revue blanche* were J.-A. Nau, whose exotic settings for verse were already establishing his reputation; Tristan Klingsor, writer of graceful songs; Adolphe Retté, who had been composing in the forest of Fontainebleau what were to be almost his final poems; and Alfred Jarry, whose acrobatics in rhyme seemed a foretaste of certain "poètes fantaisistes." Verhaeren contributed a meditation on a ruined city near the Spanish coast. "L'Ermite," one of Guillaume Apollinaire's earliest published poems, appeared in the December 1, 1902 issue.

But meanwhile in *La Revue blanche* there were no essays on poetry and only a few short bibliographical reports on current volumes of verse. The latter were often composed by Lucie Delarue-Mardrus and two of them concerned books by women writers: *L'Ombre des jours* by Mme. de Noailles, *Cendres et Poussières* by Renée Vivien. Mme. Delarue-Mardrus' volume of poetry, *Ferveur,* was reviewed by Michel Arnauld, Gide's brother-in-law.

For every literary periodical that disappeared, two or three were founded. Most of them have little interest, but one, because of the later fame of its founder, deserves brief mention.

Guillaume Apollinaire's monthly magazine *Le Festin d'Esope* had only nine numbers, which appeared between November 1903 and August 1904. Apart from Apollinaire's prose and poetry contributions,[22] the periodical is known today for having revealed another poet of talent, André Salmon.[23] Apollinaire wrote little criticism in his magazine, but in the fourth issue (February 1904) he gave his opinion that Charles Derennes seemed to him the most harmonious of contemporary poets.

Derennes, twenty years of age and recently an outstanding student of Latin and Greek at Louis le Grand, had just published his first volume,

21. *La Revue blanche* published Nicolette Hennique's *Les Rêves et les Choses* (1900), Lucie Delarue-Mardrus' *Occident* (1900) and *Ferveur* (1902).

22. "Qu vlo-v'?," "L'Adieu," "Le Retour," "La Synagogue," "Les Femmes," "La Loreley," "Passion," "L'Enchanteur pourrissant," "Schinderhannes."

23. "Féerie," "Prière," "La Rue," "La Bonne Auberge."

L'Enivrante Angoisse. Apollinaire, by the way, detested this title. What he suggested as the chief quality in Derennes, the musical cadence of his lines, is indeed a just observation. The smooth and cadenced measure of Lamartine seemed to have been captured by this young man who wrote:

> Mon cœur, ce soir, est sombre, et vide de tendresse
> Comme de roses veuf le rosier de ce mur.
> Je ne veux plus savoir d'où naît cette tristesse
> Qui sur votre front clair pose son voile obscur.
>
> ("Elégie")

Apollinaire's choice of Derennes for special commendation is indicative both of a sensitive ear, and, in the aesthetic outlook of the author of *Alcools,* of a taste for romantic poetry. Derennes sang most often of love; his tone was sentimental.

Not offering in his themes or even in his imagery much evidence of originality, Derennes yet composed so melodiously that his verse was readily accepted by magazines. *L'Ermitage* had published his "Stances" in August 1903; *La Plume* his "Elégies d'automne," "Trois Idylles," "L'Automne de Phèdre," and "Eté" between May and December of that year. In the ideas of Apollinaire, often so original and audacious, the contrary notion of respect for the past is well exemplified by his admiration for Derennes.

Examination of critical comment on current poetry during 1902 and 1903 produces meager results. The collector's item of the year 1902 in French poetic criticism was Francis de Miomandre's essay on Milosz published in *L'Ermitage.*[24] The Lithuanian poet, whose first volume, *Le Poème des décadences,* had been published in 1899, was not destined to become famous until after his death in 1939, yet Miomandre wrote, four decades earlier, what other critics would one day discover. Calling Milosz "a poet of evocation," Miomandre portrayed the complicated and intricate mind that had created *Le Poème des décadences,* pointed out the technical originality of the free rhythms and assonances, and suggested why Milosz was not merely another outgrowth of the symbolist era. Miomandre wrote other essays on writers in 1902: Paul Claudel and Camille Mauclair[25] were two he chose to study. Claudel he pronounced an indisputable genius, finding that the author of *L'Arbre* had shown how the most dogmatic form of religiosity could coexist with a rich and spontaneous imaginative power. He admired Mauclair for capturing the spirit of the times. Mauclair had been among the first to write on Stéphane Mallarmé, on Jules Laforgue, and on Maurice Maeterlinck, and in his own verse, published under the title of *Sonatines*

---

24. (Oct. 1902), pp. 260–7.
25. *Mercure de France, 41* (March 1902), 684–96; 42 (June 1902), 641–54.

d'automne (1895), had reflected many influences of the symbolist era. His lecture on Rodin, given on July 23, 1900, was the earliest of his many works in art criticism, and his book of essays *L'Art en silence,* published that same year, represented still another field in which, along with plays, short stories, and novels, he tried his skill.

Publication by Saint-Pol-Roux of *La Rose et les Epines du chemin, 1885–1900,* in 1901, brought again into the foreground the name of the creator of splendid metaphors. André Fontainas, Roux' intimate friend since the days of *La Pléiade* (1886), wrote an essay on the author of *Les Reposoirs de la procession.*[26] Roux' poetry, his play *La Dame à la faulx,* and his prose-poems, in which assonance and refrain furnished the music and arresting images the quality of poetic diction, provided Fontainas with ample material for comment. Like Camille Mauclair,[27] Fontainas felt that Saint-Pol-Roux was unjustly neglected by critics and readers, and that the idealism of the poet who had adopted for his motto "La beauté, c'est l'exaltation de la beauté" was a worthy literary example. Roux, having returned to Brittany, was no longer contributing to periodicals, but Paul Fort, the other contemporary exponent of the prose-poem, appeared in many magazines. The sixth series of his *Ballades françaises,* published in 1902, was entitled *Paris sentimental ou le roman de nos 20 ans.* In this volume Fort, using his customary form, intermediary between prose and verse, made the setting an important factor: streets, bridges, and buildings of Paris were mentioned by name; the precise time of day was described. Although the title suggests a series of romantic memories, the tonality was not that of the past. Fort appeared very much a young man of twenty, probably because some of the poems had been composed long before their publication and because the poet, recalling a particular moment in his emotional life, was able to relive vividly past experience, incorporating it in present sensations.

Paris was also the background of Paul Souchon's *Elégies parisiennes* (1902), but the southerner did not accept the city with affection. In this volume, as well as in one written two years later, Souchon appeared as the man from the provinces, more or less discontented with living in the capital but fascinated by its metropolitan charm. A third volume in which the setting was important was Henri de Régnier's *La Cité des eaux.* Versailles, its palace in a sad state of disrepair and its gardens untended, inspired the poems (sonnets, quatrains, and traditional romantic meters) of this collection. Régnier did not merely describe, he drew from the scene a series of meditations on pomp, glory, the fleeting nature of things, the power of imagination, the charm of solitude.

One volume of poetry published in 1902 was a return to the atmosphere

of 1890. Entitled *La Mort du rêve*, it was by P.-N. Roinard, a poet whose
literary career was a series of disasters, but whose lyricism was much admired by some of his contemporaries. He had been one of the figures in
the beginnings of the symbolist era, publishing *Nos Plaies* in 1886. This
first volume was a bitter series of poems expressing his resentment at the
social injustice and what he felt to be the intellectual stagnation of the age.
Roinard had derived little fame from this volume because, dissatisfied with
what he had written, he very soon tried to withdraw all copies from circulation. Then he began writing the poems which were to form *La Mort
du rêve,* but publication was delayed while he engaged in a number of
other enterprises during the years 1890–1900. With Zo d'Axa, he founded
the anarchist newspaper *L'En-Dehors,* helped organize the *Exposition des
portraits du prochain siècle* in 1894, continued to frequent societies of social
protest, and, when the French government began to take measures against
anarchists, fled to Belgium where he remained two years. His contributions to Belgian and French newspapers were considerable, but were often
unsigned. It was not until 1901 that he finally arranged for publication of
La Mort du rêve. Some of these poems had been written as early as 1886,
others were composed shortly before the volume appeared, but each part
of the work was planned as the celebration of "le rêve," man's consciousness of his nature and of the universe. Roinard personified the enemies
and friends of the dream, choosing names as peculiar as those in William
Blake's prophetic books. There are Hulter the believer, Thurrbal the fol-
lower of instinct, Fnégor the denier. Chief of the foes of the dream is
Schingult the doubter who vainly tries to confuse and destroy man's faith
in himself. The author, wretched in his own existence, found a kind of
melancholy hope in a Utopian dream of eternal insouciance and tenderness:

> Je voudrais que, sans pleur, sans fatigue et sans trêve,
> On s'aimât d'un amour toujours renouvelé,
> > Si j'avais créé le Rêve.
> > > > > ("La Voix des choses")

Sometimes, as in the lines quoted, Roinard employed regular meters, but
there were poems in free verse and others patterned after folk songs. At
times the musical intention, the interior rhymes, the assonance, the vowel
repetitions recall the period around 1887 when Stuart Merrill published
Les Gammes and Henri de Régnier *Les Sites.* The refrain in Roinard's
"Chanson de l'oseraie" will serve to illustrate the preoccupation with sound
which had played such an eminent role during the symbolist era:

> Le Râle du vent sourd
> Loure et reloure une houle d'amour.

Roinard was given a banquet by his friends on June 25, 1902, Rodin presiding. A few critics, among them Quillard, wrote enthusiastically about *La Mort du rêve,* but Roinard was never to attain even a modest degree of fame as a poet. He deserves more than his obscure niche in anthologies of poets from Normandy. His voice, that of incurable idealism and equally incurable revolt, was essentially poetic and very rich in tonality and imagery.

After *Le Deuil des primevères* of 1901, Francis Jammes wrote *Le Triomphe de la vie* in 1902. He had intended to call the latter volume *Poésie,* thinking that it expressed better than the elegies and prayers of *Le Deuil des primevères* his personal concept of lyric art. *Le Triomphe de la vie* is composed of two parts, a narrative poem "Jean de Noarrieu" and a series of twenty-six little dramatic scenes called "Existences." The story of Jean de Noarrieu's liaison with the little peasant girl who is a servant in his house, and his renunciation of this misalliance when he sees that she really loves a shepherd of her own class is certainly not a very original theme. The realistic description of rural life, the earthy and pagan atmosphere give the poem its charm, but, unless the god addressed can be construed as a sort of combination of Pan and Ceres, seem strangely at odds with the Christian poet's invocation:

> Mon Dieu, donnez-moi l'ordre nécessaire
> à tout labeur poétique et sincère.

The pagan world appeared in less degree in the descriptions of village life, "Existences." It is true that utensils, animals, and plants were given the power of speech, but their voices were quite often lifted in praise of God and censure of man. Jammes' intention in "Existences" was not unlike that of Thornton Wilder in *Our Town.* The general atmosphere of the village, with its holidays and evening gatherings, its love affairs, its opinions of world events, its selfishness and avarice as well as its generosity and forgiveness, was presented in these little scenes. Jammes accomplished the unholy matrimony of romanticism and naturalism, telling us on the one hand of the seduction of servant girls, of venereal disease, of adultery, and giving us passages describing the beauty of nature on the other. He himself is one of the actors in this poem; he is "Le Poète" and it must be admitted that this self-portrait is at the opposite pole from that of the romantic hero. True, he was not understood by his fellow citizens, but he did not complain. He meditated on a number of things, but principally on his love affairs. He reflected on Rousseau's reveries; he wondered whether Claudel had left for China; he complained, like Fantasio, of the monotony of life: "Comme toutes ces boutiques sont parallèles!"

In this volume, as in his previous verse, Jammes managed to disconcert the critics. Sometimes he used rhyme, sometimes he chose assonance, and again he simply inserted a line of blank verse. At first glance his meter appears regular but suddenly becomes capricious; the alexandrine loses or gains a syllable. His language takes an elegant form only to fall into the most trivial or even vulgar expression. This is what writers have called his "voluntary awkwardness," his "artlessness," and even his "affectation."

The volumes of 1902 which we have mentioned were by writers who were in no sense newcomers to French literature. There were in addition some first volumes by younger poets which merit passing attention. Emile Despax published *Au seuil de la lande* in a small edition of 130 copies. A candidate for the Sully-Prudhomme prize, he missed it because he had not observed rigorous Parnassian rules of versification. Later, in 1905, these same poems were published in a larger volume, *La Maison des glycines,* and won the Archon-Despérouses award. Nevertheless, this little collection of verse attracted some attention and praise. Stuart Merrill admired the youthful tone and maturity of art in the volume, contrasting it with the work of his own generation, when young poets so often presented themselves as old and tired. *Au seuil de la lande* is filled with detailed notation of rural landscapes, either transcribed from direct impression or drawn from memory. An example of this latter procedure, with the use of the conditional tense conveying an imaginary rather than real experience, is the following:

> Je rêve un soir de charme grave. Les vallons
> Seraient bleus sous le noir-violet des collines;
> Des ramiers reviendraient vers les sourdes glycines
> Bourdonneuses au vol doré des lourds frelons.
>
> ("Sonnets")

André Spire's first volume of poetry was also published in 1902. Entitled *La Cité présente,* written partly in regular and partly in free meters, it lacked the strength and irony of his later volumes. In it was the sympathy with the commoner and his emotional life that was to become the keystone of Spire's utterance, but little attention was given the volume.

In the midst of abundant lyric verse of personal confession there appeared in 1902 a strange and violent volume of entirely different character entitled *La Conquête des étoiles.* The author was F. T. Marinetti, who had been one of the editors of the short-lived *Anthologie-Revue* of Milan and Paris and who, in 1901 and 1902, was traveling about Italy giving lectures and readings of French poetry. *La Conquête des étoiles* was called an epic poem, its characters being forces of nature: winds, waves and waterspouts. Perhaps the story of the poem is merely the account of a tempest on the ocean during a day and night, but personification creates the impression of the struggle of Titans. The leader of the assault on the heavens is "La Mer

Souveraine," and a ghostly creature she is with her spongy face and her mouth which is like a "ventouse." No one in the period except René Ghil had tried to create, through clashes of words and chaotic rhythms, such an effect of violence. This volume, as indeed most of Marinetti's future productions, found a cold reception. Justifiably, the author was accused of lacking good taste, of being bombastic and, worst of all, ludicrous.

There was another powerful voice, but one much more disciplined than that of Marinetti, in the poetry of 1902. This was heard in Verhaeren's *Les Forces tumultueuses,* a volume which gathered, in free and regular meters, the thoughts of the Belgian writer on human existence. Verhaeren's vision embraced a vast historical perspective, love being presented in the forms of Venus, Mary Magdalene, and Théroigne de Méricourt,[28] and the "Maîtres" taking the characters of the monk, the military leader, the politician, the banker, and the tyrant. The author spoke of science, of religion, of woman, of convicts, of madness, and of cities, wrote a series of poems on his own nature, and collected these disparate themes in a poem addressed to a future reader:

> Heures de chute ou de grandeur!—tout se confond
> Et se transforme en ce brasier qu'est l'existence,
> Seul importe que le désir reste en partance,
> Jusqu'à la mort, devant l'éveil des horizons
> > (*Les Forces tumultueuses,* p. 176)

Some of the strength and vigor of Verhaeren's style was present in the seventh series of Paul Fort's *Ballades françaises.* Published in 1903, the poems of *Les Hymnes de feu* offered a complete contrast to the preceding collection of *Paris sentimental.* Exuberant and spontaneous Fort had often been, but his vision in this celebration of man's union with the earth was vaster and more grandiose than in his earlier work. By 1903 it was apparent that Fort, intentionally varying not only tone but theme in his successive volumes, was transferring into verse his personal experience and emotion, the folklore and history of France, and much of his reading. Already, amid general admission of his virtuosity by the critics, came discreet warnings against this dangerous facility and fecundity in utterance. But in truth Fort's volume received scarcely more than passing mention; the form of his poetry had been so often discussed, the variety of his inspiration had been so amply commented upon, that little was left to be said.

As of 1903, the poets who were held in the highest esteem were Verhaeren, Régnier, Jammes, and Moréas. M.-A. Leblond in an article of February

---

28. The revolutionary heroine. Hervieu's only historical drama, *Théroigne de Méricourt,* appeared at the same time as Verhaeren's poem.

1904,[29] commented on the universal favor that the Belgian poet, alone of the symbolist generation, enjoyed in all literary circles. Master of free and regular meters, author of many volumes ranging from the hallucinatory and visionary to the intimate and descriptive, Verhaeren had written verse which pleased almost all tastes. Régnier, dedicating the sonnets of *La Cité des eaux* to his father-in-law Heredia, and "Le Sang de Marsyas," a poem in free verse, to the memory of Mallarmé, observed a dual loyalty which gave him a wide following. Jammes, with *Le Triomphe de la vie,* had gained a public for his sympathy with his fellow men and his vision of village life. Moréas, after the publication of the six books of *Stances,* had written little poetry, but in 1903 his poetic tragedy *Iphigénie,* given in the arena at Orange in August and at the Odéon in December, brought him back into the limelight he loved so well. Paul Souchon, in "Les Trois Iphigénies," [30] compared Moréas, not unfavorably, with Euripides and Racine. Moréas was interviewed by the press and amply explained how, through the mystery of atavism, he considered that he had been able to comprehend Euripides' dramatic intentions and to make them understandable to the public of the twentieth century.[31] Moréas' neoclassicism was not for all tastes, but he presided over a small literary court at the "Closerie des Lilas" and in 1904 he was privileged to receive acclaim such as the following from the pen of Jean de Gourmont: "Encore inachevée, l'œuvre de Jean Moréas est belle: il est sans doute un des premiers, sinon le premier de nos poètes." [32]

These four poets, Régnier, Verhaeren, Jammes, and Moréas, had been concerned with the symbolist movement. Some critics chose to show how in spite of their evolution they had been indelibly marked by that experience. Others demonstrated how their development marked the end of the symbolist aesthetic. Léon Vannoz, writing in *La Revue bleue* (May 23, 1903), stated categorically that "Le symbolisme, ou au moins l'école qui a vécu sous ce nom, achève de mourir." Vannoz was examining the question from the viewpoint of prosody, suggesting that Sully-Prudhomme's rules were far too conservative, and that while the form of verse had obviously undergone change, the hermetic and vague quality of symbolist poetry had not endured. Vannoz' comments on versification brought immediate reply from Sully-Prudhomme. In a rambling and not very coherent article on "La Prose, la poésie, et les vers," (*Revue bleue,* June 27, 1903) the sixty-four-year-old Parnassian stated that the reformers of prosody were bound for oblivion because of their penury of thought and lack of art. What Sully-Prudhomme said about the users of free verse had been uttered a few

29. *Mercure de France, 49,* 289–308.
31. *Le Temps,* Nov. 25, 1903.
30. *49* (March 1904), 655–71.
32. *Mercure de France, 51* (Sept. 1904), 658.

months before concerning the first recipient of the poetry prize bearing his name; despite the accurate syllabic count of V.-E. Michelet's *La Porte d'or,* no critics, not even the most conservative, had found a kind word for its thought and artistry. There was considerable surprise that the Sully-Prudhomme award had been given to a man forty years of age who had begun writing esoteric poetry during the symbolist period and whose verse was filled with neologisms and the vocabulary of the "décadents" of the 1880's.

Sully-Prudhomme must have been content with the large amount of current poetry which attempted to convey a serious message. Mithouard's *Les Frères marcheurs,* built on the disheartening idea that suffering leads to joy; Gustave Zidler's *La Terre divine,* a series of platitudes expressing patriotic love of France; and Sébastien-Charles Leconte's *La Tentation de l'homme,* conveying the perpetual anguish of man's search for understanding were examples of verse more didactic than lyric. None of this expository poetry was succcessful either with the critics or the public; the only praise for this labored form of lyricism came from *La Revue des poètes* and a few regional publications.

The naturists should have viewed with pleasure the descriptive passages in the volumes by women. Both Mme. de Noailles and Marie Dauguet were sometimes called "poètes de la nature." But this phenomenon gave Bouhélier and his friends small cause for rejoicing. Critics were often intent on explaining that the true naturists were those who had never allied themselves with any school.

The incursion of women poets that marked the turn of the century had continued unabated. In 1902 Lucie Delarue-Mardrus with *Ferveur,* Mme. de Noailles with *L'Ombre des jours,* Renée Vivien with *Cendres et Poussières,* Marie Dauguet with *A Travers le voile,* Nicolette Hennique with *Les Douze Labeurs héroïques,* and Jeanne Perdriel-Vaissière with *Le Sourire de Joconde* attested the vitality of the feminine muse. All these writers, except Nicolette Hennique, wrote a very personal form of verse in which the first person singular was ever present. In 1903 Renée Vivien's *Evocations,*[33] Jean Dominique's *La Gaule blanche,* and a first volume by Hélène Picard, *La Feuille morte,* offered a little more variety in tone. *Evocations* with its themes of the lonely people of the earth, "la vie antérieure," passion, and remorse, recalled Baudelaire even in its diction. *La Feuille morte* bore the subtitle "poème lyrique féerique," and the strophic arrangement revealed emulation of Hélène Picard's favorite poet, Alfred de Musset. The young Belgian writer, Marie Closset, who took the pseudonym of Jean Dominique, seems the most modern of the three in her use of

33. Her *Sapho,* a volume of translations and paraphrases, also appeared in 1903.

assonance, blank verse, and Verlainian repetition of sounds. Like so many of her sister poets, she gave a series of lyric confessions, but with much modesty, and even a tonality of mystery, absent from the verse of Mme. de Noailles, Lucie Delarue-Mardrus, and Renée Vivien.

ABOUT 1904 the situation in poetry became a confused series of attempts to establish a new poetic aesthetic, one in which neither the heritage of symbolism nor of the Parnasse would be dominant. The general directions were of two kinds: the concept of poetry as part of a cosmic rhythm, and the view that verse should eschew the individual in favor of collective experience. In other words some theorists favored transcending the earthly for a kind of eternal truth, while their opponents insisted on poetry's speaking to man in terms of his general terrestrial conditions. As theories evolved, the question of technique, free verse, "vers libéré," or regular meters usually made its appearance as a secondary issue.

The main target was symbolism. The new theorists were clearly dissatisfied with the evident popularity of romantic and descriptive verse, centered in the *Revue des poètes,* yet this innocuous expression of visual sensation was not so often attacked. But the complaints against symbolism were renewed: it had not succeeded in giving a comprehensive view of life, and it had not reached the public. Such accusations found rejoinder in Quillard, who observed that symbolism must have a very strong constitution to be so often declared dead, and in Stuart Merrill, who pointed out the vanity of the new doctrines. In 1904 the chief defense for symbolism occurred in the long preface to a volume of poetry, a preface much more important than the banal verse it introduced.

Tancrède de Visan's *Paysages introspectifs* contained this seventy-nine-page essay on symbolism. Beginning with the premise that nature is the real and objective, while truth is the synthesis of the objective and subjective, he suggested that the symbolists were in search of truth, seeing oceans of mystery behind sensory perception. He was not sure that they succeeded, but he admired their goal of creating poetry in which reality was conceived as an idea and the attempt to reach the soul of things. The symbolist poet, he said, saw with his eyes closed. He spoke directly, the symbol being the necessary expression of this inner vision, rather than an artistic device. He used rhythms which could best convey the psychic processes of the human mind. One noteworthy thing in this discussion of symbolism was Tancrède de Visan's effort to relate symbolism to foreign literatures; to Emerson's statement (in the essay "Nature") that "The world is mind precipitated, and the volatile essence is forever escaping again into the state of free thought"; to Ballanche's *Orphée* in which the philosopher says, "Notre poésie est un symbole. Au fond, le symbole est une vérité que la langue de l'homme ne peut pas dire à l'oreille de l'homme, et que l'esprit dit à l'esprit"; to Novalis' pronouncement, "Alles poetische muss märchenhaft sein." All these ideas led to Visan's title, to the introspective landscapes which are truth because they combine the objective and the subjective, expressing themselves through myth and legend, distilling eternal essence from what the senses gather.

As the Parisian magazines which had encouraged symbolist poetry disappeared (the *Revue blanche* in 1903 and *La Plume* in 1904), no others immediately emerged to fill their place. Mithouard's *L'Occident* presented only a few poets in 1904: Albert Clouart, Verhaeren, Lucien Rolmer, Fagus, Ducoté, and Francis de Miomandre. The *Mercure de France,* with sixteen poets, was more representative that year, but Vallette's magazine appeared static, depending mainly on the writers who had been associated with its first decade of existence: Stuart Merrill, Verhaeren, Edouard Dujardin, Francis Jammes, Paul Fort, and Louis le Cardonnel.[1] Fagus, born in 1872; Charles Guérin, born in 1873; and Tristan Klingsor, born in 1874, were *Mercure* poets who had begun writing after the height of the symbolist movement but who had certainly felt its impact.

The *Mercure* did encourage two poets in their early twenties. One was Guy-Charles Cros, the future author of *Le Soir et le Silence* (1908) and *Les Fêtes quotidiennes* (1912). The son of Charles Cros, the poet and inventor, he had ably translated the Danish poet Sophus Claussen. He often wrote in free verse, and, like his father, experimented with rhythmic prose. Most of his poetry was tender and emotional; he was commonly called a literary descendant of Verlaine.

The other protégé of the magazine was Lucien Rolmer. Born in Marseilles, he was the author of *L'Inconstance,* a small book of poems printed in that city in 1900. Two years later he came to Paris and embarked on a journalistic career. His poetic ideal was Henri de Régnier, and his poems often had the atmosphere of remembrance of and nostalgia for the past which was in Régnier's lines. Rolmer's verse appeared in many periodicals between 1904 and 1911. After that he became something of an object of ridicule, for he enunciated a peculiar poetic doctrine of "Floralisme" or "L'Ecole de la Grâce," and even founded a little magazine, *La Flora,* to express his beliefs. He died heroically, fighting at the front in 1916. His

---

1. The *Mercure's* list also included two conservative older poets, Marie Dauguet and Pierre de Bouchard.

Chants perdus of 1907 and 1911, the two volumes in which he collected his verse, are now forgotten.[2]

The remaining periodical of that group which the old and established magazines somewhat condescendingly dubbed "revues indépendantes" was *L'Ermitage*. Its director, Edouard Ducoté, granted much space to poetry. Some of its contributors were also those of the *Mercure:* Verhaeren, Jammes, and Merrill; but in the list of twenty-seven poets who appeared in its pages in 1904 was a fair representation of the younger generation, none over thirty years of age. Charles Derennes, Albert Erlande, Ernest Gaubert, A.-M. Gossez, Marc Lafargue, Olivier Calemard de la Fayette, Guy Lavaud, Léo Larguier, François Porché, Théo Varlet, J.-L. Vaudoyer, Lucien Rolmer, and Lucien Jean were among these younger writers. Such a group represents great eclecticism, much more comprehensive than that of the *Mercure de France*. Poets of the north (Gossez and Varlet), and of the south (such as Gaubert and Erlande), adherents of free verse and of regular meter, older and younger writers were welcomed by Ducoté, and by Henri Ghéon who was one of the assistant editors.

Seemingly, in 1904, *L'Ermitage* was unique in furnishing an organ for youthful poets of diverse inspiration and technique. The one outstanding attempt that year to found a periodical for poets was inspired by the dearth of possibilities for publication by young lyricists rather than the desire to promulgate literary doctrine. The founder was the twenty-one-year-old poet Jean Louis Vaudoyer; the name of the publication was *Les Essais*. Associated with Vaudoyer were some of his young friends, like himself newcomers to literature. They were Maurice Heine, Jean de Foville, Robert Ochs, Robert Vallery-Radot, and Fernand Divoire. The group was exceedingly conservative; even though *Les Essais* offered no specific program, the poems printed in the magazine, and the comments on other writers suggest a return to the tonality of romanticism. Jean de Foville, who contributed much of the critical comment, defined the concept of poetry held by himself and his friends: "On aime une poésie humaine, familière, rêveuse et attendrie, qui recueille nos désirs et nos regrets de chaque jour."[3] These words appeared in an essay in appreciation of the work of Fernand Gregh, and it was these qualities of verse which, in the eyes of the youthful critic, explained the success that Gregh had enjoyed since the publication of *La Maison de l'enfance* in 1897. Vaudoyer was an admirer of Mme. de Noailles' work; others whom he favored were Charles Guérin and Maurice Magre, both of whom contributed to *Les Essais*. Thus the periodical represented a preference for the lyric expression of the emotions, couched in a form which

---

2. See *Anthologie des écrivains morts à la guerre* (Malfère, 1924), *1*, 589–91, for a summary of Rolmer's life and work.

3. *Les Essais, 1* (July 1904), 237.

was not overly audacious. There was even a firm admiration for the Parnassians. Although Vaudoyer, Vallery-Radot, and Maurice Heine were principally authors of personal and emotional poems, they accorded an important place to Leconte de Lisle. Especial adulation went to that sturdy pillar of the Lemerre publishing house, André Rivoire; Jean de Foville rashly likened Rivoire's style to that of Racine.[4] One suspects that the group of *Les Essais,* all being very young, preferred poetry which expressed their time of life; whence their admiration for Magre's *Poème de la jeunesse* (1901) and for Rivoire's *Songe de l'amour* (1900) and *Le Chemin de l'oubli* (1904). It is most probable that they also hoped for some encouragement from *La Revue de Paris,* where both Gregh and Rivoire held posts. Vaudoyer evidently hoped to make *Les Essais* more than a little magazine, and chose an editorial policy which would not engage his publication in arguments or theories. It is through the positive admiration expressed for those poets who had been accepted by the established periodicals (Régnier, Noailles, Guérin), and the absence of comment on those associated with the little magazines, that the reader composes a definition of the outlook of *Les Essais.* No staunch advocates of free verse, few poets whose expression passed the frontiers of emotional and personal confession, were associated with the magazine.

Thus *Les Essais* failed to provide a means for contemporary poetic expression. Its pages contained much harmonious, sincere, and beautifully correct poetry, but nothing that indicated a desire to depart from themes dear to the early years of romanticism. The incursion of modernism was confined to weakened caesura and rhymes which would not have been acceptable before the symbolist period. These poems of amatory and religious exaltation, of fervor before the spectacle of nature, and of heartbreaks, seem closer to 1830 than 1904. *Les Essais,* without ever giving a poetic credo, belonged to the phenomenon of "Néo-romantisme," expressed in the preface to André Joussain's *Les Chants de l'aurore* (1905), and which culminated in 1910 with the *Anthologie Néo-romantique* assembled by Adrien Gaignon, and the founding of Camille Beaulieu's *La Renaissance romantique.*

Vaudoyer's magazine maintained its monthly appearance until August 1905, then appeared at four irregular dates until April 1906. The familiar pattern of financial difficulties and lack of a paid staff brought an end to this periodical, which did have, however, a longer life span than most others of its kind.

The outpourings of the heart by these young poets created an impression of honesty and vividness much greater than the sterile imitations of minor Parnassians which filled *La Revue des poètes* in 1904. That magazine shared most of the technical ideas on verse that were to be observed in *Les Essais,*

4. *3* (Jan. 1905), 240.

but it had a rigid program: "Maintenir notre poésie, sans réaction, ni révolution, dans la tradition nationale." Eugène de Ribier became director of *La Revue des poètes* in 1903 and continued until 1909. In 1904 the "comité de patronage" was composed of Coppée, Heredia, Mistral, Sully-Prudhomme, Rostand, and Theuriet. These were the names the magazine celebrated, as well as those of André Lemoyne, Georges Lafenestre, Albert Mérat, François Fabré, Achille Paysant, Frédéric Plessis, and Léonce Depont, all mature men whose ages ranged between forty and eighty.

No magazine represented more clearly the cleavage between the symbolist and Parnassian traditions than did *La Revue des poètes*. It presented a great number of young authors, but only five or six attained even a modest degree of fame. A disheartening lack of originality in the poems was the result of the refusal to accept change. The section reviewing volumes of verse, instituted in 1904, gave little except encomium for noble sentiments and careful workmanship. A necrological aspect of the periodical was maintained through the years by the successive deaths of those who were the magazine's patrons and contributors: Heredia in 1905, Sully-Prudhomme, André Theuriet, Achille Paysant, and André Lemoyne in 1907, Coppée in 1908, and Albert Mérat in 1909.

When Eugène de Ribier summed up the accomplishments of *La Revue des poètes* during 1904, he was able to say that his periodical had presented verses by almost a hundred poets, and, to prove that the periodical had not been narrow-minded, he added: "Et c'est avec une vraie joie que nous avons pu tendre fraternellement la main, sans rien renier de nos principes, à des poètes comme Louis le Cardonnel et comme Emile Verhaeren."[5]

The astonishingly high figure of nearly 100 poets, compared with the meager lists of the *Mercure de France* and *L'Ermitage,* merits comment. About a third of the contributors to *La Revue des Poètes* are identifiable as middle-aged or elderly poets who are generally classified as minor Parnassians. The other two-thirds are extremely obscure because they never published books. Consultation of regional anthologies or articles reveals that many of them were teachers or journalists in the provinces, but others elude the searcher. That many poets should prefer the canons of taste and technique imposed by Emile Faguet, who was the chairman of the reading committee for the *Revue des poètes,* is not astonishing. It is regrettable, however, that by the end of 1904, the magazine should chiefly pride itself on having "discovered" Louis Mercier, Arsène Vermenouze, and Gustave Zidler. All three might be described as celebrants of rustic simplicity. Mercier, born in 1870, with *Les Voix de la terre et du temps* (1903), Vermenouze, over fifty years old, with *Mon Auvergne* (1904), and Zidler, a middle-aged professor at the Lycée Hoche, with *La Terre divine* (1903), were pre-

5. *Revue des Poètes,* 8 (Jan. 1905), 3.

eminently descriptive poets whose perfect alexandrines and octosyllabic quatrains were filled with sincere and noble sentiments, but who might be taxed with monotonous enumeration of what their eyes saw, their ears heard, and their noses smelled.

One very young contributor to *La Revue des poètes* in 1904 and 1905 claims our attention. He is Louis Farigoule, born in 1885, who had already taken the pen name of Jules Romains. He had submitted "Memnon" to a poetry contest in the magazine in 1903 and had won second place. The statue which sings at dawn represents poetry, and Romains' alexandrines describe how this magic will drive away "Les Impurs." This was not Romains' only triumph of 1903, for his first volume of verse, *L'Ame des hommes,* was accepted for publication by the Société des poètes français. It appeared in 1904. Maurice Prax, one of the editors of *La Revue des poètes,* greeted the volume with enthusiasm, noting that the author revealed himself to be a powerful singer of the modern world and a genuinely talented poet.

In 1905 Romains launched his program of unanimism with an article in the April number of *Le Penseur,* "Les Sentiments unanimes et la Poésie" and an essay in *La Revue des poètes* of September, "Sur la poésie actuelle." In the latter article, Romains indicted contemporary verse as imitative and uniform, couched in hyperbolic imagery but in reality extremely banal. He blamed symbolism for this artificiality. "On peut être sévère pour le symbolisme qui, sans produire un seul chef d'œuvre authentique, a déformé la langue française et mis à la disposition des piètres esprits un arsenal d'expressions et d'images qu'on n'accusera jamais d'être naturelles." [6]

Before Romains could broach his theory of collective phenomena as the writer's proper inspiration he was obliged to demolish two other doctrines which seemed to touch on his own through their pronouncements of synthesis and of preoccupation with one's fellow men. These were Fernand Gregh's humanism and Adolphe Lacuzon's integralism. Acknowledging that both Gregh and Lacuzon had obscurely felt the need of bringing literature closer to the common man, Romains denounced their doctrines as a bid for publicity. Their thought, he said, in no way expressed the essential feelings of modern society.

Fernand Gregh, except for some kind words in *Les Essais* and a few comments from Gaston Deschamps in *Le Temps,* had indeed received a cold reception from most contemporaries for his manifesto of humanism. The statement that he offered nothing new, that he was merely giving a name to a phenomenon which had already occurred, and the insinuation that he was an irrepressible "arriviste" had appeared repeatedly. But Lacuzon represented a more formidable rival in 1905, for his statement of belief had appeared the preceding year and had been subscribed to by Cubelier de

6. *8* (Sept. 1905), 207.

Beynac, Adolphe Boschot, S.-C. Leconte, and Léon Vannoz. S.-C. Leconte's *La Tentation de l'homme* and *Le Sang de Méduse,* of 1903 and 1905, gave him a certain amount of prestige as a poet concerned with the general aspects of human existence; Boschot's *Poèmes dialogués* of 1900 contained a philosophical note which had irritated the foes of didacticism in poetry, but which had brought praise from Emile Faguet and Gustave Lanson. Beynac was principally interested in the nature of poetic inspiration. And this little group had the advantage of possessing a critic favorable to their views, Ernest-Charles of *La Revue bleue,* and even a quarterly review of their own, *Les Poèmes.*[7] Leconte, in a preface to *Le Sang de Méduse,* and Vannoz, in an introduction to *Le Poème de l'âme,* both in 1905, confirmed the directions of Lacuzon's thinking.

Integralism and Lacuzon himself are now forgotten, but his activity helped to set off a kind of chain reaction among theorists of verse. René Ghil, easily nettled when his influence was unrecognized, and especially so when the word "integration" was opposed to "synthesis," began a new series of *Les Ecrits pour l'art* in 1905. Gregh, founding *Le Mouvement* in 1905 and *Les Lettres* in 1906, created organs for exposing his poetic viewpoint. Paul Fort guarded the interests of the symbolists by founding *Vers et Prose.*

Some of the ideas of Lacuzon, pretentious and strange though they are, bear resemblances to current ideas. Conservative in matters of prosody, for he recognized syllabic count, he yet gave almost all his attention to the question of rhythm. "Dans l'œuvre du poète, le rythme est le geste de l'âme," he had stated categorically in 1902, in the preface to his volume of poems *Elévations.* Rhythm precedes the poetic act; it is the generating force of inspiration. Raising the notion of rhythm to cosmic proportions, Lacuzon called it a part of universal vibration. The entire world is nothing more than a vast orchestration of rhythms. The poet, by integrating thought and rhythm, reveals a portion of eternity. Poetry is a transcendent form of wisdom, an ecstatic revelation of knowledge, accomplished not by synthesis (a stone aimed at Ghil's flower bed), but by a dynamic process through which a state of mind is inscribed in a symbol. Lacuzon's conclusion was as follows: the poetic symbol integrates potential knowledge; rhythm, the emotional factor, identifies this knowledge with our spiritual experience and creates poetry.

These high-flown utterances of 1904 prefigured many similar ones during the next decade: "dramatisme," "simultanéisme," "dynamisme," and "totalisme." A part of Lacuzon's theory seems indeed to descend from "la poésie scientifique" of Ghil and perhaps from the "synthésisme" of Jean

7. During 1904 four issues appeared. In addition to Lacuzon's immediate group, contributors included Léon Bocquet, Renée Vivien, Lucie Delarue-Mardrus, and Charles Guérin.

de la Hire. Integralism attained temporarily a wider diffusion than most other doctrines, in that it became the subject of a book, Jacques Rousselle's *Au commencement était le rythme* (1905), and of articles such as S.-C. Leconte's "D'un avenir possible de la poésie," printed in *La Grande Revue* in October 1905.

An opposition is immediately apparent between the pseudophilosophical credo of integralism and the doctrines which sought to bring collective mankind into the orbit of poetry. In this category is Romains' unanimism, which became, unlike integralism, a lasting literary idea. Its sources were varied; its adherents, many of them talented writers, came from several groupings. First writing poetry, they later attained fame in fiction and drama.

One of the most fruitful directions of twentieth-century poetry was that which turned from the confession of individual emotion to conscious consideration of man as a social being. Opposed to hermeticism and adornment as the foundation stone of lyric beauty, this verse sought a better understanding of man in relation to his fellow beings and to the world in which he lived. Some of its objectives had been contained in Verhaeren's poetry and even in portions of the incoherent doctrines of René Ghil and of naturism. The opposition to Mallarmé and the complaints concerning symbolist isolation in the last years of the nineteenth century were presages of the tendency, but it was a literary grouping which served to give focus and meaning to this turn of thought during the early years of the twentieth. This was the company that was to live or visit at Créteil in 1906-07, and among whom were René Arcos, Charles Vildrac, Georges Duhamel, and Jules Romains.

René Arcos' first volume of verse, *L'Ame essentielle,* was published in 1903. The title is significant in that it indicates the questing spirit which pervaded all of the author's works and indeed most of the volumes written by the group of Créteil. From personal experience and observation Arcos strove to discover not his emotional world but the pulse of humanity. Life was what interested him; *La Vie* was the name chosen by him and his friends Mercereau, Vildrac, and Valmy-Baysse for a literary magazine in 1904. Many of the poets who contributed to the periodical had a comparable vision of existence. Fernand Gregh was the author of *La Beauté de vivre* (1900) and *Les Clartés humaines* (1904), Paul Souchon of *La Beauté de Paris* (1903). Maurice Magre's *La Chanson des hommes,* published in 1898, had been prefaced by a denunciation of poets who withdrew from their fellow men. Arcos and Vildrac chose these as the worthy poets, writers who heard and recorded the cries of the crowd, who shared the emotions of both rural and city dwellers. In a word, these were poets who had social consciousness.

Such aims were not without peril for poetic beauty, as some critics observed when Magre published his *Poème de la jeunesse* (1901). In this volume poems of personal inspiration alternated with cries against social injustice, and the latter type of expression, though filled with pity for suffering humanity, displeased most of the critics. Magre, who had left his native city of Toulouse in 1898, was deeply affected, much as was Eugène de Rastignac, by the spectacle of evil in Paris. In one of the poems of the volume he evoked evening in the capital with Baudelairian horror, though not Baudelairian art:

> Tes maisons de plaisir et tes prostituées,
> La rumeur de leur rire et l'odeur de leur fard,
> Les baisers et les vins dans les orgies mêlés,
> Les rôdeuses tournant, blêmes, dans le brouillard
>
> Comme au vent de la nuit tournent les feuilles sèches,
> Les cris de la misère et de la volupté
> Font tellement de bruit que dans l'ombre ils empêchent
> La vierge de dormir, le sage de penser.— [8]

This, rather than his expression of personal emotion, was the part of Magre's poetry which brought him into the orbit of *La Vie*. Both Arcos and Vildrac favored the theme of the crowd rather than the solitary dreamer. That is why Souchon, another man from the provinces who made Paris the subject of a volume, was also of their fellowship.

This was the group which Arcos and Vildrac gathered in 1904. As Jules Romains gained prestige, certain exclusions occurred. Gregh's particular doctrine of "humanisme," Souchon's dramatic ventures which had little to do with collectivism, and Magre's decision to direct *Le Mouvement* explain in part divergencies with Arcos' and Vildrac's tacit acceptance of "La Vie unanime." It was chiefly Romains' attack against imitation, his summons to create a new kind of poetry, that alienated some of the poets of *La Vie* and attracted others. The collectivist idea was the bond which united *La Vie* to the Abbaye de Créteil.

Charles Vildrac, twenty-two years old in 1904, had chiefly been associated with the group of *Le Beffroi* until the founding of *La Vie*. His was the dream of an association of artists, craftsmen, thinkers, and writers, who would live together. Even before the discovery of the available property at Créteil he had written:

8. *Le Poème de la jeunesse*, "Paris," printed in Walch, *Anthologie des poètes contemporains*, 3, 247.

> Je rêve l'Abbaye hospitalière
> A tous épris d'art plus ou moins crottés
> Parce que plus ou moins déshérités . . .[9]

In 1904, in his twentieth year, Alexandre Mercereau had not yet published a volume. In that year his *Thuribulums affaissés* appeared under the auspices of *La Vie,* of which he was managing editor. Georges Duhamel, completing his studies in medicine, was the same age as his friend Mercereau. At this time, as he confessed in the preface to his first volume, *Des Légendes, des batailles* (1907), he was haunted by Renan's concept of the ideal human being who would be scholar, philosopher, and artist. He wished his poetry to be universal in its implication, varied in its form, and above all filled with the fervor of living.

While the denomination of "poètes unanimistes" is inept for those who frequented the Abbaye de Créteil from 1906 to 1908, posterity has so grouped them. All the poets of the Abbaye protested that their artistic beliefs were separate and individual, but the general concept of "La Vie unanime," the transference of personal emotion and experience to collective significance, so dominated the verse of Vildrac, Arcos, Mercereau, and Duhamel that they have become an "école de poètes." Romains furnished a convenient label, one which could also be applied to the early work of a poet from Grenoble, H.-M. Barzun. This writer's first collections of verse, privately printed in 1903 and 1905, had been entitled *Jeunesse* and *Adolescence.* In them he had sought to convey the enthusiasms and distress of youth, not as an individual phenomenon, but a collective one. Sympathetic with the spirit that animated the group of the Abbaye he embarked on his *Terrestre Tragédie,* a poem later amplified into five volumes on modern man, his thought, his passions, and his driving forces.

Those who were to be of the Abbaye de Créteil, despite a small degree of publicity surrounding the founding of *La Vie,* were relatively unknown in 1904 and even in 1905. Later they were to find their way into Paul Fort's *Vers et Prose* and Jean Royère's *Phalange,* a strange association for poets whose earliest work was predicated on the conviction that symbolism had been invidious in its introspection and absence of social concern. In one respect they had, from the first, been friendly toward a symbolist phenomenon, liberty in versification. This was almost sufficient reason to gain the sympathies of Paul Fort or Vielé-Griffin.

Indeed, in 1904, this question of metrics was often considered the real contribution of the symbolists. A contemporary pamphlet by a Belgian, Arthur Daxhelet, treated the movement from this point of view. Entitled "Une

9. *Poèmes: 1905,* Editions du Beffroi, 1906.

Crise littéraire," Daxhelet's essay, first published in *La Revue de Belgique,* concludes: "La crise symboliste fut utile et féconde puisqu'elle ranima la poésie française qui se mourait dans les chaînes dorées dont elle s'était elle-même chargée et qu'elle lui infusa un sang nouveau; puisqu'elle suscita, entre autres, des Maeterlinck, des Verhaeren, des Henri de Régnier que la notoriété a déjà élus et que la gloire couronnera demain." [10]

When one considers the principal volumes of poetry containing free verse published in late 1903 and during 1904, he easily comprehends the common identification of symbolism and free verse. *Le Délassement du guerrier* was by Edouard Dujardin of the *Revue indépendante* and *La Revue wagnérienne; La Chanson d'Eve* by Van Lerberghe of *La Wallonie; La Prairie en fleurs* by Ducoté of *L'Ermitage;* and *Schéhérazade* by Tristan Klingsor of the third *Vogue.* Their themes differed, ranging from philosophical meditation through love poems and bucolic descriptions to Asiatic legends, yet they all practiced the free forms which had developed during the symbolist era.

But there were, of course, symbolists who had been unaffected by the vogue of free verse. Precisely in 1904 appeared a volume of verse about half of which consisted of poems printed between 1885 and 1893 in such periodicals as *Le Scapin, Le Chat Noir, Chimère, La Plume, L'Ermitage, Le Saint-Graal,* and the *Mercure de France.*[11] The author was Louis le Cardonnel, now forty-two years of age, and an abbé, whose work had not hitherto appeared in book form. Admiration for Baudelaire, Verlaine, and Mallarmé left definite imprint on the diction and music of these poems (as on many others which Le Cardonnel piously excluded from his volume), but their form was so rigorous that it gained the approbation of the ultra-conservative *Revue des poètes* and of the intransigent critic of *Le Temps,* Gaston Deschamps.

The *Poèmes* of Le Cardonnel were much discussed in 1904, both by his symbolist friends of the 'nineties such as Retté and Merrill, and by Catholic writers such as Mithouard of *L'Occident* and the poet Armand Praviel who directed *L'Ame latine* in Toulouse. From both groups the volume received favorable comment; the artistry pleased the first, and the thought the others. In *La Revue de Belgique,* Isi Collin counted le Cardonnel's *Poèmes,* along with Van Lerberghe's *Chanson d'Eve,* among the most beautiful poetic volumes of the year.

Since many of Le Cardonnel's poems were inspired by his religious experience, they earned for their author the title of mystic, setting him apart

10. A. Daxhelet, *Une Crise Littéraire* (Brussels, Weissenbach, 1904), p. 87. In *La Revue de Belgique, 41* (June 15, 1904), 193, the wording is slightly different.

11. Thanks to the two dissertations by Noël Richard, *Louis le Cardonnel* and *Louis le Cardonnel et les revues symbolistes,* we have full documentation.

from his fellow writers. Comparable individuality was seen by a few critics in Nau's *Hiers bleus,* where ocean voyages and far lands contributed a strong exotic atmosphere. Other poets seemed to fall into more definitely established categories. Marie Dauguet's *Par l'amour* was filled with pantheistic love of nature, but so was the poetry of Mme. de Noailles. Charles Derennes' *L'Enivrante Angoisse* was the record of hopes and lost illusions, but Olivier de la Fayette's *Le Rêve des jours* was built on similar themes. Most poets were content to voice their personal outlooks on life, without pretensions of social preoccupations or philosophical significance. They were, for the moment, not so much in the public eye as were the codifiers of poetic aims. But many of them have survived longer than Lacuzon's integralism and given greater meaning to poetic art by its expression rather than its theory. The literary independence preserved by the admirers and friends of Jules Romains, their sympathy with, but not allegiance to, his ideas, were the salutary aspect of that grouping.

CHAPTER 5. A Crucial Year (1905)

In 1905 two efforts were made to discover the directions of French literary genres and to present a panoramic picture of letters. Georges le Cardonnel and Charles Vellay, in planning their *Littérature contemporaine,* decided to use the method employed by Huret in 1891, that is to question writers about current ideas and possible future evolution of poetry, the novel, the drama, and criticism. Many of the interviews were printed in the newspaper *Gil Blas* before being collected in the volume. As individual pictures of personalities these items were not without interest, but the collected answers of writers were so varied, so narrowly personal, that no clear picture could be obtained in any of the four literary fields. The Huret questionnaire had been unrewarding in most respects, but it had revealed, despite the diversity of replies, strong opposition to Parnassian description and to naturalistic realism; Le Cardonnel's and Vellay's cannot claim even such general results.

The poets' replies were exactly what could be expected from the published works of each individual. Henri de Régnier disclaimed a belief in important innovations either in romanticism or symbolism; he refused to accept the expression "renaissance classique" as fraught with significance. The poet has no social role; his task is to create beautiful verse, either in traditional or free meters. Verhaeren was opposed to the return to classicism, feeling that imitations might limit creative force and result in doing less ably what had already been well done. He believed that poetry might turn toward pantheism as its theme. Vielé-Griffin insisted on the triumph of free verse, Moréas on that of traditional meters and the return to classicism. Charles Guérin felt that poetry was gradually leaving the realm of dreams for the spectacle of nature, and that free verse was losing ground. Paul Fort explained why he felt it necessary to permit the symbolist group to reaffirm its existence by the creation of *Vers et Prose,* stating categorically that nothing had been accomplished in poetic literature which did not stem from the symbolist movement. Francis Jammes answered his questioners by referring to the disappearance of fabulous monsters from poetry and the return of domestic livestock. He and Vielé-Griffin, he thought, were the principal forerunners of rustic realism. Art was traveling toward moderation and simplicity.

The admiration expressed by a number of writers for the works of Henri de Régnier, Vielé-Griffin, Verhaeren, Mme. de Noailles, and Charles Guérin,

54

was the one positive result of the enquiry insofar as poetry was concerned. Another side of the picture was given by the portraits of masters with few or no disciples: Gregh and his humanism, Lacuzon and integralism, René Ghil and scientific poetry. Saint-Georges de Bouhélier would also have been a lonely figure had Maurice Le Blond not answered the questionnaire by stating that current literature was in accord with the principles of naturism.

Almost all the writers consulted condemned contemporary criticism, which they felt was founded on venality and favoritism. The critic who received most praise, in spite of a brief but scathing denunciation from Van Bever, was Jean Ernest-Charles. His "Samedis littéraires" in *La Revue bleue* were founded on the idea of separating the "industriels de la littérature" from true writers. The latter, he said, were few in number. Ernest-Charles announced that contemporary schools of writers were stupid, but he approved the ideas of tradition, clarity, and harmony. He did not mention Lacuzon's integralism, toward which his articles in *La Revue bleue* had appeared favorable.

The other important work on literary trends in 1905 was also the result of collaboration of two writers. Georges Casella and Ernest Gaubert, both twenty-four years of age, set about studying *La Nouvelle Littérature 1895–1905*. Casella, a native Parisian, had made three attempts to found a literary periodical: *L'Effort de Paris* (1900), *La Revue dorée* (1901), and *La Renaissance latine* (1903). While he was director of the second of these little magazines, he had published a volume of verse and a one-act play, and had contributed to several reviews and newspapers. His collaborator Gaubert, born in a village near Montpellier, had been at the age of seventeen one of the founders of *L'Aube méridionale,* the first issue of which appeared in January 1898. This little magazine, first published in Béziers, was transferred to Montpellier, and finally, in 1901, was absorbed by Henri Rigal's *Le Titan.* By 1905 both Gaubert and Casella were writing for *La Revue illustrée,* where Casella's "Chronique littéraire" had included essays on Adrien van Bever, Charles-Henry Hirsch, and Gérard d'Houville, and where the two writers collaborated on a series, "La Jeune Littérature." Gaubert had been writing some of the little monographs published by Sansot under the title "Les Célébrités d'aujourd'hui." François Coppée, Pierre Louÿs, and Jean Lorrain had been among the subjects of his study. In *La Nouvelle Littérature,* it was Gaubert who contributed most of the material relating to poetry.

The important poetic movements in the twentieth century, according to Gaubert, were Gregh's humanism, Lacuzon's integralism, and the renaissance of traditional French culture proclaimed by Louis Bertrand and others. It is not strange that Gaubert should speak of these movements, for Gregh's manifesto of December 12, 1902 in the *Figaro,* Bertrand's preface to Joachim Gasquet's *Chants séculaires* (1903), and Lacuzon's pronouncement of January 16, 1904 in *La Revue bleue* had excited much comment in the press. Gaubert, who was definitely on the side of tradition as opposed to innovation, made no claim for the success of current theories, and he was extremely skeptical about regionalism and social preoccupation as the bases of poetic art.

Faced with the difficult problem of grouping poets, Gaubert admitted his incompetence. He finally chose nine main headings: "Naturistes et Toulousains," "Symbolistes," "Indépendants," "Parnassians," "L'Humanisme," "L'Ecole romane," "La Renaissance latine," "Les Groupes provinciaux," and "Les Femmes et la Poésie."

Casella and Gaubert had announced in their preface that they considered 1905 a period of literary anarchy and confusion, and that they would reserve their highest praise for writers who had kept the national tradition of clearness, sobriety, and method. This viewpoint explains the limits of their work, for the editors excluded from discussion many of the most interesting names. Their book remains interesting today for its documentation of regionalism and for early revelation of a few poets who were to gain some measure of fame. Van Bever and Léautaud's *Poètes d'aujourd'hui* in its 1905 edition did not yet offer the names of Charles Derennes, Emile Despax, Léon Deubel, Tristan Klingsor, Philéas Lebesgue, S.-C. Leconte, Mme. de Noailles, or Paul Souchon. *La Nouvelle Littérature* considered them worthy of attention, giving biographical and bibliographical information.

Two provincial groups, besides the southerners with whom Gaubert first had been associated, were given special mention. According to Casella and Gaubert, the poets of *Le Beffroi* of Lille, under the leadership of Léon Bocquet, best carried on the traditions of Rodenbach and Samain, while in Nancy *La Grange lorraine,* with Charles Guérin, Paul Briquel, and René d'Avril, represented another strong center of regionalist activity.

Casella and Gaubert, unable to discern definite tendencies in literary criticism, did note some important current ideas: the return to reason, method, and clarity; respect for traditional form in grammar, vocabulary, and syntax; hostility toward romanticism. The basis for this choice, though it was not openly stated in *La Nouvelle Littérature,* would seem to have been the numerous articles by Charles Maurras in *La Revue encyclopédique* and those by Jean Ernest-Charles in *La Revue bleue.* The section on criticism was little concerned with poetry as a genre, but this was hardly the fault of Casella and Gaubert. The one important volume of poetic criticism thus far produced in the twentieth century was André Beaunier's *La Poésie nouvelle;* other works such as Retté's *Le Symbolisme* were largely anecdotal, or else technical, as was Robert de Souza's *Le Rythme poétique.* Remy de Gourmont's two volumes of 1896 and 1898, *Le Livre des masques,* remained one of the best critical evaluations of poetry.

Vellay and Le Cardonnel had produced an anthology of writers' opinions in 1905; Casella and Gaubert had tried to ascertain the literary spirit of their times. Neither volume was really satisfactory, and perhaps the choice of poets in the referendum published in the December issue of *Le Beffroi* reveals more about current trends of poetry than either of the books. The first six elected for the imaginary Academy of Poets represented a good cross-section of contemporary poetic ideas. Verhaeren, admired for his multiple qualities of imagination, realism, humanism, imagery, and power, had affinities with Romains, Vildrac, Barzun, and other young writers who wished to strengthen poetry both in its message and its expression. Henri de Régnier and Charles Guérin, recently the authors of *La Cité des eaux* and *Le Cœur solitaire,* were related to the host of gentler musicians whose chief source of inspiration came from memory and whose art relied on personal confession. The more enthusiastic voice of Mme. de Noailles had relationship not only with other women poets but with male writers like Souchon and Olivier de la Fayette who fervidly expressed their love of nature. Jean Moréas, by the rigorous but varied prosody of *Les Stances,* held the esteem of those who extolled tradition as the basis of lyric art. Francis Jammes, choosing simplicity and artlessness rather than noble expression, represented a poetic tonality, not devoid of fantasy, that had kinship with Fagus and Toulet. In his religious themes and in those of rusticity, he showed other affiliations.

The denomination of symbolist had not disappeared by 1905, although it had become vague. Casella and Gaubert, under the heading "symbolistes," included the names of Fort, Gide, Guérin, Hirsch, Klingsor, Ducoté, Lebey, Jammes, and Bataille. They designated as "néo-symbolistes" Tancrède de Visan, Olivier de la Fayette, and Ghéon. Allied to symbolism, according to their classification, were Segard, Degron, Chanvin, Pilon, Jaloux, Nau, Mandelstamm, and Gabriel de Lautrec. This list, questionable in many respects, was compiled from the contributors of verse to the *Mercure de France, L'Ermitage,* the last issues of *La Revue blanche,* and the initial ones of Fort's *Vers et Prose.* What determined the authors' omissions and inclusions must remain mysterious. Insisting that they were writing on "la jeune littérature," they yet spoke of some authors who by date of birth and publication of works belonged to the past; they mentioned only a few Belgian writers, excluding some of greatest contemporary interest.

Still, broadly speaking, the choice of the symbolist designation for poets welcomed by the periodical directors Vallette, Ducoté (or Gourmont and Gide), and Fort is not erroneous. The sympathies and friendships of these men were largely directed toward the poets who had been associated with the movement. What can happen when the editorial staff of a magazine undergoes radical change is well illustrated by the rebirth of *La Plume,* which occurred between February and July 1905. Karl Boès was still director, but for financial reasons he had decided to merge with another little magazine called *Europe artiste,* accepting Albert Trotrot and Ricciotto Canudo as managing editors. *Europe artiste* had been mainly concerned with aesthetic philosophy, painting, and music, rather than literature. The new series of *La Plume* reflected this direction of interest, an essay by Guillaume Apollinaire on the early work of Picasso[1] being much more arresting than any judgments on poetry. The only extensive essay on a poet, written by Olivier de la Fayette, concerned the verse of Léo Larguier. Both the author and the subject were indication of the poetic policy of the new *Plume*. La Fayette, the author of a first volume *Le Rêve des jours* (1904), and Larguier, whose second volume *Les Isolements* had just been published, both fitted into the general classification of neoromanticism. Few audacities in prosody, a tone of personal confession, and much description of nature were the common ground of their art. Although Larguier's expression tended to greater simplicity than did La Fayette's, the note of lofty idealism, expressed in harmonious and flowing meter, was the keystone of their lyricism. The other poets who contributed to *La Plume* in 1905 did not vary greatly from this pattern. Gasquet, Casella, Valentine de Saint-Point, Charles Guérin, and Marie Dauguet were all writing comparable idealistic and intimate verse. Two little poems by Guillaume Apollinaire—"Automne" and "La Fuite"—suggest the romantic ballad. The varied measures of a poem by Verhaeren stand out in the midst of offerings of regular verse.

One link with the magazine's past remained. This was Jean Moréas, whose volumes had been published by *La Plume* since 1894, and whose destiny was intimately linked with the magazine after 1891, the year of the special number on "Le Symbolisme de Jean Moréas." Almost the last volume printed by *La Plume* was Moréas' *Les Stances,* in an edition containing all six books.[2] When the magazine suspended publication on July 1, 1905, the *Mercure de France* immediately arranged with Moréas for a reprinting of *Les Stances.* This appeared in 1906, followed by new editions of Moréas' earlier work.

L'Ermitage lasted eighteen months longer than *La Plume,* its last number appearing in December 1906. During its last two years the magazine's format was larger, and Ducoté added André Gide and Remy de Gourmont as associate editors. The magazine continued to offer a good representation of poetry, much of it in free verse but mingled with samples of Parnassian

---

1. *La Plume,* No. 372 (May 15, 1905), pp. 477–84.
2. *La Plume* had printed two series of *Les Stances* in 1899 and 1901. This was the first complete edition.

technique and theme. The exotic atmosphere of Ghéon's Algerian poems, the familiar tone of Jammes' verses, the struggle between flesh and soul in Vallery-Radot's lines, the neoclassicism of Henri de Régnier's "Phrixus" (in which a centaur tells of the glimpse he had of Pegasus rising from the earth), the description of a village religious procession related in free verse by F.-P. Alibert, the celebration of October in a sonnet by Marc Lafargue testify to broad tastes in the editorial staff.

The magazine, which had printed Claudel's *L'Echange* in 1901, offered one of the most curious of that writer's poetic compositions in its July 1905 issue. This was the series of ten poems, written in 1895 in regular alexandrines, which has become known as the "Vers d'exil" since their inclusion in the *Mercure de France* edition of Claudel's *Théâtre.* These solemn lines of valedictory to Europe seemed even stranger in the middle of 1905 just after *Les Muses* had appeared from the presses of *L'Occident.* The unrhymed free rhythms of Claudel's ode were the antithesis of the regular measures of the "Vers d'exil." Vielé-Griffin probably considered the latter a youthful error on Claudel's part; at any rate he became rapturous on the subject of *Les Muses,* saying, "le mutisme de Mallarmé éclate. La force désordonnée de Rimbaud s'indigue vers un but." [3]

The magazine's section of reviews of current volumes of poetry was, on the other hand, partisan and narrow. Vielé-Griffin was supposed to make a report on poetry twice a year. He wrote three of these, but his comment was almost limited to his championship of free verse and his dislike of regular meters. During 1905 he took umbrage at an article by André Gide published in *L'Ermitage.* Writing on Heredia, Gide gave approval to traditional and free poetic techniques. Conservative poets, countered Vielé-Griffin, have so little consciousness of their natural culture that they consider it immobilized. Free verse is truly French in spirit, since it stems from the idea of unity between form and thought. Borrowing from Mithouard's imagery, Vielé-Griffin compared the asymmetries of free verse with those of the Gothic cathedrals.

Then, in February 1906, Fernand Gregh founded *Les Lettres,* and in March became one of the sponsors of *Le Mouvement,* directed by Maurice Magre. Both of these new publications pronounced against free verse, and Vielé-Griffin's principal effort became an attack against Gregh in which he was abetted by Henri Ghéon, whose *Algérie,* written in free verse, had just appeared.

Four contemporary poets received acclaim in essays which appeared in *L'Ermitage* during 1905 and 1906. Jean de Gourmont wrote on Henri de Régnier, Jean-Marc Bernard on Vielé-Griffin, Ernest Gaubert on Charles

3. *L'Ermitage, 1905 1* (June 1905), 387–8.

Guérin, and Francis de Miomandre on Jean Dominique. Jean de Gourmont stressed the complexity of Régnier's poetry; the spontaneity of emotion directly transcribed; the misty reaches of memory; dream and reality; and the variety in poetic techniques. Gaubert pictured Guérin as having reached a new height in subjective poetry by the publication of *L'Homme intérieur* (1905). Bernard's article, after a few caustic remarks directed against Gregh, Magre, and Lacuzon, dwelt on the religious themes of Vielé-Griffin's *L'Amour sacré*. The grouping of Vielé-Griffin with the Catholic poets Louis le Cardonnel, Charles Guérin, and Francis Jammes was an inevitable error on Bernard's part. Confusion of a taste for legend with religious ferver, of a distant ideal with the notion of God, were natural for Bernard's pious nature.

Francis de Miomandre's was the first important essay on the Belgian school teacher who had by 1906 signed three volumes of poems with the pen name of Jean Dominique. The reviewers of these books, including Miomandre, either were not aware that they were speaking of a woman poet or else were discreetly guarding the secret of her identity. Music and sensibility were the qualities that had been praised in brief bibliographical comments on *L'Ombre des roses* (1901) and *La Gaule blanche* (1903). Jean Dominique's third volume, *L'Anémone des mers* (1906), inspired Miomandre's essay. Not only the delicate shadings of mood and the fusion of landscape and feeling claimed his attention, but also a technical device which often appeared in the poet's alexandrines and which created a metrical disparity forbidden by tradition. A quatrain from *La Gaule blanche* quoted by Miomandre will illustrate the device, which consists in placing a word beginning with a consonant after a mute "e" at the caesura:

> Peu à peu, la poussière, légère et solennelle,
> Montera jusqu'aux lèvres, jusqu'aux yeux, presqu'au front
> De ma vie puérile et pauvre, et fera d'elle
> Une momie étroite, parfumée et sans nom.[4]

This brief survey of *L'Ermitage* has brought us to the end of 1906, but has not taken account of the founding of new magazines which espoused the cause of poetry and which absorbed to a certain degree its collaborators during its final issues. Two of the new arrivals, Paul Fort's *Vers et Prose,* a quarterly which first appeared in March 1905, and Jean Royère's *La Phalange,* a monthly magazine which first appeared in July 1906, through their longevity and breadth of interests, merit extended study. Other magazines, of minor importance because of their short existence or restricted poetic outlook, can be briefly mentioned.

4. These lines are from "Je ne sens point passer . . . ," which is included in Alphonse Séché, *Les Muses françaises* (L. Michaud, 1909), 2, 100.

In the latter group is a periodical which first appeared in March 1905, at the same time as *Vers et Prose.* Its title was *Les Ecrits pour l'art,* the name of René Ghil's periodical of 1887–1892. The founder was Jean Royère, a thirty-four-year-old poet who had just published his second volume, *Eurythmies.* A dual influence, Ghil's theories of sound-sense relationship and Mallarmé's hermeticism, dominated Royère's ideas of poetry in 1904 and 1905. Lines from one of the "Eurythmies," the twilight meditation of the poet seated near a lighted lamp and dreaming of remembered love, will illustrate these affinities:

> J'écoute à la clarté des choses endormies,
> Dans l'Espace assoupi de traînantes phalènes,
> La cendre remuer sur vos lèvres blêmies
> Et sous le plomb figé la fraîcheur d'une haleine.
>
> Vous, nul azur béant, mais une lampe amie,
> Ariane aux secrets du vivant labyrinthe,
> Venez guider l'amour dans les lacs de la crainte
> Et d'un doigt somnambule égrener les momies . . .[5]

Closer in spirit to Mallarmé than to Ghil, since his tone remained personal rather than epic, and since his technique was based on "constellations" of words (the past: "choses endormies," "la cendre," "plomb figé," "les momies"; the course of meditation: "Traînantes phalènes," "Ariane," etc.), Royère soon renounced Ghil's themes. But in 1905 he recognized Ghil as a leader. In *Les Ecrits pour l'art* he printed verse by Marinetti, and in the later numbers of the magazine poems by Arcos, Mercereau, and Vildrac attested a faith in the collectivist aim of poetry. Thus the magazine was principally an organ for the founder of scientific and evolutionary verse. Ghil had lost none of his assurance, for, in the first number, announcing the coming of a new poetic age, he concluded with these words: "J'ai été le décisif commencement moderne de ce Poète-philosophe dont d'Autres seront la suite différenciée." [6] In the year that was the life span of *Ecrits pour l'art,* Ghil had the illusion of being the leader of a school in which Robert Randau, J.-A. Nau, Edgar Boès, and Sadia Lévy were disciples, and to which he hoped to add the poets of the "Abbaye."

The first number of F. T. Marinetti's international monthly, *Poesia,* was published in February 1905. Though printed in Milan, it was from the beginning partly a French magazine. Kahn and Mauclair contributed to its first issue; in March, Mme. de Noailles, Merrill, Paul Fort, and Mistral were featured; in April, Catulle Mendès, Vielé-Griffin, and Saint-Georges

---

5. The poem is quoted in Walch, *Anthologie des poètes contemporains, 3,* 398.

6. In his *Les Dates et les Œuvres,* Ghil claimed that futurism, Verhaeren, and the poets of "L'Abbaye" all owed much to his theories.

de Bouhélier were among its poets. Marinetti was not yet the leader of the futurists, nor seemingly the megalomaniac who later used much of his periodical to extol his own work. The names of the French contributors given above testify to his eclectic tastes in 1905. Later in the year Kahn, Mockel, Saint-Pol-Roux, Henri de Régnier, Louis Payen, and Georges Casella were among the French poets in the periodical.

The catalogue of new magazines in 1905 is seemingly endless. *Le Damier,* "revue de littérature et d'art," also first appeared in March. Robert Scheffer and P.-J. Toulet were among its poets. In Marseilles Emile Sicard founded *Le Feu,* a regional magazine destined to have a long life. Sometimes devoting itself exclusively to southern literature, it often welcomed Parisian poets to contribute to its pages. Two Belgian periodicals, *Antée,* founded in June, and *La Belgique artistique et littéraire,* which first appeared in October, seemed to promise a relationship between poets of the two countries which had not existed since the time of *La Wallonie* and a few short-lived successors.

Antée, published in Brussels, was named after the Titan who retained his strength only so long as he was in contact with the earth. The founders, chief among whom were the Belgian poet Isi Collin and the prose writer Louis Piérard, announced at the very beginning their intention of including both French and Belgian writers. In the seven issues of the magazine published during 1905, Gide, Jammes, and Bouhélier were the chief French contributors. The magazine lasted until January 1908, and pursued an eclectic policy in its choice of authors. As for *La Belgique artistique et littéraire,* its second issue, in which appeared an essay by André Ruyters on Paul Claudel,[7] seemed to indicate intentions of including the two countries in its interests. Later issues showed, however, a strong nationalist feeling, save for reports on the Parisian literary scene by André Fontainas; the magazine is not important for ties with France.

In September an international congress for the encouragement of French language and culture was held at Liége. There was a literary section composed of French and Belgian writers, but the intention of closer artistic cooperation between the two countries which was the keynote of all speeches did not bear fruit. France had adopted Verhaeren, Maeterlinck, Van Lerberghe, and several others of her northern neighbors, but Belgium, already divided into Flemish and French camps, did not exactly reciprocate. A few little magazines, like the Catholic literary periodical *Durendal* and *Le Thyrse,* "la revue des jeunes," did not closely observe national frontiers.

7. *La Belgique artistique et littéraire,* No. 2 (Nov. 1905), pp. 213–21. Concerning this article by Ruyters, see Paul Claudel, Francis Jammes, Gabriel Frizeau, *Correspondance 1897–1938,* pp. 55, 71.

For example, Ansel Franz wrote on Jules Laforgue[8] and Henri Liebrecht on Albert Samain in these magazines in 1905.[9] But *Antée,* to judge by its list of contributors and its book reviews, was clearly much more a French than a Belgian publication.

At the very end of the year Toulouse was the scene of a literary grouping which created a monthly magazine devoted to poetry, and a publishing house for poems, and was the birthplace of poetic ideas which became known in 1909 as primitivism. The magazine bore the simple name of *Poésie,* and on its cover carried a quatrain by Albert Samain to indicate its literary climate. In 1909 *Poésie* was to enter into fierce combat with *Poesia,* Marinetti's periodical, which declared itself futurist at that date.

There were four founders of *Poésie.* Two were father and son, known in literature as Marc Dhano and Touny-Lérys but bearing the real name of Marchandeau. They lived in Gaillac and were friends of the aged Quercy novelist Emile Pouvillon. Pouvillon encouraged young Marcel Marchandeau to write, and indeed some small pamphlets of verse and prose had appeared in Gaillac in 1900 and 1901 signed "Touny-Lérys." He was at that time about twenty years old and was studying law in Toulouse. Then he met Georges Gaudion and Louis Estève who had already published a little magazine, *La Critique méridionale,* from January to November 1904. *Poésie* made an attempt not to be exclusively regionalistic, securing in its first four numbers poems from Jammes, Fontainas, Albert Saint-Paul, Pierre Fons, Henri de Régnier, Henry Vandeputte, Francis Eon, Vielé-Griffin, Edouard Ducoté, Léo Larguier, Léon Bocquet, and Louis Piérard. *Quelques Petits Poèmes d'amour* (1905) and *Elégie* (1908) by Touny-Lérys, and *Lampes avant le seuil* (1906) and *La Prairie fauchée* (1908) by Gaudion were some of the books printed by *Poésie.* Estève had resigned from the magazine after the fourth number.

This little magazine had a history like many others of its kind. Starting bravely as a monthly publication, it changed to a bimonthly, then to a quarterly. It lasted until the spring of 1911. It had published only fourteen issues during its five years of existence. It secured the collaboration, however, of most important poets of the time. Touny-Lérys drew his inspiration from village life and his poems are a kind of autobiography, telling of his love for his wife, his grief at the death of his mother, and his joy in rural existence. On February 20, 1907, Marcel Ballot gave a lecture in Brussels entitled "Touny-Lérys et la Poésie toulousaine." Francis Jammes composed a preface for *La Pâque des Roses* (1909), the collected volume of verse by Touny-Lérys which was published by the *Mercure de France.*

Poetry appeared to have emerged again as an important literary form in

8. *Durendal,* No. 8 (1905), pp. 481–6.   9. *Le Thyrse,* No. 4 (1905), pp. 129–37.

1905. In the founding of a periodical for regrouping the symbolists, in the establishment of reviews primarily for verse not only in Paris but in Milan, Marseilles, Toulouse, and Brussels, there was an atmosphere of ferment in favor of lyric art entirely new in the century.

The year was also an important one in the history of the *Mercure de France,* which began to appear twice a month, increasing its yearly pagination by about a third. The "Revue du mois" became the "Revue de la quinzaine" and greatly expanded its coverage of French and foreign literatures. More poems were printed, although as in the past the list of contributors remained small. G.-C. Cros, Marie Dauguet, S.-C. Leconte, Stuart Merrill, Henri de Régnier, and Emile Verhaeren each contributed poems to two issues. Of the thirteen other poets represented in the magazine during the year, three—Le Cardonnel, Herold, and Raynaud—had long been associated with the magazine, and three more—Despax, Payen, and Rolmer [10] —were authors of volumes published in 1905 by the presses of the *Mercure de France.* Vallette's magazine preserved this restricted policy of collaboration for many years.

Mithouard's *L'Occident,* through contributors such as Claudel, Ghéon, Jammes, and Vielé-Griffin, and through its acceptance of free verse, revealed affinities with *L'Ermitage* of 1905. Guy Lavaud, Fagus, and Vallery-Radot were already contributors to the magazine, but it was not until 1906, with André Suarès, Marc Lafargue, Francis de Miomandre, Verhaeren, and Henri de Régnier added to its poets, that *L'Occident* became a magazine of broad literary interest.

In 1905 the publication in pamphlet form of Claudel's *Les Muses,* and three of his poems [11] later included in *Corona benignitatis anni Dei* were the chief contributions in verse to the periodical.

Volumes of verse published during 1905 were not so striking as poems published in periodicals. It was, however, a year of first volumes by two poets whose reputation was steadily to increase, André Salmon and Charles Vildrac. Both bore the title *Poèmes.* Salmon's poems, published by *Vers et Prose,* immediately attracted attention by reason of their variety and originality. All sorts of rhythms, a strange vocabulary, poems in which hallucination, irony, and emotions alternated in importance immediately gained for him a reputation for originality. It was the Lille periodical, *Le Beffroi,* which published Vildrac's first collection. In these poems was the dream of fraternal association, the "Abbaye," that was to become a reality the next year. The presses of *Le Beffroi* were very busy in 1905. Léon Deubel's

10. *La maison des glycines; Les Voiles blanches; Madame Fornoul et ses héritiers.*

11. In letters to friends complimenting him on the three poems, Claudel called them "bagatelles" and "niaiseries" but this may be literary coquetry.

La Lumière natale, Théo Varlet's *Notes et Poèmes,* and Roger Allard's *La Divine Aventure* were among its publications. Of these, Deubel's poems attracted the most attention. Written in Italy and in Lille during one of the few times in his unhappy life when he had some money, these verses had an enthusiasm and a picturesque quality which set them apart from his earlier and later work. Varlet's *Notes et Poèmes,* like Deubel's volume, was in large part inspired by places he visited. He often put into sonnet form his pictures of Holland, England, and Italy. At other times, abandoning a Parnassian technique of description, he made his poems meditations. In such works admiration for Nietzsche often dominated his thought. Philosophical and scientific words made some of his poems appear pretentious. When his mood was somber he suggested Laforgue, but he lacked Laforgue's supreme ironic gift.

The volume of the year, so far as can be ascertained from critical reviews, was Charles Guérin's *L'Homme intérieur.* This represented what the poet had written since 1901. Most of these poems had already been printed, for Guérin had been welcomed by periodicals of all types and descriptions, claimed as a descendent of both symbolism and Parnassianism, admired for the music of his lines and the sincerity of his thought. He had sung the desires of the flesh, the pain of remorse, the longing of the spirit. The only new note distinguishing *L'Homme intérieur* from *Le Cœur solitaire* and *Le Semeur de cendres,* was the increased importance of the death theme. The poetry is grave, harmonious, and monotonous; the dramatic element in this volume is that of Guérin's preceding collections, the conflict between a sensuously pagan nature and a desire for firm religious faith. He no longer sought daring images or unusual vocabulary; his first master had been Rodenbach and his melancholy quatrains often recall that youthful admiration.

In 1905 Guérin was considered one of the important lyrical voices. After his death, two years later, when his total work was assessed, discreet comments began to appear concerning the repetitious nature of his last few volumes, and finally doubts were raised concerning his ability to renew his inspiration. Yet it is easy to see why these confessions of an anguished spirit enjoyed such current favor. *L'Homme intérieur* seemed at least more natural, less artificially literary than most of the other contemporary volumes.

Léo Larguier, the avowed disciple of Hugo and Lamartine, in *Les Isolements,* his second volume of verse, was much more eloquent and less delicate than Guérin. The theme of literary glory, the poet crowned with the laurel wreath, was an obsessive preoccupation, and his words of simplicity and humility strike a note as false as that in some of Hugo's humanitarian poems. Louis Payen, in *Les Voiles blanches,* used figures from Greek mythology (the sails in the title are those of Theseus' vessel), as symbols for interpreting his aspirations and disappointments. Emile Despax, in *La Maison des glycines,* chose a bucolic note which placed him in the lineage of the classic pastoral poets and Chénier. The Academy awarded him the Archon-Despérouses prize for this volume, the last he wrote.[12] Guérin's more direct approach, the immediate impact of his emotion, without overly patent literary devices, was what won admiration from the critics.

The publication of Claudel's *Les Muses* as a pamphlet by *L'Occident,* and its almost simultaneous appearance in *Vers et Prose,* did not receive much mention, but the few reviews were enthusiastic. Joseph Bossi, in the Belgian magazine *Antée,* found that Claudel's qualities of "permanence" and "présence" had added a new dimension to poetry. Vielé-Griffin, in *L'Ermitage,* attempted to describe this strange new form of art by comparison with two great names from the past, Mallarmé and Rimbaud. Quillard, in the *Mercure de France,* voiced his delight at the novelty of the form and expression in the poem. Fagus quoted passages from the ode in *L'Occident,* apparently finding it difficult to express his evident admiration.

Another volume which did not immediately attract attention was André Spire's *Et vous riez!* which was printed by Péguy's *Cahiers de la quinzaine.* It was not until Jean de Gourmont selected the author of *Et vous riez!* as one of the interesting "Poètes nouveaux" for an article in 1906[13] that more than passing mention was given Spire as a poet. Spire was at the time better known as a writer interested in social problems. His free verse, which was based on the oral rather than written word, was usually passed by with some mention of its absence of rhymes. Jean de Gourmont spoke of other qualities than form: the irony which was almost too violently present, and above all the dominance of ideas over emotions.

Women poets, outstanding for their numbers rather than the quality of their work, flourished in this period. At the end of 1904 Marthe Dupuy's *L'Idylle en fleur* won the annual Sully-Prudhomme poetry prize. Many of her sonnets were inspired by antiquity and she well represented the Parnassian tradition. Jane Catulle-Mendès appeared with a first volume *Les Charmes.* Her poem told in impeccable quatrains the story of her girlhood, inspiring Marcel Ballot to say in *Le Figaro* that such a complete picture of woman in a triple portrait of child, wife, and mother had not appeared since Mme. Desbordes-Valmore. Lya Berger's second volume, *Les Pierres sonores,* was praised by André Rivoire and Auguste Dorchain but dis-

---

12. Despax occupied various governmental posts in the French colonial ministry and in departmental administration. He was killed in January 1915, just after he arrived at the front lines. According to Mme. de Noailles, *La Maison des glycines* is the "chef d'œuvre inconnu."

13. *Mercure de France, 63* (Sept. 1, 1906), 5–20.

missed as a series of banalities by Pierre Quillard. Quillard was also harsh in speaking of Lucie Félix-Faure's *La Vie nuancée,* which he compared in its false elegance to the poetry of Robert de Montesquiou. In items appearing as end papers in several magazines during 1905, the profusion of women poets was noted and generally viewed with alarm, particularly when nine "femmes de lettres" founded a periodical, *La Revue littéraire,* in Montpellier. Most male critics appeared uneasy before this flood of feminine lyricism. They were conscious that it was creating a new poetic climate, but they were dismayed by its absence of discipline, by its diffuseness and copiousness, and by what they concurred in calling its "exaltation." In 1905 Charles Maurras tried to analyze several women poets in *Le Romantisme féminin,* and five years later Jean de Gourmont made the same attempt in *Muses d'aujourd'hui.* Jules Bertaut, in *La Littérature féminine d'aujourd'hui* (1909), sought to discover why the feminine writers so often produced works which were charming and interesting but almost never masterpieces. He found the defect in woman's very nature, in her inability to get beyond the prison of her emotions, in making her own feeling the absolute. But he was almost the only critic who found any formula to explain the reservations that accompanied even favorable reviews of the feminine muse. Remy de Gourmont told Vellay and Le Cardonnel in 1905 that women writers appeared currently to have more talent than men, and Rachilde slyly reported having heard that "ces poètes femelles font mieux les vers que les poètes mâles d'aujourd'hui." Whatever the attitude of the critics may have been, women poets continued to occupy an important place in all publications. One does not have to read very far in periodicals before encountering the names of Noailles, Delarue-Mardrus, Koeberlé, Nicolette Hennique, Cecile Périn, Marie Dauguet, or Valentine de Saint-Point. The publishers' lists are equally rich in women poets. One is chiefly struck by the number of sonnets they composed, and how many were on the subject of love.

The poet who had perfected another kind of sonnet, the sonnet of visual imagery and historical lore, José-Maria de Heredia, died on October 2, 1905. A huge number of articles appeared, praising the author of *Les Trophées* for his impeccable art and his noble character. But most of the obituary notices were coldly formal, giving due homage to the Acadamicien who had succeeded Leconte de Lisle in 1894. More interesting is the article by Remy de Gourmont printed in the newspaper *Le Soleil* on November 2, in which the critic, after discussing Parnassianism, avowed that he preferred the few lines where Heredia's personal emotion emerged. Emile Sicard devoted the December issue of *Le Feu* to "Hommage à Heredia," securing poems from Dierx, Régnier, S.-C. Leconte, the Belgian writer Henri Liebrecht, and several poets from Marseilles. André Fontainas wrote an essay for the *Mercure de France*,[14] and finished his evaluation of Heredia's poetic gifts by reminding readers that the symbolists had always been friendly to the author of *Les Trophées*.

Of all the events in 1905 affecting poetry and poets, the most important was the founding of *Vers et Prose*. For nine years this quarterly maintained a struggle against commercialism and offered in its list of contributors the most talented versifiers of the prewar era.

14. 57 (Oct. 15, 1905), 481–7.

CHAPTER 6. Prolongations of Symbolism: *Vers et Prose*

BETWEEN December 1906, when the last issue of *L'Ermitage* appeared, and February 1909, when Gide and his friends regrouped its collaborators in *La Nouvelle Revue Française,* was a period in which the more original poets appeared in little magazines. The *Mercure de France,* now being published twice a month, reported faithfully on current volumes of verse through Quillard but gave relatively little space to the printing of poems. The favorites were Louis le Cardonnel, Merrill, Porché, G.-C. Cros, Jammes, Régnier, and Verhaeren, all of whom were contributors before 1905. Two others, Lucien Rolmer and André Spire, were fairly frequent contributors. The former's first novel had appeared from the presses of the *Mercure* in 1905, which explains in part his collaboration. André Spire, a far more important poet, had first attracted notice when Péguy published the bitter but tender poems of *Et vous riez!* in one of the *Cahiers de la quinzaine* in 1905. These were reprinted, along with *Poèmes juifs* in a volume called *Versets* (1908), by the *Mercure.*

More important for publication of verse were three other periodicals: Paul Fort's *Vers et Prose,* Jean Royère's *La Phalange,* and Mithouard's *L'Occident.* Paul Castiaux's *Les Bandeaux d'or* and the little Belgian magazine, *Antée,* played a more modest role. All had editorial policies favoring continuation of symbolism. All except *L'Occident* accepted a new group, that of the "Abbaye de Créteil."

Between March 1905 and March 1914 there was only one magazine in Paris which consistently represented the best poetic production of the period. Directed by Paul Fort and, for the first five years, edited by André Salmon (after that by Louis Mandin and Tancrède de Visan), the periodical was named *Vers et Prose.* Its motto, the "défense et illustration de la haute littérature et du lyrisme en prose et poésie," was on the whole faithfully followed. While there were many contributions in prose, the greater part can be classified as prose-poems or personal meditations with a definite emotional note. But what set the magazine apart was its eclecticism. Paul Fort, who was friendly toward the whole symbolist generation, welcomed about him the poets who had begun writing between 1885 and 1895. André Salmon, younger and on the alert for new talent, brought into the orbit of the periodical names which were as yet unknown. Paul Fort had his own kind of Tuesday reception. Instead of choosing a place like the apart-

ment on the rue de Rome, he established himself on the terrace of the
Closerie des Lilas, the well-known café on the Boulevard Montparnasse,
and soon the tables filled with groups of writers both French and foreign.
There appears to have been little attempt, on Fort's part, at formulating
doctrine. At the beginning of the collection of ballads called *Montagne*
(1898), he had said that "penser en troupe" was unworthy of poets. In the
same foreword he had given the admonition, "Reste libre, c'est là la première
noblesse. Sois-toi." These principles seem to have guided him during his
supervision of *Vers et Prose,* where free verse was readily admitted but where
traditional meter was not disdained. Nor was this at variance with Fort's
own work. In answering Le Cardonnel's and Vellay's questions when they
were preparing *La Littérature contemporaine* in 1905, he explained the
diversity of form in his *Ballades.* His explanation went something like this:
for a long time people considered that the writer was faced with the choice
of deciding between prose and verse, but Fort rejected such hard and fast
distinctions. There is also an intermediate form, called by some rhythmic
prose, which conveys neither lyric emotion nor sober observation but something between the two. Fort claimed the right to change at will from poetic
expression to prose, using rhythmic prose as a transition. Since the poem,
in his opinion, was as much intended to be heard as read, rhythm rather
than prosody was the author's chief concern. He preferred that the utterance be close to usual spoken language, and for that reason elided "e" when
it was not a regularly pronounced syllable. He often utilized the alexandrine,
either for the effect of Mallarmé's "grandes orgues" or in simple narration.

A great number of Fort's *Ballades* were printed in the thirty-six volumes
of *Vers et Prose.* The magazine appeared as a quarterly, each volume being
well over 100 pages, handsomely but not always accurately printed. Sub-
scriptions during the first six months may have been disappointing, since
they numbered under 500, but thereafter they increased rapidly and the
magazine appears to have gained about 1000 subscribers by the end of its
first year. This was a major feat for a new periodical which in no way catered
to vulgar taste; not a little credit was due Fort, whose enthusiasm and
comity have been praised by numerous writers.

Vers et Prose, as Vielé-Griffin's prefatory words to the first issue explain,
was principally dedicated to continuation of the lyric renaissance of 1885
which rejected Parnassian and naturalist aesthetics. There was even some
effort on the magazine's part to reprint works which had received insufficient circulation during the symbolist period. Maeterlinck's "Le Massacre
des Innocents," which had appeared in *La Pléiade* of 1885; Valéry's "La
Soirée avec M. Teste," first published in *Le Centaure* in 1896; André Gide's
Poésies d'André Walter, known only to a few readers through the limited

Librairie indépendante edition of 1892, were among those literary resurrections. Other offerings from the past were Maeterlinck's defense of Van Lerberghe which had been printed in the program of Le Théâtre d'art at the first performance of *Les Flaireurs*, Jules Laforgue's "Aquarium" from *La Vogue* of 1886, some translations of Arthur Symons' poems by Verlaine, Mallarmé's "Vers et musique en France," and "Notes" by Laforgue (both from the *Entretiens politiques et littéraires* of 1892), and Van Lerberghe's story "La Grâce du sommeil" from *La Wallonie* of 1889. A few items from the past had never been printed: two letters from Rimbaud to Izambard, a variant of Saint-Pol-Roux's *La Dame à la faulx*, letters written by Van Lerberghe and Samain, some of the very early poems of Mikhaël, verse by Charles Cros, and Mallarmé's "Avant-dire" for a Reynaldo Hahn concert.

The memory of the symbolist period was also stressed by essays and poems in *Vers et Prose*. In the second issue (2, 194–203) André Salmon wrote a moving tribute to the author of *Les Amours jaunes*, the ill-starred Tristan Corbière who had been one of Verlaine's "poètes maudits" and one of Remy de Gourmont's "masques." The periodical was actively interested in collecting money for placing Verlaine's bust in the Luxembourg, Moréas writing a plea for this commemoration (*17*, 5–9) in 1909, Alfred Vallette contributing "Le Monument de Paul Verlaine" (*23*, 1–10) in 1910. Two years later the magazine printed the "Discours prononcé à l'anniversaire de la mort de Paul Verlaine" by the Armenian poet Archag Tchobanian.

Veneration for the memory of Mallarmé was shown in several ways. In 1906 Léon Dierx's poem "Valvins" was printed in the magazine. In 1910 three sonnets entitled "Le Tombeau de Stéphane Mallarmé" by Albert St.-Paul almost too successfully imitated the author of "Tel qu'en lui-même . . ." In 1912, when a commemorative plaque was placed in the rue de Rome and a banquet was given honoring Mallarmé's memory, *Vers et Prose* printed the speeches by Henri de Régnier, Vielé-Griffin, and Albert Mockel, as well as P.-N. Roinard's poem "La Rencontre radieuse" (*29*, 63–74). These speeches did not contribute very much to Mallarmean criticism, since each orator repeated what he had written long before: Régnier insisted that symbol and allusion were the bases of Mallarmé's art; Vielé-Griffin, ever sensitive on the subject of regular and free verse, explained that one should not call the individual symbolists contradictory but complementary; Mockel had apparently not found anything to add to ideas he had expressed in *Stéphane Mallarmé: un héros* of 1899. These speeches of 1912, filled with veneration for a beloved personality, were given the year of the first edition of Alfred Thibaudet's *La Poésie de Mallarmé*. Mallarmé's intimate self was about to undergo a transformation, but *Vers et Prose* did not celebrate this new critical approach.

Finally, among the dead symbolists, *Vers et Prose* honored the name of Jules Laforgue. Tristan Derème contributed in 1912 (*30*, 211–16; *31*, 104–7) an essay which was not only an appreciation of ironic humor, but also a suggestion of the influence of Laforgue on Derème's own poetry. The very last issue of the magazine (*36*, Jan.–Mar. 1914) contained a reprinting of the "Chants de Maldoror" of Lautréamont.

Between 1905 and 1913 *Vers et Prose* noted with sorrow the passing of other writers whom Fort had known since his *Théâtre d'art* venture. In 1905 Marcel Schwob, who for years had been in ill health but had courageously carried on multiple activities, was the first of these losses. Schwob's cult of Villon and his intense interest in English literature had strengthened the friendship between him and Fort. To the first issue of *Vers et Prose* he contributed a few of the short prose-poems and meditations which he was writing up to the moment of his death and which were intended for a volume entitled *Il Libro della mia memoria*. Hugues Rebell, born in 1868 and one year younger than Schwob, also died in 1905. *Vers et Prose* printed some of his prose-poems in 1906 and 1909.

In 1907 the magazine lost two more of its friends and contributors. Charles Van Lerberghe, whose *Chanson d'Eve* (1904) had received warm praise from Maeterlinck in the pages of *Vers et Prose* (*4*, 21–9), was further honored after his death by the publication of some of his letters. Alfred Jarry, often with Fort at the Closerie des Lilas, offered "La Dragonne" in 1906, and was posthumously remembered when the magazine printed fragments of *Docteur Faustroll*.

Vers et Prose suffered its greatest loss in 1910 with the death of Jean Moréas. Almost every one of the first twenty-seven volumes of the periodical contained a contribution by the author of *Les Stances*. These included the prologue of his poetic tragedy *Ajax*, some new *Stances*, and numerous meditations on travel and literature that were to become the volume *Esquisses et Souvenirs*. André Salmon demonstrated that the form and tonality of *Les Stances* were already present in *Le Pèlerin passionné* (*3*, 141–53); in 1906 Eugène Godefroy lauded the perfection in form achieved by Moréas (*6*, 109–28), and wrote his obituary notice in 1910 (*21*, 5–9). In the latter issue appeared two poems, by Georges Marlow and the Greek poet Malakassis, lamenting Moréas' death, and soon after (*22*, 35–40), Maurice Barrès offered his "Dernier Entretien avec Jean Moréas," now become famous for the romanist's final judgment that the terms "classicists" and "romanticists" were nonsense. Moréas' faithful disciple, Raymond de la Tailhède, whose poems were rare items between 1895, the date of his *De la métamorphose des fontaines,* and 1922, when his *Deuxième livre des odes* appeared, also contributed to the magazine: "Triomphe" in 1905 (*3*,

121–3), "Adolescents" and "Toi qui rêves toujours" in 1906 (*5*, 88–9), "Ode à Moréas" in 1909 (*16*, 37–9), and "Chœurs des Océanides" in 1911 (*27*, 22–4). The other adherents of the Ecole romane, Ernest Raynaud and Maurice du Plessys, contributed poems in 1907 and 1910 respectively. The association of the romanists with a magazine directed by Paul Fort was significant. Clearly the director, by the inclusion of these poets for whom traditional form was a basic principle, was attempting to suppress the quarrel concerning free verse that had been raging since 1890.

From our mid-century viewpoint, we can discern the importance of *Vers et Prose,* both in presenting new names and in giving due honor to writers who were far from well known between 1905 and 1913. André Gide, with "Ben Saada" (*1*, 20–30), "Alger" (*4*, 5–16), "Le Retour de l'enfant prodigue" (*9*, 5–28), "Bethsabé" (*16*, 5–17), "Feuilles de route" (*28*, 19–21), and Paul Claudel, with "Les Muses, ode" (*2*, 7–27) and "Connaissance du temps" (*5*, 40–61), were two of these contributors whose fame was slow in spreading.

There were also several younger poets who owed much to the periodical. Salmon and Apollinaire, between their *Festin d'Esope* of 1903 and *Les Soirées de Paris* of 1912 were kept in public notice chiefly by this quarterly. Salmon, the managing editor, wrote many articles and poems; his *Poèmes* (1905) and *Les Féeries* (1907) were published by the *Vers et Prose* presses. His friend Apollinaire appeared in the fourth issue with the poems "L'Emigrant de Landor Road," "Salomé," "Les Cloches," and "Mai." In 1907 a short story, "Le Sacrilège," in 1908 an essay on André Salmon, in 1909 the prose-poem "L'Obituaire," in 1911 the "Poème lu au mariage d'André Salmon," and in 1912 "Le Larron," "Dans le palais de Rosemonde," "La Porte," "Marie," "L'adieu," and "La Dame" were additional items in Apollinaire's bibliography. Milosz, almost unknown during the life span of the magazine, was also a contributor: "Très simple histoire d'un M. Trix-Trix" (*7*, 129–34), "A la beauté" (*12*, 98–102), "Le Vent" (*24*, 80–1), and "Méphiboseth" (*35*, 76–93).

Vers et Prose, in the majority of the poems it printed, reflected a continuation of the symbolist magazines, French and Belgian, of 1885–1900. Henri de Régnier, Vielé-Griffin, Verhaeren, Albert Mockel, Saint-Pol-Roux, André Fontainas, Francis Jammes, Louis le Cardonnel, Robert de Souza, Albert Saint-Paul, Remy de Gourmont, A.-F. Herold, and Pierre Louÿs, with Paul Fort, were the foremost contributors. The principal critics, between 1905 and 1910, were Tancrède de Visan and André Salmon. The former, whose main thesis was the discovery by the symbolists of a temporal continuity replacing ideas of present, past, and future, examined the works of several symbolists. He insisted on the unity rather than the evolution of the poets he studied. Gradually he built up, through these articles, the conclusion that symbolism had been an inevitable and natural trend in French literature. In its insistence on the subconscious and its destruction of traditional ideas of time, Visan saw a movement parallel to that of Bergson in philosophy. He felt that the form in which the poem was cast, regular or free verse, was of minor importance. In 1905 he wrote essays on Vielé-Griffin, Henri de Régnier, and Emile Verhaeren, in 1907 on Maurice Maeterlinck and Paul Fort, in 1908 on Robert de Souza, in 1909 on Albert Mockel, and finally in 1910 "La Philosophie de M. Bergson et le lyrisme contemporain."

Salmon, writing on Tristan Corbière, Moréas, and Stuart Merrill; Albert Dreyfus contributing an essay on Gustave Kahn; Maurice Gauchez, reviewing André Fontainas' critical, fictional, and poetic work, completed this gallery of names important in the history of symbolism. All were laudatory and all were tacitly striving to prove that symbolism had produced a valid poetic literature, remarkable for its simplicity and frankness, profound in its revelation of the mind in action and its "notion du continu."

Toward the end of 1908 a new grouping, formed less on an aesthetic doctrine than on friendships at the Abbaye de Créteil, began to take on importance in *Vers et Prose*. First appeared some poems by Jules Romains (*15*, 110–13; *16*, 76–8) which expressed the fraternal ideas of unanimism and which were later published in *Un Etre en marche*. Vildrac's "Une Auberge" in the April–June issue of 1909, René Arcos' "Sur la tragédie des espaces" in the following number, and Georges Duhamel's "L'Epreuve" in the last quarter of 1909 were to some degree illustrations of "la connaissance immédiate d'une âme" which was Romains' definition of great poetry.[1] Georges Duhamel, in an essay entitled "Jules Romains et les Dieux," demonstrated how the author of *La Vie unanime* had replaced divine by human considerations (*22*, 114–19), and in "Charles Vildrac et les hommes" (*24*, 194–9) and "Le Printemps de Georges Chennevière (*29*, 110–16) further stressed sympathetic understanding of man and his world as a basis of his friends' art. The part played by *Vers et Prose* in making known the "poètes de l'Abbaye," though important, appears less so when one considers the articles and poems in the *Mercure de France, Les Bandeaux d'or,* and the *Nouvelle Revue Française* which concerned these writers.

The director of the periodical, even though he avoided expressing criticism of others, contributed many of his "Ballades" to his magazine and arranged for several limited printings of selections of his work which he distributed among friends. Eight series of the *Ballades françaises* had been published by the *Mercure de France* between 1896 and 1906. Eight more, from the

1. In the lecture he gave at the Salon d'automne in 1909.

ninth to the sixteenth, entitled *Ile-de-France, Mortcerf, La Tristesse de l'homme, L'Aventure éternelle, Monthery-la-Bataille, Vivre en Dieu, Chanson pour me consoler d'être heureux, Les Nocturnes* were printed by *Vers et Prose*. A large portion of these poems had appeared in separate issues of the periodical before being assembled in volumes. Two essays by Tancrède de Visan (*10*, 94–112) and Octave Béliard (*31*, 153–6) were the only studies of Fort's work appearing in the magazine during its nine years of existence. Louis Mandin's *Etudes sur les "Ballades françaises,"* an introduction to *Mortcerf*, was published in 1909. On February 9, 1911, Fort's friends gave a banquet commemorating the publication of *La Tristesse de l'homme*. Kahn, Hirsch, Saint-Pol-Roux, A.-F. Herold, Marinetti and others gave polite speeches. The following year, after the death of Léon Dierx, *La Phalange, Gil Blas, Comœdia, Les Nouvelles,* and *Les Loups* held an election of a new Prince des poètes. Fort was the winner, with a majority of three hundred votes, and another banquet, presided over by Jean Richepin, was held in his honor on July 12, 1912. A few months later, *La Belgique française* having devoted an issue to his work, Fort departed for a series of lectures at Mons, Brussels, and Liége. His subject was "Poètes et Journaux," and his purpose was to castigate the newspapers which refused to recognize the importance of poetry, and at the same time to thank the few journalists who had accorded it a place in their columns. After Belgium, Fort visited Switzerland. At Lausanne Henry Spiess, the poet whose *Le Silence des heures* (1904), after enjoying success in his native country, was being printed by the *Mercure de France,* recited a poem in honor of the visitor. These verses were printed in *Vers et Prose* (*32*, 75–8). This is the summary of Fort's presence in the magazine; the accusation that he selfishly used the periodical for his own publicity should be somewhat discounted. Royère's and Mithouard's personalities were certainly more evident in *La Phalange* and *L'Occident* than was his in *Vers et Prose*.

One accomplishment of *Vers et Prose* was the presentation of foreign lyric and dramatic poetry in translation. Among English poets there were Yeats, Fitzgerald, William Morris, Ernest Dowson, Arthur Symons, and William Sharp. The versions made by Stuart Merrill and Professor Rudmose-Brown were well done, but a translation of Shakespeare's *Venus and Adonis* by Emile Godefroy was most unpoetic. Maeterlinck's adaptation of *Macbeth*, presented at St. Wandrille on August 28, 1909, was printed in *Vers et Prose*. The translations of some poems by Stefan George in 1905, of Hugo von Hofmannsthal's play *Elektra* in 1908–9, and of short lyrics by Richard Dehmel were the most important examples of German literature. Marinetti occasionally made translations of Carducci and d'Annunzio; Eugenio de Castro gave the magazine some French versions of poems he had originally written in Portuguese. The Danish poet Sophus Claussen, who was often in Paris and frequented the group of the Closerie des Lilas, was translated by G.-C. Cros, whose mother was Danish. A poem by the talented Norwegian writer Sigbjörn Obstfelder, who had died in 1900 at the age of thirty-four, appeared in a French version, the translator being Albert Dreyfus.

With the outbreak of World War I, *Vers et Prose* came to an end. It had probably accomplished its purpose before 1914, for the founding of *La Nouvelle Revue Française* in 1909 and new allegiances of erstwhile collaborators had lessened its importance. Tancrède de Visan's *L'Attitude du lyrisme contemporain,* which expanded many of the ideas he had expressed in the magazine, was published in 1911. In this volume the author paid tribute to symbolism, not as a school, but as an attitude or ideal in conformity with modern times. The greater part of the work was a series of studies of authors chosen as best representing the ideals of the symbolists. Paul Fort's chief aim had been to publish poems by these same authors, although, as we have seen, he desired to reveal new talents. Some of these younger writers were well on their way to fame. In 1909 Apollinaire became acquainted with Eugène Montfort of *Marges* and began writing criticisms of women writers under the name of "Louise Lalanne." At about the same time the publication of his first contribution to the *Mercure de France,* "La Chanson du Mal Aimé," opened new avenues for his energies. Publication of *L'Enchanteur pourrissant, L'Hérésiarque et Cie., Le Bestiaire ou Cortège d'Orphée, Les Peintres cubistes,* and finally *Alcools,* all between 1909 and 1913, had taken him from obscurity. With André Billy he founded *Les Soirées de Paris* in 1912, meanwhile retaining his column "La Vie anecdotique" in the *Mercure de France.*

Paul Fort's election in 1912 as "Prince des poètes" was in many ways a disservice to his reputation. Some writers, like Henri Ghéon, while professing esteem and friendship for the laureate, asked the question whether his work represented the same high accomplishment as that of Mallarmé or Verlaine. But the manner of the election and the unseemly haste with which it was carried out were the chief sources of reproof and dissatisfaction. Léon Dierx died on June 11. Jean Royère sent out a circular in the name of *La Phalange* on June 13, inviting all poets to submit their choice of successor to Léon Dierx. Five days later A. Belval-Delahaye, the leader since 1909 of a literary and artistic club called "Les Loups," sent out a form letter with a ballot on which was printed "Vote pour PAUL FORT." André Billy, offering the name of Raoul Ponchon, made an immediate effort to oppose this choice, but Fort's friends, delegating their powers to a minor poet, Georges Batault, composed a new circular on June 27. This open letter stated that the current results of the voting indicated Fort as winner and that in view of the "manœuvres d'une certaine presse" more votes ought to accumulate for the author of the *Ballades*. The other periodicals interested in the election seem to have been limited to the role of tabulating results. On July 1 Fort was declared the winner of the referendum by an overwhelming majority. But the contest had been somewhat cheapened by rivalries and mocking remarks in the newspapers. Even the banquet of July 12 was far from dignified, for it was held on a platform overlooking the amusement concessions of Luna Park. Some found this setting appropriate for honoring the poet who had drawn much inspiration from contemporary reality, but most journalists made fun of the title and the manner in which it had been gained. On the other hand, the election did suggest some appraisals of the *Ballades,* and articles like those of Georges le Cardonnel in *L'Opinion* (July 6, 1912) and of Pierre Louÿs in the popular weekly magazine *Les Annales* (July 7, 1912) were laudatory of Fort's fresh and spontaneous lyricism. By the time Mistral, in *Gil Blas* (May 1913), used the epithet "La Cigale du Nord" to describe Fort's nature, and Maurice Maeterlinck, in *Le Figaro* (April 26, 1913), called the *Ballades* an integral expression of the poetic spirit, the quarrels of the election were largely forgotten.

CHAPTER 7. Minor Poetic Groupings (1906–1910)

PAUL FORT's magazine served poetry well during the decade before World War I, but since it appeared at three-month intervals, its possibilities were limited. Several contemporary periodicals, not quite so liberal as *Vers et Prose* in their policy toward contributors but giving an important role to verse, merit comment. *Antée,* a Belgian magazine, one of whose editors, Isi Collin, had been hospitably received by French periodicals, established friendly relations between poets of the two countries. *La Phalange,* through its founder Jean Royère, combatted poetry with a social aim and defended musical and evocative verse. Mithouard's *L'Occident* continued to give lyric expression an important place, sometimes pursuing directions not unlike those of *La Phalange,* but offering a more religious and less daring form of lyricism. Finally, a literary anthology which appeared irregularly from 1907 to 1914, and which bore the name of *Les Bandeaux d'or,* deserves mention for the support it gave the writers of the Abbaye group.

There were many other periodicals that occasionally printed verse. *Le Censeur politique et littéraire,* founded on October 6, 1906 by J. Ernest-Charles, secured contributions from Verhaeren, Louis Payen, Bouhélier, Hélène Picard, and Olivier de la Fayette, but is chiefly to be remembered for its "Hommage à Charles Guérin," a collection of opinions gathered just after the death of the author of *Le Cœur solitaire.*[1] *Le Feu,* Sicard's monthly magazine in Marseilles, while principally regionalistic in character, had among its contributors Francis de Miomandre, Francis Carco, and Daniel Thaly. During 1905 and 1906 Léon Deubel, as managing editor of *La Rénovation esthétique,* made that periodical for twelve issues an organ for publication of poems by his friends of the *Beffroi* group in Lille and by Roger Frène of Toulouse. But in the spring of 1906 the magazine's Maecenas, a Russian lover of the arts, was unable to continue his subsidies. Deubel sought other ways of continuing his impecunious existence, working briefly as a private secretary, then for an insurance company.

The year 1908 witnessed further attempts at founding little magazines in which poetry was of prime interest. Louis Thomas and Emile Henriot founded *Amaryllis* in the spring of 1908. The first number of Le Mercier d'Erm's *Les Argonautes* appeared in April; July marked the founding of *Hélios,* a regional magazine in Agen to which Souchon, Jammes, Frène,

---

1. *Le Censeur,* 2 (March 30, 1907), 385–98; (April 13, 1907), 453–5.

Deubel, Derennes, and Mandin were contributors. Of these *Les Argonautes* lasted longest; it continued to appear monthly for two years, but in it were no literary directions, for Le Mercier d'Erm, a very young man from Brittany, enthusiastically welcomed contributors of all types and ages. He was particularly fond of verse by women, and Hélène Picard, Valentine de Saint-Point, Renée Vivien, and Nathalie Barney were among his frequent contributors. More noteworthy than the magazine were the evening receptions it organized every two weeks, where a heterogeneous group of novelists, poets, journalists, artists, musicians, and dramatists gathered for conversation, concerts, and readings.[2] The meetings, according to contemporary account, were noisy and often far from serious. Le Mercier d'Erm's inspiration was that of *Le Chat noir* or the "Soirées de *La Plume*," rather than the more decorous concerts and recitations of the Abbaye de Créteil, but behind the frivolity of showmanship was the desire for cultural relationships among the arts.

These magazines had only a very minor effect on the course of French poetry. But Isi Collin, Jean Royère, Adrien Mithouard, and Paul Castiaux, and the periodicals of which they were editors, were significant through the verse they printed and their critical comments on poetry and poetics. An examination of the aims and tendencies of *Antée, La Phalange,* and *Les Bandeaux d'or* may indicate the role of these magazines.

A renewal of the close bonds between French and Belgian writers that had once been provided by *La Wallonie* and *Le Réveil* was established for some three years by the monthly magazine *Antée,* first printed in Brussels, then in Bruges. The founders were Isi Collin, Louis Piérard, Joseph Bossi, and Henri Vandeputte, all of whom were eager supporters of a projected international congress for the extension of French language and culture. The congress was scheduled to be held in Liége in September 1905. The first number of *Antée* appeared four months earlier and indicated its eclectic and international intentions by its list of contributors. From France there were Claudel, Gide, Jammes, Mme. de Noailles, Bouhélier, and Vielé-Griffin.[3] Belgium was represented not only by the founders but by Elskamp, Maeterlinck, Mockel, Van Lerberghe, and Verhaeren.

2. Florian-Parmentier, who attended these meetings, listed some seventy frequenters of the *Argonautes* group. *Histoire contemporaine des lettres françaises de 1885 à 1914* (Paris, Figuière, 1914), pp. 350–2.

3. All these did indeed contribute something to *Antée.* Some of Gide's "Feuillets" from Cuverville appeared in No. 2 (July, 1905), pp. 66–8; Claudel sent only translations of poems by Coventry Patmore which were printed in the eighth issue. But many other French poets did become contributors to *Antée.* Among them were Delarue-Mardrus, Guérin, Deubel, Régnier, E. Jaloux, Eugène Montfort, Miomandre, Touny-Lérys, Vildrac, Ghéon, E. Raynaud, M. Dauguet, Carco, Suarès, L. Mandin, H. Martineau, Léo Larguier, Cécile Périn, Merrill, Alibert, and Klingsor.

Antée had no set program. The name *Antée* suggested the general literary premise that the valid artist, even as the Titan, should remain in contact with the earth. Isi Collin quoted a remark by Vielé-Griffin to indicate this tenet: "c'est de sol franc et ferme que le lyrisme doit prendre l'essor." Joseph Bossi's admiration went to poetry that maintained a definite relationship with the exterior world. But the magazine did strive not to follow a narrow pattern. Although Ernest-Charles, in an article extolling St.-Georges de Bouhélier, vigorously combatted symbolism in favor of naturism,[4] the book reviews in the magazine always treated the symbolists with great respect. Moréas spoke out against free verse, but his article was followed by a poem in free meters and a response to his article in the form of a "Lettre ouverte à Moréas" by Maurice de Noisay was printed in an ensuing issue.[5]

Certain comments in the magazine are worthy of note in that they forecast opinions which would later be generally accepted. In August 1905 Joseph Bossi found "présence" and "permanence" to be dual characteristics of Claudel's work, indicating the combination of the human and the eternal, of the real and the mystical, which gave special quality to his plays. In July 1906 Louis Piérard analyzed *L'Echange*. An essay on Max Elskamp by C.-L. Philippe (March 1907) was one of several attempts to lure the erstwhile poet from his obstinate silence. Stuart Merrill's article (June 1907) on the poetry of Arthur Symons was one of the first attempts to define the effect of symbolism on the English poet's verse.

Vielé-Griffin wrote a somewhat bitter essay entitled "Entretiens sur le mouvement poétique" for *Antée* in 1907.[6] The first part of his discussion was on "La Terreur symboliste," in which he reviewed the incomprehension of the press toward poetic innovations during the last years of the nineteenth century. Auguste Dorchain and Gaston Deschamps, two widely read newspaper critics who were determined enemies of free verse, were his special targets. Then Vielé-Griffin went on to describe how symbolism, and especially free verse, triumphed in spite of the French Academy, in spite of journalists and reactionary poets. He closed with a section ("La poésie vivante") which was largely a list of poets who used free verse.

The polemic tone of Vielé-Griffin's article is to be attributed in part to a controversy of 1906 in which he had been involved. Fernand Gregh founded in that year the magazine *Les Lettres* and in its pages indicated that he considered the case for free verse to be lost. Vielé-Griffin wrote an open letter to *Les Lettres,* and Gregh replied publicly in a caustic and condescending way. Thus the "Entretien" is not a fair or illuminating essay on poetry.

4. *Antée*, No. 18 (Nov. 1906), pp. 513–28.
5. No. 19 (Dec. 1906), pp. 633–9; No. 21 (Feb. 1907), pp. 947–52.
6. No. 24 (May 1907), pp. 1277–89.

Antée ran into financial difficulties about the middle of 1907 and was forced to suspend publication with the June number. In January 1908 a single issue of a new series was published. To the very last, *Antée* kept to its policy of including French contributors; in the final number Vielé-Griffin voiced his disapproval of Moréas in a "Causerie sur le classicisme," while Alibert and Lavaud offered poems. Meanwhile two Parisians, André Gide and Eugène Montfort, were considering either transferring *Antée* to Paris or creating a magazine with a new name. Their endeavors ended in the founding of *La Nouvelle Revue Française.*

What *Antée* had undertaken to accomplish was continued by *Les Visages de la vie,* founded in Brussels November 24, 1908 by a group of admirers of Verhaeren. Charles Dulait, Christian Beck, and Jean Dominique were among those who organized a public demonstration held at the Théâtre du parc in the Belgian capital, and who planned the simultaneous appearance of a periodical which would be favorable to new ideas rather than academic traditionalism, and which would be open to French as well as Belgian writers. Between November 1908 and September 1911, twelve issues of *Les Visages de la vie* were printed, two of them being double numbers. Charles Dulait had edited the periodical almost singlehanded, and his death on August 30, 1911 at the age of twenty-seven ended the little magazine. But during its difficult and precarious existence, *Les Visages de la vie* had brought together a certain number of French and Belgian poets. French contributors included Michel Abadie, Saint-Georges de Bouhélier, Francis Carco, Fernand Gregh, Guy Lavaud, Philéas Lebesgue, Sebastien-Charles Leconte, Louis Mandin, Louis Thomas, Touny-Lérys, Cécile Périn, and Vielé-Griffin.

Jean Royère's monthly magazine *La Phalange* first appeared on July 15, 1906. At that time about thirty-five years old, Royère had written two small volumes of poetry, *Exil doré* (1898) and *Eurythmies* (1904). During 1905 he had assumed the editorship of René Ghil's second series of *Ecrits pour l'art,* but finding the author of the *Traité du verbe* too dogmatic a theorist, he resigned in order to found his own periodical. He is remembered today for a sentence in which he epitomized his approval of poetic obscurity ("Ma poésie est obscure comme un lis"[7]) and for his theories which have taken the name of "néo-Mallarméisme." His career as editor of *La Phalange* lasted until 1912, and during this time several unknown poets achieved recognition through his magazine.

The word "symbolism" was kept very much alive by Royère in *La Phalange.* He found in Verhaeren's *La Multiple Splendeur* an interesting mingling of naturalism and symbolism (No. 6, Dec. 1906). He entitled an essay on Robert de Souza's *Où nous en sommes,* "Un manifeste symboliste" (No. 7, Jan. 1907), and in the course of his article took occasion to attack

7. Preface to Royère's *Sœur de Narcisse nue* (1907).

Fernand Gregh's theory of humanism. Royère, in his poetic preferences and in his enunciated theories, took the view that poetry should not attempt to be easily understood or appeal to the masses. Rather should it be filled with "notations neuves," analogies, and intuitive mystery. Royère employed the terms "concrète" and "sensible" to indicate what he regarded as necessary attributes of poetry. The abstract and the didactic were to be excluded from verse, its beauty residing in these two watchwords of the symbolists: music and suggestion. Probably no one ever took more literally than Royère the pronouncement that naming an object suppresses three-fourths of the enjoyment of a poem. Commonly, in his lines, a detail of landscape, a moment of the day, or a personal reflection lies hidden in metaphor and imagery.

Royère and the group of *Phalange* believed in great liberty in versification. Among the older poets who contributed selections of free verse to the magazine were Gustave Kahn, P.-N. Roinard, Tristan Klingsor, Robert de Souza, Francis Jammes, André Spire, and Vielé-Griffin; among the younger group were Charles Vildrac, Daniel Thaly, and Elsa Koeberlé. Royère, writing in March 1910 an essay "Sur la poésie actuelle," [8] spoke of the triumph of free verse, voiced his admiration for the rhythmic prose of Péguy's *Mystère de la Charité de Jeanne d'Arc,* and deplored the persistent prejudice against innovation. He was particularly bitter against Charles Maurras and the "monarchistes" who, he said, had waged war against beauty by their insistence on traditionalism.

The poets whom Royère particularly admired have not attained a place of first importance, but they are not without interest or talent. One of the frequent contributors to *La Phalange,* John-Antoine Nau, was the subject of several of Royère's essays.[9] Nau (whose real name was Antoine Torquet) was no longer a young man, having been born in 1860, but his wandering existence while he was on the crew of a sailing ship, his frequent changes of residence, from Martinique to Spain, from Spain to Brittany, and from Brittany to Algeria, and his innate timidity had resulted in only sporadic appearances in French publications. Vanier had published his first book of poems in 1897, and his novel *Force ennemie* had won the Goncourt Prize in 1904, but it was while Royère was editing the *Ecrits pour l'art* in 1905 that Nau's verses came to his attention and secured his instant admiration. Many of Nau's contributions to *La Phalange* were lyrics on northern Africa, but even when his settings were Provence or Brittany, the inveterate worshiper of the ocean succeeded in giving an exotic note to his verse. For this reason he has sometimes been placed in the lineage of Leconte de Lisle,

8. *La Phalange,* No. 45 (March 1910), pp. 381–6.

9. The first article on Nau by Royère appeared in *La Phalange* in September 1907 (No. 15, pp. 348–54).

but such an association of names is faulty. Nau used many combinations of rhythms, observed none of the rules of caesura, and often employed assonance instead of rhyme. But the tone of his verse, even more than the form, separated him from the Parnassian leader. Nau never really described for description's sake; his poems were filled with his personal emotions and feelings; he was not looking at a landscape but, as it were, living it.

A man much younger than Nau, but like Nau a poet of the sea, was another of Royère's favorites.[10] This was Guy Lavaud whose busy career as lawyer and governmental employee always left a margin of time for poetic creation. Titles of two poems he contributed to *La Phalange* in 1907, "La Floraison des eaux" and "La Dernière Elégie," sum up the principal aspects of his poetic talent. He was the poet of water, whether the fountain, the stream, or the ocean; he was moreover an elegiac whose verse seems constantly to develop and expand Vigny's melancholy as voiced in the last lines of "La Maison du berger":

> Après l'eau des ruisseaux,—ô notre enfance neuve,—
> Le blanc ruissellement des torrents, puis des fleuves,
> Et l'immobilité des lacs couleur de perle,
> Après le triste étang où stagnent les eaux vertes,
> Où vas-tu, ma Folie, courber ton doux visage?
> Ta tristesse fuira en pleurs dans quelles glaces!
> (*La Floraison des eaux,* "Or, l'étang d'Elseneur, IX")

Besides Nau and Lavaud, fairly regular contributors to *La Phalange* were Viélé-Griffin, André Spire, Julien Ochsé, Léo Loups, Paul Castiaux, Emile Verhaeren, Albert Mockel, Georges Périn, Louis Mandin, and Jules Romains. Less frequent in its pages were poems by Francis Jammes, Louis de Gonzague-Frick, Henri de Régnier, Léon Deubel, Charles Vildrac, André Fontainas, L.-P. Fargue, Tristan Derème, and Paul Claudel. Royère himself not only contributed much verse but most often wrote the book reviews on poetry, and it was he who set the tone of the magazine. His personal tastes were well illustrated by the lecture and readings he gave on October 20, 1908 at the Salon d'automne. Mallarmé and Verlaine were his choices among the older poets; a wide representation of the symbolists included Valéry, Charles Morice, Henri de Régnier, Van Lerberghe, Mockel, Merrill, Fontainas, Souza, and Roinard. The third and youngest group included Lavaud, Apollinaire, and Gabriel Mourey.

In his preface to *Eurythmies* (1904), Royère spoke of "une collaboration décente avec Stéphane Mallarmé—lequel par malheur je n'ai pas connu." By this he meant, he went on to explain, that his poetry, like Mallarmé's,

10. See *La Phalange,* No. 16 (Oct. 1907), pp. 348–54.

demands as much initiative from the reader as from the writer. Three years later, in his preface to *Sœur de Narcisse nue,* he iterated his debt to Mallarmé, ending on these words: "Si Mallarmé fut calme, c'est que l'émoi surnaturel exige le quasi-silence. L'âme, si elle est émue, atteint au paroxisme par la sérénité." Finally in 1923, writing a preface for *Quiétudes,* he stood firm on his earlier ideas. The attribute of the French mind is not clarity but depth. To seek simplicity and logic is not to understand the true nature of poetry. That had been revealed by Baudelaire and Mallarmé.

Thus Royère's ideas came to be known as "néo-Mallarméisme," and indeed the name of Mallarmé did receive much attention in *La Phalange.* Vielé-Griffin in 1907 wrote on Mallarmean discipline, in 1908 A. de Bersaucourt published a letter of Mallarmé, and André Fontainas his memories of Mallarmé as a teacher. Thibaudet offered two extracts of his *La Poésie de Mallarmé* in the December 1910 and January 1911 issues of *La Phalange.*

Royère's antipathy toward poetry with a social aim was most violently expressed when he had occasion to speak of Fernand Gregh and humanism. But he was equally harsh toward Moréas and the Ecole romane. He accused the romanists of having composed only "discours latins." In symbolism, which to his way of thinking had found a way of escaping from books and plunging poetry into the deep wellsprings of nature, he saw the proper climate for lyricism. In the age of classicism, he found two authors, La Fontaine and Racine, whom he regarded as exceptions to the spirit of their epoch and as ancestors of Mallarmé and Vielé-Griffin.[11]

Apollinaire was interested in Royère's theories. He wrote an essay on him in the January 1908 issue of *La Phalange,*[12] and in a lecture ("La Phalange nouvelle" given on April 25, 1908 in the Salon des artistes indépendants) he said of Royère's work: "L'auteur de *Sœur de Narcisse nue* a droit à toute notre admiration, car son ouvrage s'approche tellement de la perfection que, sur ce point avant tout, il est incomparable" (*La Poésie symboliste,* p. 192). Other important critical essays in the magazine include Stuart Merrill's study of Albert Mockel (May 1907), Vielé-Griffin's of Verlaine (July 1908), Toussaint Luca's of Signoret (September 1908), Jean Florence's of Paul Claudel (November 1908), and Guillaume Apollinaire's of Paul Fort (March 1909). Alfred Jarry's death was commemorated in an article written by Louis Lormel.

Both Vielé-Griffin and Robert de Souza were exponents of a theory of

---

11. Royère became particularly incensed on the question of classicism in 1910 when René Fauchois, lecturing to the students of the Odéon, attacked the plot of Racine's *Iphigénie.* Royère classified Fauchois as a "barbare ridicule." Lasserre and Maurras he called "barbares intelligents." Each time a critic proposed the word "clarté," Royère countered with "profondeur."

12. No. 19, pp. 596–600.

free verse for *La Phalange*. The former entitled one of his essays (No. 17, Nov. 15, 1907, pp. 415–22) "Une conquête morale," and this victory was precisely that of freedom in versification. Souza, in "La Pensée lyrique" (No. 42, Dec. 1909, pp. 97–108), "Du rythme en français" (No. 56, Feb. 1911, pp. 102–36), and "Notre Rythmique et la Tradition" (No. 60, June 1911, pp. 511–13) seconded Royère's and Vielé-Griffin's attitude toward freedom in prosody.

Royère had stated in the first number of *Phalange* that he was founding the periodical because no magazine worthily represented the conquest in poetic expression made by Mallarmé. His critical comments in the magazine were almost all determined by his admiration for hermetic qualities and rare words. Robert de Souza's book *Où Nous en sommes* (1906) was the occasion for his first long article entitled "Un Manifeste symboliste." While praising Souza, Royère tried to demolish Fernand Gregh. His placing of some extracts from recent poems by Gregh which had appeared in *La Revue de Paris* for comparison with a poem by de Souza, extracted from the 1893 volume *Fumerolles,* was a none-too-convincing form of criticism. By this, however, Royère strove to prove that Gregh was inferior to de Souza.

For eight years Royère's likes and dislikes dominated the critical comments in *La Phalange*. Loyal and perhaps overly laudatory toward poets he admired, he was brutal in his disdain. He gained enemies by his truculence. He accused the *Mercure de France* of failing to keep its promise to uphold an ideal; he stated that the Ecole romane had succeeded only in aping Latin poets; he called Henry Spiess an "écrivain suisse et poète ridicule"; he berated under the title "Monsieur Louis le Cardonnel" the abbé who had renounced his early symbolist verse. Faithful to an aversion of long standing, in June 1910 he called Gregh's *La Chaîne éternelle* a fine example of servile imitation and platitude. The tone of certain end papers in the magazine, signed "Intérim," was even more caustic. One reads in the May 1909 number: "Les décalcomanies de M. Bonnard, les faux gestes de M. Gregh, les bariolures de M. de Bouhélier." It is true that these phrases were printed in a moment of anger. Eugène Montfort had written an insulting article in *Les Marges* [13] in which he pictured Royère, René Ghil, and Robert de Souza as aging writers who somehow imagined they were still eighteen years of age and living in 1890. "Intérim," who was most likely Royère, had reason to feel offended and answer in bitter terms. Montfort read "Intérim's" note, but expressed no contrition. Of Royère he said, "C'est un pion de Carcassonne qui se croit artiste. Il fait du Mallarmé—mais Mallarmé sourirait." [14]

While Royère expended much of his energy in combatting Gregh, Abel Bonnard, Charles Maurras, and Maurice Magre, he was quick to come to the

13. No. 14 (March 1909), pp. 70–4.   14. No. 16 (July 1909), p. 11.

defense of poets he admired. In 1910, when Henri Clouard called Verhaeren and Vielé-Griffin "Les Mauvais Maîtres," [15] Royère countered with an article, "La Critique négative," in which he demonstrated that the Belgian poet was not a mere purveyor of sensations, nor Vielé-Griffin the prisoner of words that Clouard claimed they were. Robert de Souza remained for Royère "un de nos plus purs poètes," René Chalupt the best lyricist in the tradition of Samain and Régnier, and his two favorites, Nau and Lavaud, the most talented of their times. Although he detested poetry with social implications, he praised the "Abbaye" group, and Romains, Duhamel, Vildrac, and Arcos were important contributors to his magazine. He was more interested in the liberties in prosody and the imagery than in the ideas of these poets. Indeed, a large part of Royère's admiration was for "vers libristes." "Sur la poésie actuelle," the essay printed in the March 1910 issue of *La Phalange,* was almost entirely devoted to the champions and enemies of free verse. The enemies were Charles Maurras and the royalists who had been calling for a return to classicism. The champions were presented as Vildrac and Duhamel, particularly because of their *Notes sur la technique poétique* (1910); Mithouard by reason of his policies in directing *L'Occident;* Robert de Souza and André Gide whose *Nouvelle Revue Française* appeared friendly to innovation.

An amicable attitude existed between *L'Occident* and *La Phalange.* Many poets were frequent contributors to both magazines (Vielé-Griffin, Robert de Souza, and Guy Lavaud, for example). The critical articles and notices often expressed the same point of view (Jacques Rivière in *L'Occident* in 1907 and Jean Florence in *La Phalange* in 1908 extolled Paul Claudel; Francis Jammes and René Chalupt were given a good press), but despite these points of contact each periodical kept its distinct personality. François-Paul Alibert, Fagus, Jean de Bouchère, Suarès, Robert Vallery-Radot, Maurice de Noisay, Francis de Miomandre, and Marc Lafargue were attached to the group around Mithouard. Different as they were, they represented the fusion of sentiment and intelligence, the intrusion of philosophical thought, the religious preoccupation that the director of *L'Occident* favored. In *La Phalange* were Louis de Gonzague-Frick, C.-A. Cantacuzène, Léon Tonnelier, Tristan Klingsor, Roger Frène, S.-C. Leconte, André Spire, Louis Mandin, Léo Loups, Stuart Merrill, Elsa Koeberlé, Touny-Lérys, Jules Romains, and Henri Franck, besides the three favorites, Nau, Lavaud, and de Souza. Such a varied list, to which could be added the names of the "Abbaye" group, is seemingly at odds with Royère's critical comments in the magazine. Exoticism, bucolic simplicity, fantasy, preciosity, social preoccupation, free verse, and regular meters, all were blended pell-mell in the

15. *Revue critique des idées et des livres, 11* (Oct. 10, 1910), 61–79.

magazine. What becomes of Royère's neo-Mallarméism, of his ideas of hermetic verse?

Here arises the complex question of Royère's personality. The dogmatic, often overbearing critic was the most tolerant of men in his capacity as director and editor. *Une campagne littéraire,* a little pamphlet by Valery Larbaud, tells us that his close friends often felt that Royère was too eclectic and too generous in accepting copy for *La Phalange.* His reply, that his only concern was to combat mediocrity and banality, explains the contradiction between names of certain collaborators and Royère's opinions. Although reproving S.-C. Leconte's admiration for Leconte de Lisle and Heredia, he found sufficient talent in the poet to accept his works.

Royère's interest in innovations and his loyalty to his friends more than once brought mockery from critics. One of the early regular contributors to *La Phalange* who excited some hilarity was Louis de Gonzague-Frick. His neologisms gave his poems a style not unlike that of Adoré Floupette. In "Refuge," a work of sixteen lines, the words *intactile, exitiale, illécébrant, spelonque,* and *innascible,* and in "Déréliction," *perflabile, nugace,* and *plagoncule,* furnish examples of the author's love for rare vocables. Another of Royère's close associates, Robert de Souza, toward the end of 1911 had the unhappy idea of offering a monthly contribution, "Le Poème du jour." Written in free verse, these items were somewhat like a "Gazette rimée," and recounted such events as rape, accidents, prize fights.

L'Occident between 1907 and 1910, like *Antée,* was a forerunner of *La Nouvelle Revue Française,* not by reason of Mithouard's philosophical theories, but for the attention it accorded writers who were to become famous through the new magazine. First of all there was Claudel, the writer Gide wanted more than any other for the *Nouvelle Revue Française.* The 150 copies of *Partage de midi,* not put on public sale but printed by the "Bibliothèque de l'Occident" at the end of 1906, did not of course reach a wide public. But *Partage de midi* inspired an essay by Eugène Marsan,[16] and a copy of the play borrowed from Gabriel Frizeau led Jacques Rivière, in February 1907, to write a letter to Claudel. This marked the beginning of an important literary friendship. *L'Occident* printed Rivière's long essay "Paul Claudel, poète chrétien."[17] This was a landmark in criticism of Claudel, for Rivière touched on many aspects of the writer's art and thought. The bringing together of diverse things by the mere fact of their coexistence; the primitive and living imagery of nature; the rhythm of the phrase based on that of breathing; the representation of man earth-bound but constantly rising in his thought toward heaven; the failure of man's arrogance, illus-

16. *L'Occident, 11* (June 1907), 279–92.
17. *12* (Oct. 1907), 158–76; (Nov. 1907), 210–20; (Dec. 1907), 267–75.

trated in *Tête d'or* and *La Ville;* the presence of God in the human heart, as portrayed in *La Jeune Fille Violaine,* were principal points of Rivière's discussion.

Claudel did not contribute many poems to the magazine that was spreading his fame. A "Ballade" in 1908, a "Hymne de la pentecôte" in 1909 constituted his contributions.

Another favored collaborator of *L'Occident* who later became associated with *La Nouvelle Revue Française* was F.-P. Alibert. Born in 1873, Alibert was the author of several pamphlets of verse published in his native city of Carcassonne. His volume *Le Buisson ardent* was printed by the "Bibliothèque de l'Occident" in 1907. André Suarès, Jammes, and Vielé-Griffin, all esteemed by Gide, and all contributors to *La Nouvelle Revue Française,* were in Mithouard's group. Others of course, including Mithouard himself, never became identified with the Gide periodical. Guy Lavaud, who founded a review of his own in Nice in 1908, *La Revue des lettres et des arts,* collected in his circle a number of the writers of *L'Occident* and *La Phalange* who did not become collaborators of *La Nouvelle Revue Française.*

One of the minor periodicals which gave poetry a large place in its pages was *Les Bandeaux d'or* (1907–14). Its director, Paul Castiaux, was from Lille, and in 1900, as a young man of twenty, he had helped found *Le Beffroi* in his native city. The first number of *Les Bandeaux d'or* appeared in April 1907. The periodical was to be an anthology of prose and poetry compositions by young writers. Théo Varlet, one of Castiaux's friends from the *Beffroi* group, and like him from Lille, immediately joined the *Bandeaux d'or.* Both Castiaux and Varlet were great travelers and their trips inspired much of their verse. Varlet visited England, Holland, Germany, Switzerland, Greece, Italy, and southern France, and while his poetry cannot be called descriptive, it does consist of meditations in definite geographical settings. He wrote verse in both free and regular forms. Castiaux composed many of his poems during trips to Holland, Brittany, and the Mediterranean. He was much more enthusiastic than Varlet; his verse was usually a celebration of existence and of the world in which man is privileged to behold the grandeur of the sea, the rich panorama of changing landscapes. Almost all his poems were in free meters, and the poet who seems to have inspired him most was Verhaeren.

Les Bandeaux d'or was scarcely recognized as a periodical, for its numbers appeared at irregular intervals, some bearing dates and others only the "fascicule" numeral. Printed in Arras, the little anthology found its way to Paris, where it was mentioned either for the contributions it had secured from Régnier, Verhaeren, Vielé-Griffin, and Albert Mockel, or for its support of the Abbaye group. It is this latter affiliation that gives it importance. Not only Arcos, Duhamel, and Romains, but Roger Allard, P.-J. Jouve, and Luc Durtain were among its contributors. Allard's *Vertes Saisons* (1908) was printed at L'Abbaye. Luc Durtain, whose real name was Dr. André Nepveu, won the admiration of Romains in 1908 with his collection of poems *Pégase*. Jouve, a native of Arras, was during the years preceding the war accounted one of the confirmed disciples of unanimism.

These were the magazines, other than *Vers et Prose,* where poetry chiefly flourished until the founding of *La Nouvelle Revue Française.* The preponderance of names from the symbolist period and the appearance of a younger group intent on giving poetry a social meaning are the principal directions to be discerned. But there is another side to the picture. Critical comments on poets rarely appeared unless a published volume inspired them. What were the books of verse during 1906–10 which claimed attention?

CHAPTER 8. Books and Reputations (1906–1910)

IN VIEW of the publisher's natural desire not to lose money on the books he prints and the limited public for poetry as contrasted with the novel or even the drama, it is remarkable how many collections of verse, year after year, found their way into print in twentieth-century France. From correspondence of the period, one suspects that often the poet or his friends paid costs of publication, but the works did appear. During the years 1906 to 1911, the presses of the *Mercure de France* issued most of the important volumes. Alfred Vallette, the astute director, is reported to have driven hard bargains, but his house was much esteemed. Almost all these books of poetry were by writers who had built their reputations during the symbolist period. The two most celebrated were Henri de Régnier and Emile Verhaeren. The former was writing a good many novels, also published by the *Mercure,* but *La Sandale ailée* (1906) and *Le Miroir des heures* (1910) collected the poems which had first appeared in many periodicals, from little regional magazines to the *Revue des Deux Mondes.* Verhaeren's *La Multiple Splendeur* (1906) was a first edition published by Vallette, but he also reprinted three collections which had appeared in Brussels: *Les Heures Claires* of 1896, *Les Visages de la vie* of 1899, and *Les Heures de l'après-midi* of 1905. From the defunct *La Plume,* Vallette obtained rights for Moréas' *Les Stances* which he promptly reprinted in 1906, and in the following year he presented new editions of Moréas' early work under the titles of *Premiers Poèmes* and *Poèmes et Sylves.* Collecting some small pamphlets, either privately printed or published under the auspices of *L'Ermitage* or *L'Occident,* Vielé-Griffin gave the *Mercure* in 1906 a volume entitled *Plus loin.* During that same year Jammes' *Pensée des jardins,* containing both prose and verse; *L'Eglise habillée en feuilles;* and a larger volume, *Clairières dans le ciel,* containing most of the poet's verse since 1902, were printed by the *Mercure.* There were also lesser poetic luminaries inherited by the publishing house. Tristan Klingsor had begun his association with the *Mercure* press in 1895, Saint-Pol-Roux in 1893, André Fontainas in 1894, and Stuart Merrill in 1897. Klingsor's *Le Valet du cœur* (1908), Roux's *Les Féeries intérieures* (1907), Fontainas' *La Nef désemparée* (1908), and Merrill's *Une Voix dans la foule* (1909) continued that relationship.

One poet of the old guard deserted the *Mercure.* This was Paul Fort, whose collections of *Ballades françaises,* after *Coxcomb* (1906), bore the imprint of *Vers et Prose,* the periodical he had founded. On the other hand, the press added one voice from the past when it published the *Poésies complètes* (1908) of Emmanuel Signoret, who had died in 1900. During his lifetime, Signoret's work had appeared from the press of *La Plume* or his own *Saint-Graal.* André Gide's admiration for the dead poet, expressed in a preface, was in large part responsible for the publication of the collected poems.

These, the symbolist poets of the 1890's, formed the solid basis of the *Mercure*'s production. The other volumes of verse from this publishing house were relatively few and extremely diverse in inspiration and technique. Léo Larguier's *Jacques* (1907) recalled Lamartine's *Jocelyn,* while Cécile Sauvage's *Tandis que la terre tourne* (1910) had the tenderness and emotional quality of Marceline Desbordes-Valmore. Touny-Lérys' *La Pâque des roses* (1909), in its tonality of intimacy and simplicity, reflected the influence of Francis Jammes who composed a preface for the volume. The *Mercure* also presented two poets who had earlier appeared in the *Cahiers de la quinzaine.* One was François Porché whose *A chaque jour, comme j'ai pu, comme il m'advint* (1907) was an enlarged edition of a Péguy pamphlet.[1] Leaving France to teach French language and literature in Russia that same year, he continued to send poems to Parisian periodicals. These verses, almost all inspired by impressions of his travels in the Baltic countries or by his sojourn in Moscow, were collected in *Au loin, peut-être . . .* (1909).

André Spire's *Et vous riez!* which had attracted some attention when it appeared in the December 20, 1905 issue of the *Cahiers de la quinzaine,* formed the basis of a larger volume entitled *Versets* which the *Mercure* published in 1908. This was, for two reasons, the most unusual of that publishing house's offerings. The form, which took no account of syllabic count and almost never contained rhyme, was entirely built upon sonorities and rhythmic groupings of spoken speech. The periods of the sentences were relatively short, punctuation frequent, the lines determined by these pauses. Spire's thought was often bitter or ironic, and the nervous tension of his utterance reflected this state of mind. Paul Claudel's more ample measure, and Vielé-Griffin's embellished lyric pattern gave totally different effects from this direct and passionate voice. Repetition of words and of sounds accounts in part for the emphatic tone, often comparable to that of Walt Whitman, but less verbose and more concentrated in its effects.

Spire's poetry was emotional, but the emotions always sprang from ideas. Indignation at social injustices, expression of the longings and anguish of the Jews, and revolt against the forces that keep the individual from attaining a free existence animated this verse. Like Jules Romains, Spire was a

---

1. *Les Cahiers de la quinzaine,* V⁰ série, No. 17 (June 9, 1904).

poet of collectivity, but his voice was often the prophetic voice of the Old Testament. Furthermore, the sympathy of Spire reached out and took the crowd into his embrace, while Romains usually remained the central figure of the group with which he sought association.

Romains became one of the poets of the *Mercure* publishing house in 1910, when his thin volume, *Deux Poèmes,* and a larger one, *Un Etre en marche,* appeared. Here again the physical form of the poems assumed importance. In *Deux Poèmes* were "Le Poème du Métropolitain" and "A la foule," the first composed in 1904 and the second in 1909. Almost all the early poem was written in short paragraphs and lines, unrhymed, which might suggest the influence of Whitman or Claudel. Romains denied, in a note, any such sources, explaining that both authors were unknown to him in 1904. The poem of 1909 was an ode in which the writer (or rather speaker) addressed the crowd. Its lines were of nine and twelve syllables, but with little regard for caesura and only occasional rhyme. The actor de Max had recited this poem at the Odéon in March 1909.

Un Etre en marche, Romains' full-length volume of 1910, was not well received by the critics. A series of poems telling of an excursion into the country by a group of boarding school girls bore the curious title of "Poème épique." The other heading in the volume, "Poème lyrique," was more understandable, for the poems in that division concerned Romains' personal observations during a day in Paris. It was not difficult to discover that the dual purpose of the author was to give, through the school girls, an idea of collective thought, and, through his poetic diary, to establish the relationship between the individual and his surroundings. Evidently some readers felt that this plan vitiated spontaneity. There were many meters in the volume and great variety in stanza form, but syllabic count was kept. The most salient phenomenon came in the last words of lines, for Romains often used words that cannot be defined as rhymes, blank verse endings, or even assonance. He was replacing rhyme by repetitions in phonic effects he considered much more subtle and arresting. A series such as "descend," "centre," and "entrer" or "glissent," "frissons," and "gonfle" will illustrate this recurrence of consonant or vowel.

Neither of these volumes by Romains added substantially to his fame. He was well known by 1910, partly because of the relative celebrity of the Abbaye de Créteil. The title of his collection of verse, published by the Abbaye press in 1908, had caused comment on his philosophy. He was known as the poet of *La Vie unanime* and represented as the leader of other poets of the Abbaye group. Duhamel's *Des Légendes, des batailles* (1907), Vildrac's *Images et Mirages* (1908), Allard's *Vertes Saisons,* all published at Créteil, were popularly considered examples of work by his disciples.

Thus the *Mercure* was not only the publishing house of the symbolists but also of some poets who represented a range from romanticism to modernism, with techniques both traditional and new. Other publishing houses sometimes printed volumes of verse with a wider sale, but no other had so long a list of distinguished poets. Fasquelle, with volumes by Droin, Lucie Delarue-Mardrus, Bonnard, Gojon, Gregh, and Mandin, remained conservative. Sansot, with Georges Périn, Strentz, Beauduin, Marinetti, Abadie, Erlande, and Vallery-Radot, was more eclectic. Besides poets who were content to transfer their personal emotions into verse, were the more tumultuous and violent voices of Beauduin, the "poète paroxyste," and of Marinetti, the futurist.[2] Calmann-Lévy published in 1907 a volume which had wide popularity, Mme. de Noailles' *Les Eblouissements*.

Besides the volumes of the *Mercure,* those of *Vers et Prose, L'Occident, La Phalange,* and *Le Beffroi* deserve mention. Paul Fort's poetic works (*Ile-de-France*, 1908; *Mortcerf*, 1909; and *La Tristesse de l'homme*, 1910) and those of his co-editor André Salmon (*Poèmes*, 1905; and *Les Féeries*, 1907) were the principal offerings of *Vers et Prose*. But when the presses of the Abbaye de Créteil ceased to operate in 1908, Fort welcomed two of that group, publishing in 1909 *L'Homme en tête* by Duhamel and *Premier Livre des prières* by Romains. This was only a temporary affiliation; after 1910 most of the group were associated with Figuière.

Unlike Paul Fort, the directors of *La Phalange* and *L'Occident* did not immediately collect their periodical contributions into volumes. Royère's *Sœur de Narcisse nue* (1907) was his only work published by his magazine. But he printed J.-A. Nau's *Vers la fée Viviane* (1908), Guy Lavaud's *Du Livre de la mort* (1909), Léo Loups' *Les Lévriers* (1908), and Philéas Lebesgue's *M. de Boufflers* (1908). All these publications of *La Phalange* were little pamphlets rather than volumes and contained seventy-five pages or less. Royère's preface to *Sœur de Narcisse nue* contained the sentence "Ma poésie est obscure comme un lis," an expression which became better known than the author's verse. Lavaud's little book was an elegiac series of poems written at Aigues-Mortes during the mortal illness of a woman he loved. Léo Loups' verses, set in his native Algeria, all filled with descriptive local color, belonged to the exotic currents of the time.

L'Occident was also the publisher of a volume by Guy Lavaud. *La*

---

2. Beauduin was only briefly associated with the Sansot publishing house. In 1908 he founded his own periodical, *Les Rubriques nouvelles,* and issued his volumes from that press. Marinetti's French publisher was Sansot until the first World War. The noteworthy volumes in the French language were *La Vie charnelle* (1908), a book of poems; *La Conquête des étoiles* (new edition, 1908); *Mafarka le Futuriste, roman africain* (1909); *Enquête internationale sur le vers libre* (containing the first futurist manifesto and published in 1909); *Le Futurisme* (1911); *Le Monoplan du pape* (1913).

Floraison des eaux (1907) was not essentially different from *Du livre de la mort,* save that it was more symbolic. In the two works the central figure was woman weary of life and on the point of death. In *La Floraison des eaux,* she represented the poet's soul and the setting was a legendary Elsinore rather than Provence. But the imagery, in which water plays such a large part, and the long cadences of alexandrines offered resemblance with the *Livre de la mort.* The most important poetic publications in the *Occident* list were Jammes' *Rayons de miel* (1908), eclogues which began his series of *Georgiques chrétiennes,* and Claudel's *Cinq Grandes Odes* (1910).

There were also several regional magazines or printing houses which issued volumes of verse. The most important were Sicard's *Le Feu* in Marseilles and Bocquet's *Le Beffroi* of Lille and Roubaix. The former printed a first volume by Francis Carco, prose-poems entitled *Instincts* (1908). The latter's most noteworthy publication was Vildrac's *Le Livre d'amour* (1910), but the list of the "Editions du *Beffroi*" was impressive in length and included the names of Deubel, Lafon, Pergaud, Syffert, and Varlet.[3]

Although the list was highly selective, the poets and volumes mentioned thus far represented the most important elements of the poetic scene between 1905 and 1910. Just at the end of the period appeared a work which brought another name into the ranks of poetic masters. The author was Péguy and the work *Le Mystère de la Charité de Jeanne d'Arc.* Péguy, known since 1900 for his prose in *Les Cahiers de la quinzaine,* suddenly emerged as a poet. The *Mystère,* a work of about 250 pages, was the sixth number of the eleventh series of the *Cahiers* and bore the date January 16, 1910. Only a few close friends knew the relationship of the work with the first part of a dramatic trilogy, *Jeanne d'Arc,* signed Marcel et Pierre Baudouin, which had appeared in 1897 in a huge volume of almost 800 pages (many of which were blank, in order, as Péguy had explained, to permit the reader to think while turning them). Péguy, a student at the Ecole normale in 1897, had collected the money for printing the *Jeanne d'Arc* from his school-mates, but had not told them "Pierre Baudouin" was his pen name.[4] In the *Mystère,* published thirteen years later, much of the text was taken directly from the first play of the Jeanne d'Arc trilogy. The presentation on the page was quite different, however, since the *Mystère* contained occasional passages in which separate paragraphing of short sentences formed what are known as Péguy's "litanies."

The *Mystère de la Charité de Jeanne d'Arc* gained immediate admiration.

3. Volumes by these poets published by *Le Beffroi* include *Poèmes choisis* (1909), *Poèmes provinciaux* (1910), *L'Herbe d'avril* (1908), *Les Brumes de la vie* (1907), *Notations* (1906).

4. The actual amount of collaboration between Marcel Baudouin and Péguy in the writing of *Jeanne d'Arc* is still uncertain. Baudouin died in 1896.

André Gide sent copies to several of his friends, among them Jammes and Claudel, and wrote some laudatory words concerning the work in the March 1910 issue of the *Nouvelle Revue Française*. Barrès tried to obtain the Grand Prix de littérature for Péguy. During the years from 1910 to 1914 Péguy's poetic reputation became firmly established. His death in action on September 5, 1914, was the beginning of a kind of apotheosis.

For many readers, *Les Grandes Odes* and the *Mystère de la Charité de Jeanne d'Arc* represent the apogee of poetic attainment during the first decade of the twentieth century. Both works were filled with religious fervor, however questionable Péguy's political and social views appeared to certain of the Catholic clergy. Péguy's words of 1908, "J'ai retrouvé la foi—je suis catholique," were explained in his essay "Notre Jeunesse" of July 1910, and expressed during the following years in other "mystères" and in a profusion of short and long poems. Both Claudel and Péguy became identified with a form of lyricism which was closer to the prose-poem than to verse. The "verset" of Claudel, and the "litanie" of Péguy cast into shadow the rhymed couplets, quatrains, or other more regular forms that both authors also practiced. Péguy's repetitive effects were often called tautological, but both authors were acclaimed for having brought religious poetry to new heights.

Certainly Péguy and Claudel gave religious poetry a vast and general significance which made their predecessors shrink in stature. Jammes, after Claudel had persuaded him to become a practicing and militant Catholic in July 1905, adopted a more pious tone in his poems but chiefly painted himself in his verse as the rustic poet living in harmony with nature and God. Louis le Cardonnel's *Poèmes* of 1904, which some had hailed at the time of their publication as the greatest mystical writing since *Sagesse,* were mainly concerned with emotions inspired by sojourns in monasteries, by meditations, or by the consciousness of past error or present weakness. Charles Guérin, in his last volume (*L'Homme intérieur,* 1905), scarcely transcended his individual struggle between doubt and belief. The poetry which appeared in *Le Temps présent,* a little magazine founded in 1907 by Francis Caillard and Louis Chaîne, was almost always religious in tone and distinguished by little save its piety. François Mauriac's first volume (*Les Mains jointes,* 1909) had as sponsor *Le Temps présent,* but these poems of youthful religious experience differed little from lyrics by André Lafon or Armand Praviel.

The new dimensions brought to religious poetry by Claudel can be readily perceived. Péguy's work is more difficult of definition. The dramas and the *Grandes Odes,* with the usual imagery in which the concrete and visual attained a spiritual meaning, and with the vision which embraced sky, oceans, and continents or historical perspectives from the antique to the modern, set Claudel apart from the lyricists who voiced their personal anguish and joy in matters of religious import. But Péguy offered no such spatial or temporal breadth, no such arresting figures of speech. Madame Gervaise, who was the lyric voice in the *Mystère de la Charité de Jeanne d'Arc,* and whose long monologue filled the entire *Porche du mystère de la deuxième vertu* (1911), spoke a very simple and direct language. Whether she was expounding the passion of Christ or the divine gift of hope, she did not rely on ornamentation for poetic beauty. Her devices were simpler: accumulation and repetition. A short passage from the *Mystère de la Charité de Jeanne d'Arc,* where Madame Gervaise developed the "mater dolorosa" theme in hundreds of lines, contained the principal elements of Péguy's technique:

> Si elle avait su elle aurait pleuré toujours.
> Pleuré toute sa vie.
> Pleuré d'avance.
> Elle se serait méfiée.
> Elle aurait pris les devants.
> Comme ça elle n'aurait pas été trompée.
> Elle n'aurait pas été trahie.[5]

Péguy apparently cast overboard one of the accepted tenets of modern poetry, that of concision. Repetition and amplification were considered dangerous; they were faults rather than virtues. Péguy was and is still sometimes called wearisome and verbose. On the other hand, these developments of thought, these shadings of meaning, built up a forceful impression which has its admirers.

The year 1910 marked the beginning of poetic fame for Claudel and Péguy. It was also the end of a career of one of the most widely known of contemporary poets, Jean Moréas. He died on March 30, and was accorded a kind of official funeral with speeches by Louis Barthou, the minister of justice, by Léon Dierx the "Prince des poètes," by Maurice Barrès, and by Ernest Raynaud. The *Mercure de France,* which had become Moréas' editor after the demise of *La Plume,* was engaged at the time of his death in printing an important essay by Marcel Coulon, "L'Unité de Jean Moréas."[6] Soon afterward the magazine presented a necrological article by Pierre Quillard on April 16, and Ernest Raynaud's nineteen sonnets, "L'Apothéose de Jean Moréas, poète français," on September 16. During the course of 1910, newspapers and magazines printed many articles on Moréas. The tenor of these was that the author of *Les Stances* had successfully shown the value of principles of prosody established during the sixteenth and seventeenth

5. Charles Péguy, *Œuvres poétiques complètes* (Pléiade edition), p. 98.
6. *84* (March 16, 1910), 193–215; (April 1, 1910), 431–50.

centuries and had left a work of definite value and great beauty. An example of fervid admiration was that of J.-M. Bernard. He issued in July 1910 a special number of *Les Guêpes,* a little magazine he had begun publishing in Valence in 1909. Entitled "A la mémoire de Jean Moréas," this issue contained articles by Barrès, the Tharaud brothers, Eugène Marsan of *La Revue critique des idées et des livres,*[7] and the novelist Marcel Boulenger. The substance of these articles was not different from the general commemorative articles published elsewhere. Moréas was a picturesque figure and much that was said about him was anecdotal rather than critical. For J.-M. Bernard and for Barrès, Moréas' championship of the Greek heritage in French literature was his greatest claim to fame.

When the Parnassian poets had died (Heredia in 1905, Sully-Prudhomme in 1907, Coppée in 1908), articles commemorating them had had a dignified, official tone that was entirely different from what was written about Moréas. The author of *Les Stances,* by the time of his death, represented a dual literary personality: the poet who had successively been associated with *La Plume, Vers et Prose,* and the *Mercure de France,* and the journalist whose writings had appeared in several Parisian newspapers. He wore the officer's rosette of the Legion of Honor and at the same time was the frequenter of the Closerie des Lilas and the Café Vachette where a heterogeneous group of artists and writers pursued a tradition of informality that had existed since the days of Verlaine. His sharp repartee, his travel diaries, his literary essays, and his drama *Iphigénie,* as well as his lyrics, furnished the material for those who wrote about him. Rightly, his commentators conveyed the impression that France had not only lost a writer of some worth but also a personality. Long after his death, some of his friends, such as Coulon and Raynaud, were still penning their memories of him, for a renewal of interest in his writing occurred after the appearance, in 1920, of a posthumous book of the *Stances.*

Moréas, much in the public eye, spent his time in the midst of Parisian literary activity, presenting a very different case from a poet who died three years before him, in March 1907. Charles Guérin, only thirty-four years old at the time of his death, was seldom in Paris, and spent almost all of his life in his native Lunéville or nearby Nancy. Articles in 1907 concerning him contained some of the fervor, some of the sense of a great loss to French poetry, that were inspired by the death of Moréas. Those who admired his poetry represented a wide range of literary beliefs, from Gaston Deschamps of *Le Temps* (the archenemy of the symbolists) to Pierre Quillard and Remy de Gourmont.

7. Marsan's long essay published in *La Revue critique des idées* on June 25, 1910 (pp. 459–92) was typical of the articles extolling Moréas as defender of French tradition.

Like Moréas, Guérin represented an evolutionary process in his poems. *Les Syrtes* and *Les Cantilènes* had been written by the author of *Les Stances*. The poet of *L'Homme intérieur* had begun with *Fleurs de neige* and *Joies grises*. In both poets the search for rare words and musical evocation had yielded to preoccupation with form. Guérin recognized this. Speaking in *L'Homme intérieur* (1905) of his early poetry, he said:

> J'étais libre alors du souci
> D'atteindre à la forme parfaite;
> Pourquoi ne suis-je pas ainsi
> Resté naïvement poète?
> ("On trouve dans mes anciens vers," p. 36)

This renunciation of what Guérin called "fraîcheur" and "négligence" had its compensations. Guérin, sharing this honor with Henri de Régnier, became a contributor to the *Revue des Deux Mondes*[8] as well as to the *Mercure de France*. The poet who had first been called "un poète décadent lorrain," was compared to Vigny and to Sully-Prudhomme. In 1885 Guérin had dedicated *Le Sang des crépuscules* to Rodenbach and Mallarmé. In 1901 he dedicated *Le Semeur de cendres* to José-Maria de Heredia. *Le Cœur solitaire* of 1898 was revised by Guérin, and in its 1904 edition six poems which took liberties with rhyme or meter were struck out, while eighteen poems of impeccable form were added.

Guérin's *L'Homme intérieur* (1905) was the last book of verse which appeared during his lifetime. Particularly through this volume he gained a number of new admirers among Catholics. His "inquiétude religieuse," already patent in *Le Semeur de cendres,* was made more acute by his illness. This aspect of his verse had attracted Jammes even before the turn of the century. Jammes and Guérin had become fast friends, and on the latter's death it was Jammes who went to Lunéville to classify Guérin's papers and manuscripts. The wide following and admiration that Guérin had gained may be easily perceived in the forty-five paragraphs of homage gathered by Ernest-Charles in *Le Censeur*. In newspapers and magazines, Henry Bordeaux, Gaston Deschamps, François Coppée, Fernand Gregh, René Boylesve, and Francis Jammes were among the authors who composed essays that were not mere obituary notices, but expressions of literary admiration.

Guérin, who had kept the *Mercure de France* as his publisher but had also won favorable comment from *Le Correspondant* for his religious verse and from *Les Lettres* for his clarity of expression, occupied a place at the time of his death not unlike that of Samain in 1900. A poetic expression of

8. Guérin first appeared in the *Revue des Deux Mondes* in the issue of February 15, 1900. Henri de Régnier made his debut in that magazine the following year. This may seem a dubious honor: the poet who appeared most frequently in the magazine was Léonce Depont.

personal emotion, filled with images which suggested rather than stated, a form which obeyed the traditional rules of versification, and a tonality which was intense rather than grandiose gained the greatest amount of approbation. The ovation Guérin received in 1907 and 1908 was unique in the first decade of the century. In the *Mercure de France* alone, articles by Jammes on April 1, 1907, by Fernand Baldenne (Baldensperger) on May 15, 1907, and by Paul Delior on December 1, 1907, were devoted to him.

Even if allowances are made for writings composed immediately after the death of a poet, the claims in 1907 for Guérin's greatness contrast strikingly with his later obscurity. Calemard de la Fayette died in 1906 at the age of twenty-nine; Charles van Lerberghe in 1907, when he was forty-six; and Renée Vivien in 1909, in her thirty-second year. Each had a small circle of admirers, but none had won a wide public. La Fayette, the author of *Le Rêve des jours,* had stayed within the tradition of the minor Parnassians, but had chiefly contributed to more liberal magazines such as *La Plume, L'Ermitage,* and the *Mercure de France.* His friends saw to it that a posthumous volume of his manuscripts, *La Montée,* was published in 1909. Van Lerberghe, a Belgian, with close associations among the group of *Vers et Prose* and with the *Mercure* where his *Chanson d'Eve* had appeared in 1904, practiced free verse. This endeared him to some, but of course brought censure from Fernand Gregh and other conservatives. Evaluation of Renée Vivien's verse was made difficult by the subject matter of her poems. Generally credited with a rare talent for creating beautiful images and musical lines (a judgment which appears valid enough), she never gained approbation because of her overt expression of Sapphic love.

The relative security of poetic reputations made during the symbolist period, and the uncertainty concerning the worth of young writers, was evident in several programs of lectures and poetic readings which occurred in 1907 and 1908. In the early years of the century there had been many "Matinées poétiques" in Parisian theaters, but since Catulle Mendès and his secretary Louis Payen usually arranged the programs, the poetry given was limited to that of Parnassian tradition. But the series of later years were taken over by speakers more sympathetic to symbolism and free verse: Edmond Pilon, Robert de Souza, P.-N. Roinard, Guillaume Apollinaire, V.-E. Michelet, Jean Royère, Gustave Kahn, and Albert Mockel.

The general picture of poetic endeavor in 1907 was well represented by two of the poetic programs given in October at the Salon d'automne. Edmond Pilon [9] spoke on "Quelques aînés," choosing Moréas, Régnier, Vielé-Griffin, Verhaeren, Kahn, Morice, Mockel, and Maeterlinck to represent the

9. Pilon was neither a Parnassian nor a symbolist. His *Maison d'exil* (1898), published by the *Mercure de France,* had placed him briefly in the symbolist orbit.

older group. Robert de Souza, entrusted with the subject of new lyricists, dwelt principally on fifteen names. Two were women: Mme. de Noailles and Mme. Perdriel-Vaissière, whose *Les Eblouissements* and *Celles qui attendent* had just been published. Other poetic volumes of 1907 (Fernand Fleuret's *Friperies,* Maurice de Noisay's *Le Bon Adieu,* Léon Bocquet's *Les Cygnes noirs,* and André Salmon's *Les Féeries*) explain inclusion of their authors in Souza's program. André Spire and Tancrède de Visan, two of the speaker's friends from the *Vers et Prose* group; André Joussain, somewhat in prominence as a defender of neoromanticism; Paul Castiaux, who had begun publishing the literary anthology *Les Bandeaux d'or;* Jules Romains, not yet the author of *La Vie unanime* but well known in the Créteil group; Louis Payen, a perennial organizer of poetic readings; and the Swiss poet Henry Spiess, whose first volume of serious verse *Le Silence des heures* (1904, 1905) had been well received in France, also figured in this program. Souza, whose polemic essays in defense of symbolism and free verse in *Vers et Prose* had been published in 1906, tried to give a broad representation of current writing. His choice was not striking except for the variety in techniques represented.

Three lectures on poetry given in April 1908 in the Salon des artistes indépendants bore the general name of "L'Après-midi des Poètes," suggested by Mallarmé's eclogue. Later in the year these three talks were published under the title *La Poésie symboliste.* The lecturers were P.-N. Roinard, who presented "Les Maîtres et les Morts," V.-E. Michelet, who discussed "Les Survivants," and Guillaume Apollinaire, who discoursed on "La Phalange nouvelle."

Roinard's impassioned speech was the description of a heroic combat waged by symbolist poets against tyrannical influences. The chief enemy had been naturalism: Zola, Maupassant, and Daudet. Hugo, "le plus verbeux des poètes," had jealously opposed younger writers. No less hostile had been the Parnassians, whom Roinard did not cite by name, "car il faut rendre silence pour silence!" Roinard's concept of the symbolist period was one of broad revolt against tradition. The formation of the Société des artistes indépendants with its formula of "sans jury ni récompenses," the growth of anarchy with Zo d'Axa and Malato, were for him two other manifestations of liberating force.

But the chief matter of Roinard's discourse was the presentation of poetry by writers now dead who had been forces in the lyric renascence of 1885. Their masters had been Gérard de Nerval, Alfred de Vigny, Baudelaire, Tristan Corbière, then Villiers de l'Isle-Adam, Rimbaud, Laforgue, and Mallarmé. With the name of Mallarmé, Roinard burst into a true panegyric: "Au-dessus de notre jeunesse, nous n'eûmes que Mallarmé, l'esprit le plus

haut, le cœur le plus noble, le visage le plus souriant, la main la plus pater-
nelle que nul ait pu rêver, 'sagesse égale bonté,' l'homme que quelques-uns
d'entre nous aimèrent plus qu'aucun autre homme et qui partit subitement
en un jour de détresse inoubliable . . ." [10] There were four poets who had
died in 1907 to whom Roinard paid homage by recitation of their verse.
They were Charles Guérin, Alfred Jarry, Albert Thomas, and Charles van
Lerberghe. The first three were overtaken by death at thirty-four; the Belgian poet was some ten years older. But these relatively short lives and the
even briefer spans of Jules Laforgue (1860–87), Albert Aurier (1865–92),
Edouard Dubus (1863–95), Ephraïm Mikhaël (1866–90), Emmanuel Signoret (1872–1900), and Jules Tellier (1863–89), served to maintain Roinard's
contention that idealistic and unselfish poets are often martyrs whose early
death may be attributed, if not to poverty, at least to disillusion.

V.-E. Michelet, who during the early 1890's had been editor of *Psyché,*
an esoteric magazine with literary pretensions, had known many poets of
the symbolist period. His lecture on the "Survivants" contained a representative choice of poets, beginning with Régnier, Vielé-Griffin, Merrill,
Saint-Pol-Roux, Paul Fort, Quillard, Kahn, Louÿs, Moréas, Raynaud, passing on to more recent arrivals in the poetic world, and ending with the
recitation of a poem by Germain Nouveau.

The emotional speech by Roinard, the calmer retrospective survey by
Michelet, were completed by Guillaume Apollinaire's discourse on poetry in
1908. He too acknowledged the importance of the symbolists, and in a more
categorical manner than his fellow speakers: ". . . tous ceux qui, depuis
1895, ont créé de la poésie doivent de la reconnaissance aux maîtres aimés du
Symbolisme." [11] His point of departure was the group of the naturists (Maurice Magre, Saint-Georges de Bouhélier, and Paul Souchon) and certain
later poets whose work seemed in harmony with that school (Derennes,
Despax, Ernest Gaubert, and Lucien Rolmer). In speaking of naturism,
Apollinaire was careful to indicate that these poets, even when they spoke
against symbolism, were definitely in its debt. After talking on naturism,
Apollinaire made little attempt to classify poets, giving, in a few descriptive
adjectives, the characteristics of each author's works. Naturally considerable
space was given to his own associates in *Le Festin d'Esope* and *La Phalange.*
Henri Hertz, the author of *Quelques vers* (1906), André Salmon (*Poèmes,*
1905; *Féeries,* 1907), Nicolas Deniker, and Max Jacob were four of Apollinaire's intimate friends, while the group of *La Phalange,* which Apollinaire
called "cette jeune revue qui, presque seule, défend en France la cause du
lyrisme," was abundantly represented.

10. Roinard, Michelet, Apollinaire, *La Poésie symboliste* (L'Edition, 1909), p. 73.
11. Ibid., p. 135.

Apollinaire, despite his words concerning *La Phalange,* did credit Fort's *Vers et Prose,* Castiaux's anthology-magazine *Les Bandeaux d'or,* and Bocquet's *Le Beffroi* with fostering the cause of poetry. The Lille magazine had published the early volumes of Théo Varlet (*Notes et poèmes,* 1905; *Notations,* 1906), Léon Deubel (*Vers la vie,* 1904; *La Lumière natale,* 1905; *Poésies,* 1906), and Paul Castiaux (*Au long des terrasses,* 1905). These were three of the authors whom Apollinaire grouped around Bocquet's publication. Still another poet who had been fostered by *Le Beffroi* was Charles Vildrac, and his name naturally suggested to Apollinaire one of the most curious and in a sense the most fecund of collective artistic endeavors, the Abbaye de Créteil. The group of the Abbaye had been dissolved less than three months before Apollinaire gave his lecture, but the activities of the fourteen months of its existence were still fresh in the public memory, thanks to numerous newspaper articles and the publications that had come from the Abbaye press. Apollinaire inserted in his lecture a reading of poems by Vildrac, Duhamel, René Arcos, Mercereau, and Vanderpijl to illustrate activities of this group, having already spoken of Jules Romains in the section devoted to *La Phalange.*

Apollinaire recalled to his listeners the names of many other poets who were not allied with any particular group or periodical, but reserved special praise for two, André Spire and W.-O. Milosz. The irony and pathos of Spire appeared to him powerful enough to change the foundations of empires, "et même des républiques," while Milosz possessed "un lyrisme si évocateur, qu'il ne faut pas hésiter à le placer entre les premiers des nouveaux poètes." [12]

This pattern of lectures and reading of poetry was repeated six months later at the Salon d'automne of 1908. This fall series, called "concerts de poésies," was given on October 20, October 27, and November 3, 1908, by Royère, Kahn, and Mockel. The director of *La Phalange* proposed to treat poetry which was not simple, which aimed at a chosen audience, which did not obey tradition, and which as he said was "transfigurative." Most of his choices were from the symbolist period (Verlaine, Mallarmé, Valéry, Charles Morice, Régnier, Van Lerberghe, Mockel, Merrill, Fontainas, Souza, Roinard), while the others were largely poets from his own magazine (Nau, Lavaud, Ochsé, Apollinaire, Mourey).

Gustave Kahn's title was "Quelques Poètes nouveaux," and while he did not speak of so many poets as had Apollinaire earlier that year, he chose some of the same ones for comment. Charles Vildrac and Mercereau from the Abbaye group, Paul Castiaux of *Les Bandeaux d'or,* Georges and Cécile

12. Ibid., p. 231. The author of *Les Sept Solitudes* had contributed "A la beauté" to *Vers et Prose* two months before this lecture.

Périn, Edmond Pilon, and Alfred Mortier were the principal subjects of his discussion. Obviously a very personal selection, this assortment of names did not give the panoramic sweep that Apollinaire had succeeded in achieving.

Of far more interest was Mockel's subject "La Tradition populaire," in which the speaker grouped poets who had utilized folklore and legends in their lyrics. These included Klingsor, Elskamp, Georges Gaudion, Kahn, Fort, Merrill, Herold, Régnier, Verhaeren, and Vielé-Griffin. Mockel, the author of *Chantefable un peu naïve* and *Clartés,* the critic who had studied the verse of Vielé-Griffin and Henri de Régnier in *Propos de littérature* in 1894 and that of Verhaeren the following year, had been intimately associated with Belgian and French poetic groups during the symbolist period. In his lecture he was examining one of the aspects of that period most closely akin to his own poems where legend held an important role.

In 1909 a series of "Séances littéraires" was offered during October and the first week of November. This time, instead of so much time being devoted to the past,[13] the contemporary literary scene received attention. Jules Romains spoke on "La Poésie immédiate," his discourse being summed up in the sentence: "Toute grande poésie me paraît être la connaissance immédiate d'une âme." Henri Ghéon, the critic of the recently founded *Nouvelle Revue Française,* delivered a speech on "Le Mouvement dans la poésie française." This was a defense of free verse, and Ghéon chose André Spire and Charles Vildrac to illustrate the vitality of that technique. Albert Dreyfus spoke on contemporary German poetry, particularly on Rilke and Stefan George.

The lecture on contemporary poets in the series of 1909 was given by Georges Périn. This thirty-six-year-old writer, the husband of the poetess Cécile Périn, was the author of *Les Emois blottis* (1902) and *La Lisière blonde* (1906). After the founding of *La Phalange* he became a frequent contributor of poems to that periodical. His verse, which had at first been regular, became more daring in form after 1905.[14] Half of the poets whom he presented in his 1909 lecture were fellow contributors either to *La Phalange* or to *Vers et Prose* where some of his verse also appeared. Jean Royère, Guy Lavaud, J.-A. Nau, Louis Mandin, Léon Deubel, Emile Cottinet, Edouard Gazanion, the late Olivier Calemard de la Fayette, Mme. de Saint-Point, Julien Ochsé, and Jean Clary were in this group. Périn's intent was to include only poets who were relatively unknown and, as he implied, unjustly neglected. The exclusion of the Créteil group and of Spire, Salmon, Apollinaire, Alibert, Carco, and Gonzague-Frick from his discussion did not give

---

13. Albert Mockel, however, delivered a lecture on Charles Cros.
14. These poems were collected in *Le Chemin, l'air qui glisse* (1910).

a very fair picture of the younger poets, even in the limited circle of Fort's and Royère's magazines. Today his choice reads like a list of writers destined like himself to near oblivion.

A new grouping of writers, occurring in 1909, the year of this lecture by Périn, profoundly altered the poetic scene. This was effectuated by *La Nouvelle Revue Française,* which took talents from existing circles and discovered new ones.

ANDRÉ GIDE, after his editorship of *L'Ermitage* with Remy de Gourmont during 1905 and 1906, had dreamed of creating a periodical which would accomplish the aims he had envisioned for that magazine. These were the offering of a means of expression for young writers of talent, and an eclectic policy which would depend on only one criterion, that of fine writing. The Belgian magazine *Antée* partly fulfilled this wish; Gide seriously considered bringing that magazine, suffering from financial difficulties in Brussels, to Paris. During 1908 he and Eugène Montfort decided to create a new name, *La Nouvelle Revue Française*, Montfort, who between 1903 and 1908 had composed twelve numbers of *Les Marges,* a one-man periodical which appeared at irregular intervals, was to be director. On his staff were to be Gide, Jean Schlumberger, Jacques Copeau, and Henri Ghéon.

A first number appeared on November 15, 1908, but the contents of this issue led to a rupture between the director and his staff. Montfort, not consulting his colleagues, had accepted and printed articles which were not to their liking. Chief among these was an essay by Léon Bocquet, accepting as valid J.-M. Bernard's conclusions concerning Mallarmé's literary impotence. Montfort immediately resigned his directorship and set about finding a staff for a new series of *Les Marges*.

A regrouping followed. A committee composed of Jacques Copeau, André Ruyters, and Jean Schlumberger formed the new directive staff of *La Nouvelle Revue Française*.

Gide preferred to remain a force behind the scenes, abetted by his old friend Henri Ghéon of the *Ermitage* days. He had secured promise of collaboration from Verhaeren, and had written to Jammes and Claudel, "les deux seuls qui nous importent vraiment," [1] to assure himself of their contributions.

The first issue prepared by Gide and his friends appeared in February 1909. The previous number, disowned by the new editors, did not count in their eyes; they numbered their issue "No. 1." Copeau's province was the theater, Ruyters' the novel, and Schlumberger shared with Ghéon the realm of poetry. Gide did not wish to have a critical column, but he later included many literary judgments in a "Journal sans dates." In the first three issues his important contribution was "La Porte étroite."

1. Francis Jammes et André Gide, *Correspondance 1893–1938* (Gallimard, 1948), p. 256.

Jacques Rivière, whose essay on Claudel in *L'Occident* had apparently escaped Gide's attention, first met the author of *Le Retour de l'enfant prodigue* in December 1908. Gide spoke of a possible collaboration in *La Nouvelle Revue Française,* promising to read what Rivière had written on Claudel. Impressed by the young man's talent, he accepted Rivière's book review of Suarès' *Le Bouclier du Zodiaque* for the April 1909 issue of the *Nouvelle Revue Française*. This began the collaboration of the future director with the magazine.[2] Meanwhile Gide's letters to Jammes and Claudel had borne fruit. The April number contained Paul Claudel's "Hymne du Saint-Sacrement" and that of December "Trois hymnes" on St. Paul, St. Peter, and St. James. Jammes' poem to Paul Claudel, "Lettre à P.C., consul," was presented in the July issue, and in December appeared his poem in free verse entitled "La Vie."

The founding of *La Nouvelle Revue Française* created several eddies in the literary world, and especially in poetic groupings. Eugène Montfort, his directorship of the new magazine having come to immediate disaster, resolved to make *Les Marges* a true magazine, securing Marc Lafargue and Guillaume Apollinaire as critics and contributors of poetry. He proposed to issue at least six numbers a year, but left the dates of publication flexible. The first number of the new series appeared on January 15, 1909, and Montfort accomplished what he had set out to do, for six or seven issues did appear every year until publication was interrupted in 1918 by the war. In 1909 Apollinaire wrote articles on Raoul Ponchon and Alfred Jarry, and a series on "La Littérature féminine." His comments on women writers were signed Louise Lalanne. Under this pen name he amused himself with the creation of a feminine style and with frank judgments which might have appeared satirical if signed by a man. Marc Lafargue, now in his thirty-sixth year, had been associated in the last years of the nineteenth century with the group of *L'Effort* in Toulouse, and later had appeared in several Parisian magazines. His verse, collected in *Le Jardin d'où l'on voit la vie* (1897) and *L'Age d'or* (1903), was filled with description of nature and written in regular meters. His first critical articles in *Les Marges* were devoted to two minor poets of his own generation, Delbousquet and Gasquet. In 1910 Fort, Guérin, Henriot, Merrill, Guy Lavaud, Moréas, Klingsor, and Olivier de la Fayette were the poets he considered.

A certain coolness existed for a time between *La Nouvelle Revue Française* and the *Mercure de France*. Some conjectures are possible to explain this aloofness. Two of Gide's poets, Jammes and Verhaeren, had contracts with Vallette. As early as 1909, the new periodical was considering becoming a

2. The third volume of the Rivière-Alain Fournier *Correspondance* furnishes exact details on Rivière's relationship with the *N.R.F.*

publishing house and especially wanted six authors, of whom these were two.[3] When Gide, nursing a dislike patent since the days of *L'Ermitage,* wrote an ironically biting essay on Remy de Gourmont's hatred of Christianity and lack of modesty (*N.R.F., 3,* April 1910, 425–37), relations were probably embittered. Montfort utilized this article as the point of departure for a diatribe against Gide. This appeared in *Les Marges* on May 15, 1910.[4] The *Mercure* thereafter faithfully reported on current issues of *Les Marges,* but sedulously ignored *La Nouvelle Revue Française.* Gide apparently wished to soften the harshness of his attack on Gourmont, for in November 1910 he spoke with admiration of an article that Remy de Gourmont had written, and explained that in spite of his reservations about Gourmont's outlook, he considered him one of the most original and intelligent minds of the age. The following issue of *La Nouvelle Revue Française* contained an unsigned note, however, which spoke of the adulation that Gourmont demanded in the circle of the *Mercure de France.* The breach remained, less overt, but definitely there.

Gide was friendly with Mithouard and consequently with *L'Occident.* That magazine, which in 1910 was appearing months later than the dates on its covers (to the point that it had to skip the year 1911 in its series in order to become chronologically correct), was in 1910 the publishing house for several collaborators of *La Nouvelle Revue Française.* From the presses of *L'Occident* appeared *Les Odes* of Claudel, *Le Retour de l'enfant prodigue* by Gide, *Le Buisson ardent* by F.-P. Alibert, and *Epigrammes romaines* by Jean Schlumberger.

The beginnings of *La Nouvelle Revue Française* were much more noteworthy in the publication of prose, fiction, and criticism than in poetry. In 1910, essays by Jacques Rivière on Debussy, Gauguin, and Baudelaire; Jean Giraudoux's story "Jacques L'Egoïste"; Valery Larbaud's *Fermina Marquez;* and a memorial issue on C.-L. Philippe far outweighed any contributions in verse. The first act of Claudel's *L'Otage,* in the December number, offered the double interest of poetry and drama, but many of the contributions of verse were by poets of secondary importance: Claude Lorrey, Elsa Koeberlé, Gabriel Mourey, Julien Ochsé, Ambroise Raynal, Albert Erlande, Lucien Marié, and Henri Aliès. Gide and Jammes had quarrelled early in 1910.[5] The poet of Orthez sent his contributions to other periodicals. Nor did the expected collaboration of Vielé-Griffin with the *Nouvelle Revue Française* materialize.

3. The others were Claudel, Gide, Suarès, and C.-L. Philippe.

4. Both Gide and André Ruyters published, in *La Nouvelle Revue Française,* rebuttals of Montfort's article.

5. The story of this quarrel is traced in the notes by Robert Mallet in *Jammes et Gide, Correspondance 1893–1938.*

But Gide retained Claudel and Verhaeren. The former's "Magnificat," one of the "Grandes Odes," and "A Philippe," a poem dedicated to the memory of C.-L. Philippe, as well as the act from *L'Otage* appeared in the magazine during 1910. During that year ten of the poems that were later collected in Verhaeren's *Les Heures du soir* (1911) were printed in the periodical. F.-P. Alibert, André Spire, Henri Ghéon, Mme. de Noailles, J.-L. Vaudoyer, and Guy Lavaud (all either contributors to *L'Ermitage* during Gide's editorship of 1905–06, or to Mithouard's *L'Occident*) completed the list of poets, save for a noteworthy contribution signed "Saintléger Léger." This twenty-one-year-old student of political science and law, whom we know better under his pen name of Saint-John Perse, was a friend of Rivière and Jammes. Like them he was an admirer of Claudel. Indeed the form of his verse was much like Claudel's "verset," and the impassioned utterance of the "Eloges" he was composing suggested at times the revolt, the irony, and the ecstasy of Rimbaud. What were Claudel's reactions to this verse? Sollicited by Gabriel Frizeau to help Léger in his diplomatic career, he spoke in his letters only of that problem in relation to the young man, at least in the correspondence so far published.

In *La Nouvelle Revue Française* the criticism of volumes of poetry was largely entrusted to Jean Schlumberger and Henri Ghéon, although Gide in his "Journal sans dates," expressed some opinions, notably his enthusiasm at reading Péguy's *Mystère de la Charité de Jeanne d'Arc,* and his disgust at the mediocrity of Edmond Gojon's *Le Visage penché* (1910) and Maurice Levaillant's *Le Temple intérieur* (1910). Usually Ghéon and Schlumberger reviewed verse in which they found some merit, and Gide's denunciations of Gojon, an avowed disciple of Heredia, and of Levaillant, an editor of *La Revue des poètes,* furnish significant examples of the poetry that the magazine generally considered beneath its notice.

Applause in the magazine went to Fort, Verhaeren, and Klingsor. The influence of Laforgue on André Salmon's *Calumet* and Tristan Derème's *Petits poèmes* was approvingly noticed. Ghéon was particularly interested in the "Abbaye" writers. He did not consider *Notes sur la technique poétique* by Duhamel and Vildrac a satisfying contribution to the art of free verse, nor did he find Romains' *Un Etre en marche* sufficiently lyrical. But when he read Romains' prose in *Puissances de Paris* and the verse of Duhamel's *Selon ma loi* and Vildrac's *Livre d'amour,* he was impressed not only by the ideas but by their expression. He concluded that Romains was no poet but a fine writer of prose, that Duhamel's verse was unmusical but successful in its intense feeling, and that Vildrac was a true poet.[6] In these writers, according to Ghéon, was a similarity of outlook and purpose that bound

6. N.R.F., 4 (Dec. 1910), 786–95.

them much closer than earlier literary groups. Romains might think in terms of groups, and Vildrac and Duhamel in terms of individuals, but their achievement was that of giving poetic meaning to modern everyday life.

In 1912 Ghéon formally assumed the post of poetry critic for *La Nouvelle Revue Française,* Schlumberger devoting himself exclusively to reviews of novels. With this change came a definite critical outlook on poetry in the periodical. In 1911 Schlumberger, reviewing *Poèmes* by Pol Simonnet, *Humus et Poussière* by Porché, *Le Miroir des heures* by Régnier, *Le Masque de fer* by S.-C. Leconte, and *La Maison pauvre* by André Lafon, had largely contented himself with the style and tonality of the volumes. Ghéon's interests were wider: ideas and influence were of equal importance with technique. The background of Rimbaud, Laforgue, and Barrès (of the *Culte du moi*) in L.-P. Fargue's *Tancrède,* belatedly appearing in a volume after thirteen years, and the fusion of mood and landscape in Guy Lavaud's *Des Fleurs, pourquoi* . . . were concisely and concretely analyzed by Ghéon.

In February 1912, Ghéon expressed his beliefs concerning poetry. The problems which he found most interesting were related to symbolism, the freeing of verse from didacticism, eloquence, and abstract analysis with the concomitant danger of obscurity. Attributing chiefly to the symbolists' interest in English poets the introduction of elements of dream and music in French verse, Ghéon stated categorically: "Toute la poésie présente doit aux symbolistes tribut."[7] Another opposition which claimed Ghéon's attention was that of spontaneity versus artistic workmanship. He was led to consider this theme by Jean-Richard Bloch who had revived *L'Effort* under the name of *L'Effort libre* in Poitiers. Bloch, in the November 1911 issue had written an essay, "Le Cas Paul Fort," praising the author of the *Ballades françaises* for having remained a popular poet in the period when tendencies favored art for a small and learned public. Meanwhile Bloch was collecting poems by contemporaries which represented affinities with this virile, direct, and modern style of the *Ballades.*

Richard Bloch's *Anthologie de l'Effort* appeared in January 1912, with a preface he himself had written, in which he proposed Fort, Verhaeren, and Whitman as the inspiring forces for certain modern poets. These were Aliès, Arcos, Chennevière, Duhamel, Franck, Georges Périn, Romains, Ghéon, Marguerite Gillot, Spire, and Vildrac. Ghéon, a voluntary contributor, certainly sympathetic with the tendencies represented in the anthology, nevertheless opposed Bloch's exclusive championship of poetry which tried to reach the common man. In Ghéon's eyes verse should be of many types, according to the temperament of the poet and the subjects that inspire him. Thus while he accepted the form of Moréas' *Stances* as fitting for the

7. 7 (Feb. 1912), 276.

thought and age of its author, he deplored imitation of it in André Mary's
Le Cantique de la Seine, Ghéon had especial sympathy and admiration for
those of his own generation, but there were few of them in poetic publications of 1911 and 1912. Verhaeren's *Les Plaines,* part of *Toute la Flandre,*
appeared in Brussels, and his *Heures du soir* was printed in Germany by the
Insel Verlag. In 1912, however, Crès was the publisher of his *Blés mouvants,*
and this gave Ghéon the opportunity to develop the theme of broad variety
and constant renewal in Verhaeren's genius. Vielé-Griffin's *La Lumière de
la Grèce* (1912), which had received grudging praise from Emile Faguet,
found in Ghéon an ardent champion.

Ghéon, like Gide, was irked in 1912 by militant Catholicism.[8] In truth, *La
Nouvelle Revue Française* presented in its early years a real division of opinion. In 1912, while the magazine was printing Claudel's "L'Annonce faite à
Marie," Jacques Rivière's "De la foi," and a review praising Péguy's poetry,
Ghéon attacked an article by Jammes in the Catholic newspaper *La Croix.*
The author of the *Géorgiques chrétiennes* had made a categorical statement
which offended Ghéon: "La littérature immorale est celle qui est en désac-
cord avec les lois de l'Eglise catholique, c'est-à-dire avec la vérité et par con-
séquent, l'ordre et la beauté."

Ghéon, although first professing his esteem for Jammes' talents, developed
a response denying any necessary alliance between faith and literary beauty.
With a certain malice, pretending to defend Jammes against an unfavorable
report on the *Géorgiques chrétiennes* by Faguet in *La Revue,* Ghéon quoted
many of the most dubiously artistic of Jammes' couplets. Ghéon's article,
which offended not only Jammes but Claudel,[9] closed Jammes' affiliation
with *La Nouvelle Revue Française.*

Two of the most famous items in criticism were printed in *La Nouvelle
Revue Française* in 1912. The first was Paul Claudel's "Arthur Rimbaud,"
which became the preface of the Paterne Berrichon edition of the *Œuvres*
of Rimbaud. The second was a series of three unpublished letters written by
Rimbaud himself; one of these was the celebrated "Lettre du voyant." It was
only by chance that Gaston Gallimard (who in 1911 had become director of
the publishing house of *La Nouvelle Revue Française*) did not get the
contract to publish the works of Rimbaud. Berrichon, irked at Remy de

8. During the first World War, Ghéon became a convert to Catholicism.

9. Gide, during 1912, was concentrating on the writing of *Les Caves du Vatican,* and was
publishing nothing in the *Nouvelle Revue Française.* When he saw that Claudel had given the
first part of his "Cantate à trois voix" to the *Revue de Paris* instead of his own periodical, he
hastily wrote to Frankfort where Claudel was stationed. His letter, which has not been preserved, apparently asked whether Claudel was displeased with the staff of *La Nouvelle Revue
Française.* In a reassuring reply Claudel expressed his regard for the editors of Gide's periodical,
but a letter he had written to Jammes proved he was angry at Ghéon.

Gourmont's unkind words in *Le Temps* concerning his late brother-in-law, was on the point of breaking an agreement with the *Mercure de France*. Vallette, knowing the growing interest in Rimbaud's work, promised that Gourmont would be less hostile in the future.[10] Berrichon was placated and left the publishing rights with the *Mercure*.

By 1912 the *Nouvelle Revue Française* press was beginning to assume some importance, thanks to the energy of Gaston Gallimard.[11] Claudel's new play *L'Otage* (1911), his translation of Coventry Patmore's poems (1912), *L'Annonce faite à Marie* (1912), *Cette Heure qui est entre le printemps et l'été* (1913), and a new edition of the *Cinq Grandes Odes* (1913) were the first of a long series of volumes from the *N.R.F.* press. Vielé-Griffin's *La Lumière de la Grèce*, Georges Duhamel's *Compagnons*, and Henri Franck's *La Danse devant l'arche* were three of its lyric offerings in 1912. In that same year it published the volume of prose-poems bearing the title *Poèmes*, which began Léon-Paul Fargue's fame in that literary form. While prose works like those of Gide, Schlumberger, Suarès, and the posthumous publications of C.-L. Philippe were wider in their appeal, these beginnings in publication of poetry were outstanding for a struggling new magazine.

The *Mercure de France*, more firmly established, continued to produce an important portion of published volumes of verse. Jean Cocteau's *La Danse de Sophocle* (1912), Jammes' *Géorgiques chrétiennes* (1912), François Porché's *Humus et Poussière* (1911), and *Prisme étrange de la maladie* (1912), S.-C. Leconte's *Le Masque de fer* (1911), Ferdinand Herold's *La Route fleurie* (1911), H.-M. Barzun's *Hymne des forces* (1912), Louis Mandin's *Ariel esclave* (1912), and Louis le Cardonnel's *Carmina sacra* (1912) were among its publications.

Except for Figuière where a few volumes by the Abbaye poets had recently been printed (*Ce qui naît,* by René Arcos; *Le Livre d'amour,* by Charles Vildrac), these two publishing houses, the *Mercure* and the *N.R.F.,* were the true strongholds of poetic production in 1911 and 1912. Rivalry between the older and newer organizations was incessant but on the whole friendly. The *Mercure* put Rimbaud's *Œuvres* on sale in 1912; the *N.R.F.* printed Mallarmé's *Poésies* (the last edition having been Deman's volume of 1899) in 1913. Albert Thibaudet's important volume of criticism, *La Poésie de Stéphane Mallarmé,* was issued by the *N.R.F.* in 1912; a few months later the *Mercure* published Paterne Berrichon's *Jean-Arthur Rimbaud, le poète*. Between the magazines themselves, in the domain of criticism of poetry, a

10. See Remy de Gourmont, *Promenades littéraires,* 4ᵉ série, pp. 26–8, for the remarks which so offended Berrichon.

11. Information on the early years of the *N.R.F.* is found in Jean Schlumberger's *Eveils* (Gallimard, 1950), pp. 184–223.

new relationship was established. In February 1912, Quillard, who had written almost all reviews of poetry in the *Mercure* since 1900, suddenly died. Georges Duhamel, currently being published by the *Nouvelle Revue Française,* took his place. Duhamel was a much more aggressive critic than Quillard had ever been. The author of *La Lyre héroïque et dolente,* closer to the Parnassians than to the symbolists in the regular form of his verse and his love of antiquity, was yet friendly to technical innovations and even hermetic verse. The calm tone of his reports, although gently ironic at times, was quite different from the direct censure often employed by Ghéon and Duhamel.

The literary dislikes of these two critics were very different. Ghéon was especially irked by poetry that was too didactic, too prosy, or too eloquent. He had attacked the lack of lyricism in Romains' poetry, and in 1912 he dwelt on the didacticism of H.-M. Barzun's *Hymne des forces,* on the prosaic utterance of Charles Troufleau's *Entre les murs,* and Albert Londres' *La Marche à l'étoile.* He was acidly critical of the poet of "paroxysme," Nicolas Beauduin, who had published seven volumes of poetry between 1908 and 1913,[12] and who directed a literary quarterly, *Les Rubriques nouvelles,* during that period. Beauduin, a great admirer of Victor Hugo and Emile Verhaeren, relied on violence of imagery and sonorous diction for his effects, but for Ghéon these represented merely confusion and bombast.

Ghéon was a partisan of personal emotion; if he accepted poetry with social or epic aims, it was because the poet had somehow retained the expression of his individual mood; that is what had charmed him in Duhamel's *Selon ma loi* (1910).

For Duhamel, poetic dangers lay elsewhere. The dangers of simplicity in language, exemplified by Paul Géraldy's *Toi et moi;* of facility, in Hélène Picard's *Nous n'irons plus au bois;* of triviality, in Henry Dérieux's *Le Regard derrière l'épaule;* and of triteness, in Louis le Cardonnel's *Carmina sacra,* were among these. But Duhamel's chief complaint was that nine out of ten published volumes of verse, as of 1912, gave one the impression that all novelty ceased with romanticism. Although approving much in lyrical form and expression that stemmed from symbolism, he was unfriendly toward propagation of poetry of that period which was closest to romanticism, and is perhaps best represented by Albert Samain.[13] The poet who merely strives to interest the public in his sentimental and emotional life, as did Maurice Magre in *Les Belles de nuit* (1913), is not accomplish-

12. *Le Chemin qui monte; Les Triomphes; La Divine Folie; Les Deux Règnes; Les Cités du verbe; Les Princesses de mon songe; Les Sœurs de silence.*

13. Samain's continuing influence was shown in Alcide Ramette's *Clartés au crépuscule,* published by *Le Beffroi* in 1912.

ing his mission. But introspection may be accompanied by ideas of more general import, and when Duhamel spoke of the impact of Baudelaire, Laforgue, Mallarmé, Verlaine, Rimbaud, or Verhaeren on later generations, it was not in a tone of disfavor. He discovered their influence in many places: in G.-C. Cros' *Les Fêtes quotidiennes,* in Francis Carco's *La Bohème et mon cœur,* in Tristan Derème's *Le Poème de la pipe et de l'escargot,* in Philéas Lebesgue's *Les Servitudes,* in Dominique Combette's *Les Pèlerins d'Emmaüs,* and in Guillaume Apollinaire's *Alcools.* Vildrac's spontaneity and discreet music were learned, he said, from the symbolists. Deubel's posthumous volume *Régner* (1913) was a complicated heritage of Baudelaire, Verlaine, and Mallarmé.

In one respect Duhamel emulated his predecessor Quillard. He apparently tried faithfully to review as much of current poetic production as possible. In this he differed from Ghéon, whose choice was much more limited and dictated seemingly by personal taste and distaste. Duhamel's method was fruitful in that he revealed many talents during the two years preceding the first World War. One of these was P.-J. Jouve. Jouve had been associated with the Abbaye group and helped Castiaux as co-editor of *Les Bandeaux d'or* between 1907 and 1910. He collected his verse in *Les Muses romaines et florentines* (1910), *Présences* (1912), and *Parler* (1913). The latter two volumes, in which Duhamel approved the search for understanding of self, of environment, and of fellow men, marked the beginnings of Jouve's literary fame although they did not represent his true stature. His style, which had first felt the influence of Mallarmé, then of Moréas, had become personal.

There was one volume of verse which found especial favor with Ghéon. This was Guillaume Apollinaire's *Alcools* (1913), a book representing thirteen years in its composition, so diverse in subjects and techniques that it defied definition. The mingling of popular diction and literary language, the erudition hidden in the poems, and the free and regular meters both disconcerted and charmed the critics. They looked for literary ancestors and emerged with names as different as Rimbaud, Verlaine, and Moréas. Both Ghéon and Duhamel agreed that here was a poet whose spontaneity and personality placed him apart.

Ghéon was among the first of the critics to speak at length of "la poésie fantaisiste," a form of expression which did not attract Duhamel since he felt it lacked ideas. Francis Carco's *La Bohème et mon cœur,* Henri Hertz's *Les Apartés,* Tristan Derème's *Le Poème de la pipe et de l'escargot,* and René Bizet's *Le Front aux vitres,* all published in 1912, found in Ghéon a sympathetic reader. The note of irony or insouciance, especially when suggestion of Laforgue or Verlaine was present, he found refreshing in a period when philosophy and sociology were invading poetry. One of the "fantai-sistes" he frankly detested: J.-M. Bernard's attempts at polished language and wit in *Sub tegmine fagi* suggested to him a continuation of the deplorable poetry of the Chevalier de Parny. Ghéon never claimed that "poésie fantaisiste" could attain greatness; this he reserved for two other poets, Claudel and Péguy, and for two of their books, *Cette Heure qui est entre le printemps et l'été* and *La Tapisserie de Notre-Dame*. Ghéon, soon after his outburst against Jammes' Catholic dogmatism in 1912, either had a change of heart which was to culminate in his conversion during World War I, or else determined to become more circumspect. His praise of Claudel's *Cantate à trois voix* is even understandable in the interests of solidarity among the group of the *N.R.F.*, and his championship of Péguy's work was not in disaccord with that of Gide. But sincere literary admiration, rather than practical reasons, appears to have formed his opinions. The force and vigor of Péguy's alexandrines in the *Tapisserie,* and the fervor and broad vision of Claudel's "versets" were the matter of his criticism. He avoided the religious aspect of the poems, and stressed the talent of the writers.

That Ghéon approved the regular and monotonous alexandrines of Péguy's *Tapisserie de Notre-Dame* comes as something of a surprise, since generally he was favorable toward free meters and variety in rhythm. He noted with pleasure new liberty in versification in Charles de Saint-Cyr's *Toute Mon Ame* and in Jean Dominique's *Le Puits de l'azur,* and he deplored the metrical strictness of J.-L. Vaudoyer's *Poésies (1906–1912)*. What Ghéon apparently approved was the general suppleness of Péguy's talent, which found a completely free form for the *Mystères* and chose a strict and rhymed meter for the *Tapisseries*. This versatility was what delighted him in F.-P. Alibert's *Le Buisson ardent,* published by *L'Occident* in 1912.

There was one kind of poetic volume which Ghéon and Duhamel, like the critics of other literary magazines, did not discuss. This silence on their part was counteracted by a certain amount of publicity in the newspapers, for the books in question had won prizes or official recognition. In 1912 Edmond Gojon's *La Grenade* was awarded honors by the French Academy, Emile Ripert's *La Terre des lauriers* won the national prize for poetry, and Charles Clerc's *Les Oasis* received the Sully-Prudhomme prize for poetry. This phenomenon of the prize-winning book of verse, which, to win the prize, seemingly had to be completely devoid of any novelty, was an annual event. Now and then a brief sentence about the mediocrity of such recipients was penned by the critics of literary magazines.

The *N.R.F.,* during 1913 and 1914, was disappointingly incomplete in reports on books in general and particularly on poetry. The reason is clear: the monthly periodical could afford to print only a certain number of pages.

Regular contributions such as Suarès' "Chronique de Caërdal" were supplemented by installments, in many pages, of Gide's "Les Caves du Vatican," of Alain-Fournier's "Le Grand Meaulnes," and of Claudel's "Protée." What should have been a critical essay became "Notes" or "Notules." The best critical writing in the magazine was done on broad literary questions by Albert Thibaudet in a series of "Réflexions sur la littérature."

The *Mercure de France,* on the other hand, appeared twice a month, and Duhamel gave a fairly complete account of contemporary poetry until the war forced suspension of the magazine in August 1914. Not only these book reviews, but a considerable number of longer essays on poets and poetry, published in the magazine during the 1912–14 period, are worthy of extended comment.

THE IMPRESSIVE number of articles on poetic matters in the *Mercure* during the three and a half years preceding World War I may be ascribed to several factors, but three chief ones are deaths to be commemorated, the maturity of certain poets of the 'nineties of whom it was possible to make a retrospective evaluation, and the perennial desire to find out poetic directions. A rough division of articles into necrological, retrospective, and contemporary may give meaning to this material.

The essays on Moréas, numerous after his death in 1910, were continued. Maurice de Noisay, writing on "L'Esprit de Jean Moréas" was merely anecdotal, but Marcel Coulon, in "Moréas 'dévoilé,' "[1] sought to give the psychological background of the writer's work. Coulon saw in Moréas a complete egoist who accomplished an evolution toward utter unselfishness and who even learned abnegation. In this change, from *Les Syrtes* to *Les Stances,* Coulon discerned not contrast but unity. The pursuit of the beautiful and the ideal, the attention to self which led to comprehension of others were the effective forces in this unification. André Fontainas, studying Moréas' *Iphigénie,* produced an article comparing the modern work with the plays of Euripides and Racine.[2]

The deaths, in 1912, of Léon Dierx, the "Prince des poètes," and of Pierre Quillard, the critic of the *Mercure,* also provoked commemorative articles. Dierx, aged and ailing, had read his poem "Valvins" during the unveiling of a memorial plaque in the rue de Rome only a few days before his death. This event, symbolizing through the personal esteem which had existed between Mallarmé and Dierx a tolerance for divergent poetic aesthetics, served as the point of departure for most obituary notices. In the *Mercure,* however, Henry Dérieux sought to prove that Dierx had been less close to the art of Leconte de Lisle than to that of Baudelaire, and that his prosody went farther in the direction of liberty than was generally suspected.[3] The election of Paul Fort to succeed Dierx as "Prince des poètes" was adroitly celebrated in the magazine by a translation from the Danish of Sophus Claussen's "Le Voyage au pays de Paul Fort."

Pierre Quillard's obituary was written by a poet almost exactly his con-

1. *Mercure de France,* 90 (March 1, 1911), 5–24; (March 16, 1911), 277–99.
2. 97 (June 16, 1912), 768–76.   3. 95 (Jan. 16, 1912), 225–42.

temporary, A.-F. Herold. The writer and his subject were sympathetic in literary outlook. Both were conservative in versification and both were so imbued with the passion of ancient literatures that they had represented the impact of symbolism only in diction and in evocative imagery.

The suicide of Léon Deubel in June 1913 brought to the attention of the Parisian press a poet chiefly associated with regional magazines such as *Le Beffroi*. Deubel's miserable existence, relieved only by two short periods when inheritances permitted him to indulge his passion for travel, his burning of his manuscripts before he threw himself into the Marne, and the theme of certain of his poems in which he lamented his chronic poverty tended to give obituary articles the tone of lament for a Chatterton, a poet-martyr. In the *Mercure*, Louis Pergaud, the poet of the *Beffroi* group who had often befriended Deubel, wrote a biography of the dead writer and discussed his extant work.[4]

In the periodical the bulk of critical articles on poetry concern those who began writing during the last fifteen years of the nineteenth century. Henri de Régnier was the most distinguished of the group. The author of eighteen volumes of prose and poetry, he became in January 1911 a member of the French Academy. An event such as this called for commemoration, since before Régnier's admission there were only three poets among the forty immortals: Rostand, Aicard, and Richepin. G. Jean-Aubry composed the essay on Régnier, dwelling on the author's cool aloofness which was tempered by the tonality of melancholy.

Duhamel, in the issues of December 16, 1912 and January 1, 1913, was the author of an essay on Paul Claudel. First treating the philosophical and poetic works of the author, he devoted his second chapter to the dramas. The subject was timely, for the first performance of *L'Annonce faite à Marie* at the Théâtre de l'œuvre had occurred on December 20, 1912, at last giving the public an opportunity to judge the dramatic possibilities of the printed plays.

That Henry Dérieux should write in the *Mercure* of 1913 about Stuart Merrill, and that in February 1914 "La Mysticité et le lyrisme de Max Elskamp" by Francis de Miomandre should appear in the periodical seems anachronistic. These two poets, nearly contemporaries, were about fifty years of age, and almost everything they had written had been composed during the 1880's and 1890's. But Merrill's volume of 1909, *Une Voix dans la foule,* as well as his occasional contributions to magazines, had revealed a radical change from personal to universal themes, a humanitarian pity and sympathy sharply in contrast with the verse of his youth. Max Elskamp, on

---

4. Pergaud also arranged a selection of Deubel's verse under the title of *Régner,* and wrote a preface for the book. An article on Deubel appeared in Bocquet's *Les Destinées mauvaises.*

the contrary, could be said to have accomplished his poetic work in 1898, the date of the publication of his *Louange de la vie*. From then on, despite an encouraging group of friends and admirers, Elskamp kept silent for nearly a quarter of a century. In 1913, when the religious themes of Claudel and Péguy were assuming real prominence, the name of Elskamp, the eccentric recluse of Antwerp, the collector of rosebushes who refused all invitations to contribute poetry to magazines, was resurrected as a precursor of the Catholic literary revival.

Other retrospective essays in the *Mercure* reveal the constant importance which the magazine accorded to the poetry of the end of the nineteenth century. Ernest Gaubert recalled Pierre Louÿs' *Astarté* (1891) and *Chansons de Bilitis* (1894), Paul Escoube examined the verse and prose writings of Jules Laforgue, and Marcel Coulon contributed an essay entitled "Le Symbolisme d'Ephraïm Mikhaël." In addition Paul Escoube was the author of "Paul Verlaine et l'amour," and Marcel Coulon devoted two essays to "Le Problème de Rimbaud." The Verlaine monument, dedicated in the Luxembourg gardens on May 28, 1911, inspired an article by Ernest Raynaud. In this essay Raynaud took occasion to castigate those critics who deemed Verlaine's work of little importance and outdated in theme and expression.

In July 1914, the *Mercure* printed an essay on Adrien Mithouard, the director of *L'Occident*. The author of the article was Charles Morice. These two names, Morice and Mithouard, represent a lost cause insofar as the aesthetics of poetic art are concerned. From the beginning of the century Mithouard had been campaigning for a "renaissance gothique" in which literature would find its true source in the Middle Ages rather than in Greco-Latin inspiration. During 1911 Morice, in the pages of *Paris-Journal,* had proclaimed an analogous theory, stressing, it is true, the idea of synthesis of various cultural influences. But his fecund literary career, beginning with the essay *Paul Verlaine* of 1885 and *La Littérature de toute à l'heure* of 1889, and continuing after his death in 1919 with the publication of volumes of prose and poetry, remained strangely unsuccessful. Morice, like Mithouard, interpreted the tonality of mystery in symbolist poetry as a tendency toward religious consciousness. Even though his conversion to Catholicism came late, about 1911, he had used the term "mystique" and had lectured on the religious message of poetry as early as 1892. Like Mithouard, he had a national or patriotic sense which refused the domination of French literature by foreign influences. Since 1919, which is also the date of Mithouard's death, both men have been almost entirely forgotten. Their poetry and their literary theories have left little trace.

Thus the *Mercure,* in the years preceding the first World War, seemed chiefly concerned with the past rather than the present state of poetry.

Moréas, Maeterlinck, Régnier, Verlaine, Dierx, Laforgue, Merrill, Mikhaël, Signoret, Elskamp, and Verhaeren furnished the subjects of critical essays; all were names which suggested the period of origin of the periodical and which brought the reproach that the magazine was not sufficiently alive to contemporary ideas. An essay now and then would seem to oppose this accusation; such a one was Georges Batault's "Les Tendances de la poésie contemporaine" which appeared in the September 16, 1912 issue of the *Mercure.* Seeking current poetic directions, Batault discovered only what had been apparent a decade before. Poetry had ceased to be pessimistic, he said, and was now characterized by interest in everyday things. Love of the present and hope for the future were the favored themes. The names he adduced to support his statements were chiefly those of writers who began writing during the symbolist period: Régnier, Verhaeren, Vielé-Griffin, and Jammes. The younger poets he named were Mme. de Noailles, G.-C. Cros, and Georges Duhamel.

The inclusion of Duhamel's name among those long associated with the *Mercure* is not strange, in view of his assumption of the duties of poetry critic for the magazine. Between March 1912 and August 1914, Duhamel twice a month contributed essays on poets or poetry to the *Mercure,* speaking with a vigor quite different from the gentle tone adopted by Quillard during his later years. Duhamel obviously wished to give complete coverage of his subject and he mentioned hundreds of volumes. But having quickly discovered an almost universal lack of poetic originality, he made harsh judgments. His volume of 1914, *Les Poètes et la poésie,* almost entirely taken from his chronicles of the *Mercure,* revealed what he thought worth salvaging from his survey of the current poetic scene, as well as his displeasure at slavish imitation of past masters. With sharp sarcasm he set about to prove that Jean Aicard was the epitome of mediocrity, that Louis le Cardonnel's *Carmina sacra* were filled with trite metaphors, that the descendants of the Parnassian tradition seemed to find their subjects by thumbing through the pages of proper names in the *Petit Larousse,* and that poets who chose their sentimental experience as the theme of their work were somewhat ridiculous. His friendship with the groups of Créteil, of *Les Bandeaux d'or,* and of *Vers et Prose* account to some degree for his laudatory tone in speaking of Jules Romains' *Odes et Prières,* Luc Durtain's *Kong Harold,* P.-J. Jouve's *Présence* and *Parler,* Paul Castiaux's *Lumières du monde,* and four different volumes by Paul Fort. But Duhamel showed great respect for Emile Verhaeren, Francis Jammes, and Vielé-Griffin. He treated René Ghil with deference, in spite of the fact that he found him impossibly obscure. What Duhamel demanded in true poetry was the presence of intellectual activity; for that reason he was suspicious of the "poètes fantaisistes." He was willing to say that they charmed the reader, but not that they could become great. He required a sense of unity, the impression of a serious message. Jean Cocteau possessed a "détestable talent"; despite its originality, Apollinaire's *Alcools* reminded him of a curiosity shop. The intellectual quest, which he discovered in Henri Franck's *La Danse devant l'arche* or Jouve's *Parler,* gained his admiration.

In addition to the fifty-odd articles on poetry, Duhamel contributed to the *Mercure*[5] his long study on Paul Claudel, the poet, the philosopher, the writer, the dramatist. Published as a volume in 1913, this work was a landmark in Claudelian criticism.

What Duhamel's presence on the staff of the *Mercure* could have meant in relation to the poetic aims of the group of Créteil is difficult to ascertain. The war intervened, and for five years, even though the *Mercure* suspended publication for only a few months after the outbreak of hostilities, the post of poetry critic remained vacant.[6] But one article of 1913, entitled "A propos de quelques poètes modernes,"[7] and written by René Arcos, is worthy of attention since it focused on the poets who were loosely called "Unanimistes." For Arcos, the great influences on good modern poetry were those of Baudelaire and Verlaine. Rejecting the inspiration of books, conscious of having a personal message, preferring concision to superficial adornment, the true twentieth-century poet is profoundly concerned with his fellow beings. Arcos praised Romains and Vildrac for their principles of order and equilibrium; he commended Duhamel for the variety of his inspiration. The fervor of these poets, he stated, stemmed from their affection for humanity. But Arcos was against the idea of literary schools; he emphasized the diversity of expression in the poets he had been studying. He indicated his admiration for *Les Grandes Odes* of Claudel, and terminated his article by regretting that space had not permitted him to speak of Spire, Fargue, Varlet, Georges Périn, G.-C. Cros, and "beaucoup d'autres qui ont tant de titres à notre respect."

It seems likely that Duhamel and his friends, although sharing certain general concepts of poetic art, would never have made a concerted effort to dominate the *Mercure.* Their refusal to bear the name of "Unanimistes" and their insistence on their individuality precluded such intentions. But the *Mercure,* at the time of the outbreak of the first World War, was making some effort at separation from the poetic past. In January 1914 an article by the erstwhile director of *Les Rubriques nouvelles,* Nicolas Beauduin, was presented to the readers of the periodical. Beauduin suggested that mod-

5. *Mercure de France, 100* (Dec. 16, 1912), 673–702; *101* (Jan. 1, 1913), 45–73.

6. In the spring of 1919 Duhamel resumed his task for a few issues, expressing his discouragement at the quality of war-inspired verse and saluting Romains' *Europe* as the poem which best expressed the tragic sense of the times.

7. *Mercure de France, 105* (Oct. 16, 1913), 696–713.

ern poetry was antipodal to complaining sentimentality. It was a summons to action and to life. It looked forward rather than backward. Thus far Beauduin was not in complete disagreement with Duhamel or Arcos. The dislike of the group of Créteil for the poetry of Albert Samain and Henri de Régnier, for the lyricism of dreamy retrospect, had been amply demonstrated. But Beauduin went much farther, and in doing so associated his name with the ideas of futurism, or of what he called "paroxysme." Not only fervor but tumult and violence, he said, were the modern sources of inspiration. Whereas the group of Créteil remained essentially on the level of man's everyday existence, Beauduin tried to give his poetry a grandiose and prophetic note by including legend, religious history, and philosophical concepts in some of his poems, and by accumulating a mass of sensations in others. An admirer of Walt Whitman, Victor Hugo, and Verhaeren, he sought sonority and power. His concept of poetry bore some relationship to that of Henri-Martin Barzun, who was the author of a dramatic poem, *L'Hymne des forces* (1911), and whose general title for his volumes was *La Terrestre Tragédie*. Both Beauduin and Barzun favored great liberty in verse forms, the former often writing free verse with end-rhyme, the latter sometimes suppressing the rhyme. This could be called a heritage of the symbolist period, but the two poets represented rather a reaction than a continuation of symbolism. Their themes tended toward the cosmic, their style toward sonority. Abstract nouns, adjectives suggesting magnitude, verbs of dynamic power were the principles of their diction. Barzun strove to make his poetry dramatic; Beauduin endeavored to combine in his verse many aspects of human existence. Like René Ghil, they felt poetry should eschew the little emotions of daily existence in favor of epic breadth. Unlike Ghil, they spoke clearly and even bluntly. The *Mercure* issued Barzun's books after the Abbaye de Créteil ceased publishing. Beauduin's volumes were published by his own magazine, *Les Rubriques nouvelles* (1908–12).

Apart from book reviews and articles on poetry, the publication of verse in the issues of the *Mercure* gives some clue to the periodical's policy. During the years 1911–14 few of the contributors belonged to the older group associated with the magazine's beginnings. André Fontainas, Louis le Cardonnel, Francis Jammes, Stuart Merrill, Tristan Klingsor, and Francis Vielé-Griffin were the chief survivors from the end of the nineteenth century. Poets born between 1875 and 1885 furnished most of the lyric compositions. Paul Castiaux, G.-C. Cros, Fernand Divoire, Georges Gaudion, François Mauriac, François Porché, André Salmon, Cécile Sauvage, Henri Thuile, Fernand Benoît, Alfred Droin, J.-L., Vaudoyer, Pierre Camo, and Vincent Muselli were the principal names among these poets, twenty-five to thirty-five years of age. Finally there were a few writers who, because of other occupations, had arrived tardily on the poetic scene. The most notable was André Spire, born in 1868, but little known for his lyric talent until 1908.

The list of younger poets suggests the eclectic but conservative policy that had become the *Mercure*'s. True, free verse and regular meters were equally acceptable to the periodical. The themes of the verse remained largely the notation of personal emotion in the setting of daily life in France or in foreign lands. What particularly strikes the reader is the number of poets represented in the magazine for whom the *Mercure* press was the publisher. Castiaux' *La Joie vagabonde* (1909) and *Lumières du monde* (1913), Cros' *Les Fêtes quotidiennes* (1912), Porché's *Humus et poussière* (1911), and *Le Dessous du masque* (1914), Sauvage's *Tandis que la terre tourne* (1910), and Camo's *Les Beaux Jours* (1913) were among such publications.

On the other hand, the *Mercure*'s list reflects a friendly attitude toward other magazines. Castiaux had been particularly associated with *Le Beffroi* and *Les Bandeaux d'or,* Gaudion with *Poésie* of Toulouse, Salmon with *Vers et Prose* and currently with *Les Soirées de Paris,* Porché with *Les Cahiers de la quinzaine.* The reader of the magazine senses that the printing of poems was a minor preoccupation of the editors. The relative mediocrity of what was offered was offset to some degree by the activity of the publishing house itself. Claudel's plays in a four-volume edition during 1911 and 1912, and Apollinaire's *Alcools* in 1913 were from the presses of the *Mercure.* Such works redeem in part the magazine's pages of innocuous stanzas by Alfred Droin, Marie Dauguet, Elsa Koeberlé, and Vincent Muselli.

Poets, as in the past, found a kind of haven in the little magazines. Charles Calais and Victor Rocca founded *Le Cahier des poètes* in Nice in November 1912 and had among their contributors Carco, Derème, Fagus, Klingsor, Toulet, and Salmon. Catholic poets such as Claudel, le Cardonnel, and Jammes offered their poetry to the *Cahiers de l'amitié de France* during 1912. Henri Martineau's *Divan* offered hospitality to Vérane, Emile Henriot, Francis Eon, Toulet, Porché, and Derème. Louis de Gonzague-Frick founded *Les Ecrits français* on December 5, 1913; among the poets were Salmon, Apollinaire, and Carco. *Les Facettes,* founded by Léon Vérane in Toulon during the fall of 1910, counted among its contributors Derème, Toulet, Carco, Georges Périn, Klingsor, and Dérieux. Lucien Rolmer's *La Flora,* which appeared between 1912 and 1914, was especially given to publication of its founder's poetry, but also printed verse by Roger Frène, Vaudoyer, and Gonzague-Frick. Henri Strentz, with several friends, envisioned a magazine, to appear six times a year, which would give a large place to verse. Their venture, *Les Horizons,* made its first appearance on February 15, 1912, but survived only one year, offering poetry by Georges Périn, Léon Vérane, Fagus, Jules Romains, and Théo Varlet. Ricciotto Canudo was the

director of *Montjoie!,* which first appeared in January 1913, with poetry by
L.-P. Fargue, but lasted only a short time.

Another poet who attempted to give lyric art a more important place was
Roger Frène. With Michel Puy, he founded *L'Ile sonnante* at the end of
1909 and managed to keep the periodical alive until December 1913. A
four-year life span was unusually good for the little magazines which featured poetry; *L'Ile sonnante*'s list of contributors included almost all the
names cited in the preceding paragraph. Of comparable importance for the
publication of verse was *Pan,* created as a bimonthly by Jean Clary and
Joël Dumas in Montpellier in 1908. In 1909 Clary moved to Paris, and *Pan,*
bearing the appellation "revue libre," began appearing every month. The
ambitions of the little magazine were lofty. It wished to have an international scope and to accord equal weight to prose and poetry. But Clary,
a poet himself and the author of two volumes, *D'or et de soleil* (1908) and
Quelques Lames de la mer sauvage (1910), gave much attention to publication of verse. Between 1909 and 1913 Allard, Beauduin, Canudo, Carco,
Cottinet, Dauguet, Divoire, Fort, Mandin, Mercereau, Nau, Ochsé, Pergaud,
Georges Périn, Vérane, and Varlet were among his contributors.

These little magazines, representative of a larger group,[8] were created in
large measure for poets. The established magazines, such as the *Mercure,*
were granting so little space to verse that the poets themselves bravely attempted to create outlets for their expression. The usual painful story of lack
of money filled the brief existence of these periodicals, but the contributions
represented a fair cross-section of the best lyric art of the period. One of
them, because it published some of the best known poems of Apollinaire,
and because it represented such close relationship between poetry and pic-
torial art, is of unusual interest. This was the *Soirées de Paris,*[9] of which
twenty-seven numbers appeared between February 1912 and July 1914. The
campaign in support of Picasso, Matisse, Henri Rousseau, Picabia, Braque,
and Fernand Léger makes the periodical noteworthy in the history of art,
while the publication of poems which became part of *Alcools* and of *Calligrammes* gives it importance in the chronicles of poetry. Apollinaire directed
Les Soirées after November 1913 and accepted poems by Cendrars, Hertz,
Strentz, Royère, Muselli, Divoire, and Jacob. The last number (No. 26–27)
of the magazine contained examples of Apollinaire's "idéogrammes lyriques"
which elicited some amused or sarcastic comments before the advent of war
silenced commentary.

8. In 1912 alone one could mention the first appearance of *Comme il vous plaira, Les
Feuilles de mai, L'Olivier* of Nice, *Les Marches de Provence, Le Parvis* (founded by the poet
Jacques Noir), *Les Poètes, La Vie,* and *La Revue de France et des pays français.*

9. André Billy, in his *Apollinaire vivant,* and in the preface to Pierre Seghers' anthology of
Apollinaire's verse, has related the story of *Les Soirées de Paris.*

CHAPTER 11. Poetic Doctrine (1912–1914)

DURING 1912 Alphonse Séché undertook to define *Les Caractères de la poésie contemporaine*.[1] Comparing his task with that of André Beaunier, who had weighed the results of symbolism in 1902, Séché found that the intervening decade had added so many complications and confusions that it was hazardous to make generalizations. He emerged with four guiding principles of contemporary poetry. The first was fantasy, with the presence of familiar style, the reminiscences of folk tunes, burlesque humor, and ingenuous confession. Séché quoted Cocteau, Klingsor, Salmon, and Bonnard to illustrate this type of light and witty verse.

A second characteristic, which Séché did not succeed in defining but which he felt had its origins in Baudelaire and Verlaine, was modern poetic sensitivity. In the verse of François Porché, Henri Bataille, and Alfred Mortier, the critic discerned an uneasy, questing, and complicated state of mind in harmony with twentieth-century problems. The absence of figures of speech and of declamation set these confessions apart from romanticism. Profound psychological shadings were concealed beneath simple utterance.

Séché's third division was given to the union between art and science, the communion between poet and humanity. Here he spoke chiefly of Verhaeren and Jules Romains; these represented the poets who celebrated modernity in its thought, its heroes, its discoveries. Their eyes looked toward the future rather than the past; disdaining their narrow personal experience, they spoke of cosmic problems.

The fourth tendency of modern verse, as given in *Les Caractères de la poésie contemporaine,* was the "renaissance classique." In 1912 such a subject was inevitable, for Charles Morice had conducted an inquiry into "Une Renaissance de l'idéal classique" in *Paris-Soir* during 1911, and at the same time Gaston Picard, in the sporadic issues of *L'Heure qui sonne,* and Gaston Sauvebois, in Beauduin's *Rubriques nouvelles,* had protested vigorously against neoclassicism as servile imitation of the seventeenth century, but had praised it as a return to order, harmony, and equilibrium. The death of Moréas in March 1910 had contributed to renewed discussion of neoclassicism and indeed of free verse and the definition of French mentality.

Séché made no complete analysis of the conflicting opinions concerning the meaning of neoclassicism. A large part of his discussion concerned Beau-

1. Published in 1913.

124

duin's prognostications of dynamic and "paroxyste" poetry as elucidated in *Les Rubriques novelles*. Beauduin employed the term neoclassicism in a particular sense: it was a protest against the superficial lyricism of the romanticists, the servile reproduction of the world as practiced by the Parnassians, and the musicality of the symbolists. The neoclassicist, according to Beauduin, would be distinguished by his unshaken faith in life and by his energetic action. Séché did not accept Beauduin as a real force in literature. Rather did he see in a fusion of neoclassicism and unanimism a possible future direction.

Fantasy, modern sensitivity, cosmic awareness, and neoclassicism scarcely give a satisfying picture of French poetry, especially since Séché often chose obscure writers for his illustrations, and seldom spoke of the most daring innovators. The concluding chapter of his book, which treats of the poet's attitude toward nature, is finally resolved by dividing the lyricists into two groups. Women poets sing of love, men celebrate the hero.

Other efforts to determine general directions of poetry were no more rewarding than Séché's conclusions. Florian-Parmentier's *La Littérature et l'Epoque* (1914), useful as a reference book on poetic manifestoes, assures us that poetry seemed to be accomplishing a synthesis of Parnassian naturalism, symbolist idealism, and impressionist naturism. Henri-Martin Barzun, in *L'Ere du drame* (1912), was convinced that sentimental sources of inspiration were no longer valid. He too spoke of synthesis, of the simultaneous presence of individual and universal forces, and of the dramatic quality that conflict between these elements will give to poetry. The following year, in a pamphlet entitled *Poétique d'un idéal nouveau,* he reproached the young generation for not having created a form of expression in keeping with the times. With symbolism and free verse twenty-eight years old, Barzun suggested that innovations were long overdue. His solution for the problem was "le chant simultané et polyrythmique." This took the form, as one can see from poems in his magazine *Poème et Drame,* of choruses typographically arranged like opera librettos. For example, a workman, a mechanic, an engineer, and an inventor tell of their contributions to the creation of the airplane. Barzun's "simultanéisme" produced some acrid comments in periodicals, critics asking whether the separate voices were to speak at the same time, thereby creating an unintelligible cacophony, or in series, thus destroying the simultaneous quality Barzun sought. But during 1913 Barzun found some adherents, notably Fernand Divoire and Sébastien Voirol.

Barzun's point of departure had been the negation of individual sensitivity as a theme for modern verse. This aspect of poetry was the subject of a book by Jean Dornis (Mme. Guillaume Beer), *La Sensibilité dans la*

poésie moderne 1885–1912, a long work hopelessly confused in its presentation. While the author's chapter headings would seemingly indicate a directive principle, the mass of notations on love, on philosophical or religious
aspiration, and on social preoccupation led nowhere. Possibly the author's
central theme was a question: whether the forces of symbolism were still
vital or whether they were exhausted. In any case she avoided coming to
conclusions, and mingled names and dates in a curious fashion. She did
believe that personal sensitivity was still a vital force, and in this she presented a contrast to Barzun.

The most precise and satisfying remarks on poetic trends in 1912 are to
be found in a small pamphlet by P.-J. Jouve. *Les Directions de la littérature
moderne,* although some of its remarks are derived from Jouve's long association with the poets of the Abbaye, conveys a true picture of a new poetic
style. According to Jouve, lyric expression had become the direct, spontaneous transcription of inner vision, unencumbered by adornments, couched in
simple terms, and revealing the deep emotion of living man. "La poésie immédiate" of Jules Romains and "l'expression nue" of Georges Duhamel had
proposed somewhat the same idea, but in this essay Jouve was speaking of
impressions received from his reading rather than pleading a cause. That
poetry had simplified its expression, casting aside superfluous images which
in the early years of the century were the hallmark of Samain and Guérin,
was undeniable. Directness in style and the interest in everyday things with
its attendant optimism constituted something more important than poetic
form. More than one writer in 1912 was aware of this. Georges Batault, in
an essay in the *Mercure de France,*[2] concluded by saying that the new subject of poetry was life, revealed in the love of present things and hope for
the future.

In French newspapers, however, not questions of style or manner of utterance but the manifestoes and the quarrels among poets were considered
good copy. In *Le Temps,* between April 23 and June 4, 1912, appeared the
results of an inquiry conducted by Emile Henriot. His question, "Existe-t-il,
à votre sens, une 'jeune école littéraire,'" drew almost universally the answer that there were a great many so-called schools but that they represented
what was most perishable and ridiculous in the domain of art. True, a few
writers spoke in favor of a particular belief. Jean Royère replied that since
nothing valid had replaced it, symbolism necessarily must be the only living
school of poetry; Beauduin explained how "paroxysme" surpassed both
romanticism and symbolism in not remaining fettered to sensations; Romains gave an explanation of "unanimisme"; Henri Clouard found in
"L'Ecole romane" the only indication of new orientation in French lit-

2. "Les Tendances de la poésie contemporaine," 99 (Sept. 16, 1912), 298–325.

erature; and Mauriac spoke of the religious currents in poetry as exemplified by Claudel, Jammes, and Péguy. Apart from Catholicism, Mauriac discerned only two important groups: the neoclassicists in *La Revue critique des idées et des livres* and the inventive group of the *Nouvelle Revue Française*. Those of the first alignment, he said, were too distrustful of inspiration, while those of the second were overly suspicious of common sense.

Henriot interspersed his own comments among the replies he received and his opinions drew vigorous protest. *La Renaissance contemporaine,* through its director, Robert Veyssié, and *L'Heure qui sonne,* through Gaston Picard, objected to being identified as "revues paroxystes." Duhamel refused to be considered a disciple of Romains. When Henriot published in 1913 the results of his inquiry under the title *A quoi rêvent les jeunes gens,* he appended some of the letters of protest.

What Henriot tried to do in *Le Temps,* Alfred de Tarde, under the pseudonym "Agathon," attempted in *L'Opinion,* and Jean Muller and Gaston Picard in *Comœdia.* Agathon's conclusions, in "Les Jeunes Gens d'aujourd'hui," were that writers in 1912 were interested in humanity and that perhaps humanism best described current directions. Muller and Picard were forced to conclude in "Tendances présentes de la littérature française" that young writers had not brought forth any new literary formula.

Each inquiry among writers had produced a hopelessly confused picture and many personal and conceptual antagonisms, but the vigorous and combative tone of the answers gave evidence of general discontentment about current letters. Some criticis, particularly among those who were called neoclassicists, appeared intent on destroying everything that the nineteenth century had offered in lyricism. Henri Clouard, for instance, wrote *Les Disciplines,* a little book in which he denounced the perils of romanticism, naturalism, and what he called "l'impressionnisme symboliste." In his demonstration of the literary and social need for a classical renaissance, he proclaimed intelligence the only salvation. His admiration for Anatole France, Barrès, and Maurras might offer some hope for prose writing, but his invocation of Moréas as the guiding light for lyric art gave scant hope for poetry.

These are the results, and disappointing they are, of attempts by Frenchmen to see clearly into the poetic tendencies of 1912. An appraisal by an English poet, made in the same year, is on the whole more satisfactory. F. S. Flint, in the August 1912 number of Harold Monro's *Poetry Review,* wrote a long essay on "Contemporary French Poetry." [3] Introducing his subject by a backward glance at symbolism and the advent of free verse, he spoke of Henri Ghéon, Jean Royère, André Spire, the Abbaye (Barzun and Mercereau); of *Les Bandeaux d'or* (Paul Castiaux and Théo Varlet), Lucien

3. *The Poetry Review, 1* (Aug. 1912), 355–414.

Rolmer, Beauduin, Jean Thogorma, Florian-Parmentier; of three women poets: Cécile Périn, Valentine de Saint-Point, and Berthe Reynold; of Tancrède de Visan, Henri Hertz, and finally of Marinetti. He mentioned in passing some fifteen other contemporary poets whom he considered equally worthy of his attention. Although Flint tended to place poetic schools in the foreground (and small wonder, since his chief consultants were Mercereau, Florian-Parmentier, and Arcos), he saw each poet as an individual. His general conclusion, which reflects some of Barzun's ideas, is: "The confluence of the streams of romantic, parnassian, and symbolist verse which carried them into the twentieth century seems to be bearing them on to that province of their art where poets speak the language of inspiration and intuition to assembled men: poetic drama" (p. 362).

In 1913 Flint, remaining loyal to Harold Monro who founded the quarterly *Poetry and Drama,* composed four "French Chronicles" which supplemented what he had written in 1912. Aware of the debate between Clouard and Thibaudet, he discussed the two definitions of classicism: on the one hand the imitation of seventeenth-century style, which was sometimes advocated in *La Revue critique des idées et des livres* and in *L'Action française,* and on the other, simple need for restraint and equilibrium, which was suggested by many poets.

Flint had read Emile Henriot's book *A quoi rêvent les jeunes gens.* In the replies by French writers he observed the important place occupied by Francis Jammes and Paul Claudel. By the end of 1913, having studied a large part of Claudel's published work, Flint concluded that "Paul Claudel is undeniably a great poet in every sense," though he reserved the title of the greatest lyric European poet for Verhaeren.

H.-M. Barzun's article "Du Symbole au drame," presented in the second issue of his *Poème et Drame,"* attracted Flint's attention. The arbitrary division of French poets into the "intuitifs" and the "visionnaires," the first group continuing Rimbaud, Laforgue, Verlaine, and Mallarmé, the second finding its leadership in Paul Adam, Verhaeren, and Claudel, did not strike Flint as implausible. He exhibited, however, no wholehearted enthusiasm for any group, and was much less impressed by Marinetti's futurism than was his colleague Harold Monro.

Interest among the English poets in the activities of their French neighbors remained constant until the outbreak of World War I. Monro's *Poetry and Drama* ran into financial difficulties, but a new periodical, *The Egoist,* was founded in January 1914. One of its editors was Richard Aldington, and it was he who gave a report on French poetry in the June 15 issue of the magazine.[4] Modestly claiming to be less well read in French verse than his

4. *The Egoist, I* (June 15, 1914), 221–3.

friends F. S. Flint and John Gould Fletcher, he offered a little anthology of poetry by six French authors. His choice is interesting for the light it sheds on the literary relationship between the imagists and their French contemporaries. Luc Durtain's "Tonneins," that simple equation of the individual personality and the town, was, Aldington said, a fine poem. The irony and gaiety of G.-C. Cros' "Une Tristesse de Canapé," the impressionist technique of Spire's "Ligurie" and "Provence," the exact rendering of mood in P.-J. Jouve's "Paix de vivre," and the typographical audacity of Apollinaire's "Tombe d'Henri Rousseau" gained his approval. He regretted that space did not permit his quoting in their entirety poems by Blaise Cendrars and Max Jacob, but he gave a fragment illustrating the latter's strange rhymes. A few lines from Beauduin's "L'Ame du siècle neuf" were prefaced by Aldington's comment that "M. Beauduin is not without power, and in France he has succeeded in attracting a great deal of attention." Aldington appears to have been suspicious of the numerous French schools of poetry, but as a champion of free verse he followed closely what Romains, Barzun, and Beauduin were writing. He even translated an article on "Paroxysme" for *The Egoist*.[5]

These English writers on contemporary French poetry are in some ways unsatisfactory. Their discussion was limited to periodicals and books which chanced to come into their hands, and those poets who were vigorously declamatory assumed an importance not justified by their work. Occasionally an English periodical, striving for close literary bonds with France, resorted to reports from Frenchmen. The most important of these was *Rhythm,* founded as a quarterly in the summer of 1911, but published as a monthly magazine during 1912. John Middleton Murry, its editor, made Francis Carco and Tristan Derème his French contributors, the former being entrusted with prose and the latter with poetry. In addition, through the Parisian art dealer Clovis Sagot, Murry secured permission to reproduce art works by Picasso, Herbin, and Chabaud. The English public was informed about such magazines as *Les Bandeaux d'or* and *L'Ile sonnante* by Murry himself, but it was Tristan Derème who wrote an "Esquisse de la poésie française actuelle" as well as essays on Francis Carco, Jean Pellerin, and Roger Frène. While Derème represented a biased approach to poetry of his time by reason of his dislike of the neoclassicists and neoromanticists, and his predilection for the "fantaisistes" (among whom he placed Carco, Pellerin, and Vérane) and for the "indépendants" (Frène, Puy, Deubel, Salmon, Mandin, Spire, Lavaud, and Périn), he did acknowledge the importance of Romains and the poets of the "Abbaye." He minimized the value of the noisy creators of schools. Derème found the sources of modern verse in

5. *1* (Aug. 15, 1914), 313–16.

Baudelaire, Verlaine, Mallarmé, and Corbière. Among living poets, he named as masters Jammes, Fort, Régnier, Verhaeren, Merrill, Vielé-Griffin, Kahn, and Maeterlinck. He was pleased with the individual liberty that the contemporary writers were demanding.

Implicit in Derème's displeasure at attempts to form poetic schools was an attack on Henri-Martin Barzun and Nicolas Beauduin. These two poets made the last important attempts before World War I to formulate a doctrine for lyric expression, and we have seen how often their names occurred in critical articles on poetry. Barzun's *L'Ere du drame*, which he called an "Essai de synthèse poétique moderne," was printed in 1912 and codified his earlier endeavor at creating a poetic drama in *La Montagne* of 1908 and a dramatic poem in *Hymne des forces* of 1912. This presentation of speaking characters, such as the poet, the hero, and the prophet, with supporting hymns and choruses, tended to direct poetic art toward epic rather than lyric form. Derème, despite Barzun's assertion that he was not establishing a poetic school but rather bringing together various poetic currents, was alarmed at Barzun's tendency to leap into grandiose and universal themes. For Derème, this spelled the end of personal lyricism.

Barzun's "Dramatisme" was no less grandiose than Beauduin's "Paroxysme." The latter's poetic doctrine, which was printed in Jean Muller's and Gaston Picard's *Sur les Tendances présentes de la littérature française,* was later condensed in an article of which we have spoken, and which appeared in 1913 in the *Mercure de France*. This was the moment when Beauduin's name became really important. A new quarterly, *La Vie des lettres,* which he founded in March 1913, was the official organ of "paroxysme." Finding that recent poetic schools, and especially that of Jules Romains, had represented too narrow and incomplete a doctrine, Beauduin proposed a synthesis of groups which believed in enthusiasm, in courage and strength, and in the modern age of machines. His definition of the tendencies of such poetry was summed up in "spontanéité lyrique, lyrisme actif, vision directe du réel, pathétique de la plénitude, objectivation des états radiants de l'âme, effort vers la plus vaste vie . . ."[6] Excluding the Abbaye group from his admiration, he praised the work of some forty-five writers ranging from Bouhélier, Royère, and Bocquet to Milosz, Apollinaire, and Salmon.

Beauduin's poems, many of which appeared in *La Vie des lettres,* are without exception demonstrations of his enthusiasm for modern life. They are documents of a theory, but they are singularly monotonous in their exuberance and uninteresting in their diction. "Le Poème des trains," "Odes des poètes à l'aviateur," "Exultation en aéroplane," "Vision de la cité future," and "Hymne du travail" indicate by their very titles the relationship

6. *La Vie des lettres, 1* (March 1913), 173–4.

that Beauduin's verse had with that of Marinetti, the Abbaye group, which he disdained, and other poets of his time. In October 1913 his most ambitious chant, "L'Homme cosmogonique: poème paroxyste," appeared in *La Vie des lettres*. In three cantos, "La Beauté moderne," "La Naissance d'un dieu," and "Les Identifications," he celebrated man in possession of the universe. His talent was far inferior to his theme, as can be easily seen in the two following quatrains:

> Tout l'univers est moi-même,
> Tout rayonne en mon extase;
> Le soleil qui monte au ciel
> Est mon âme qui voyage.
>
> Je suis dans l'éther dompté,
> Dans la fougue des machines,
> Dans la force des léviers,
> Dans les fluides électriques.[7]

But this voluble mediocre poet was a real force in his time. He favored assonance in place of rhyme, but was extremely generous in matters of prosody. In *La Vie des lettres* he assembled a distinguished group of contributors. Among the poets were Régnier, Verhaeren, Vielé-Griffin, Royère, Jammes, Rolmer, Edouard Guerber (Jean Thogorma), Fernand Divoire, Henri Hertz, and Paul Fort. Among prose contributors were Gide, writing on Verlaine and Mallarmé, Gaston Sauvebois on neoclassicism and the literary aspect of French imperialism,[8] Tancrède de Visan on Bergson and modern art, Jean Muller on religious themes in contemporary letters, and William Speth on Verhaeren. Beauduin constantly stated that his efforts tended toward creating a synthesis in literary currents of his age, but his denial of the Abbaye group as a literary force seems to contain overtones of personal ambition to become a leader, as indeed does the care with which he cited in notes newspaper references to himself or to "paroxysme."

Against the vast epic tendencies of a Barzun or a Beauduin existed the equally strong current of personal verse, whose characteristics were humor, irony, and subtle nuances. Those who wrote in this manner were especially eager to claim originality. Some repudiated the past. For instance, at the end of 1913, Francis Carco undertook the curious demonstration of anti-symbolist tendencies among young poets.[9] In his eyes, the critics had for some years misjudged Apollinaire, Salmon, Deubel, and Mandin. Delicate

---

7. *3* (Oct. 1913), 404.
8. A timely subject because of Louis Estève's book *Une Nouvelle Psychologie de l'impérialisme*, 1913.
9. *Les Marges*, No. 44 (Dec. 1913), pp. 258–63.

shadings and mysterious overtones had made these poets seem to be descendants of the symbolists, and had blinded readers to their roles as innovators. Naturalness in expression, more directness, less uncertainty, vacillation, and anguish—these were for Carco the indications of waning symbolist influence. His choice of young writers to illustrate the new tendencies, although obviously dictated by his associations with *Le Divan, Les Facettes,* and other periodicals, was a partial confirmation of what Clouard was preaching in *La Revue critique des idées* and of what J.-M. Bernard had announced in *Les Guêpes*. But Carco's poets (Tristan Derème, Jean Pellerin, J.-M. Bernard, Léon Vérane, René Bizet, and Robert de la Vaissière), all loosely associated with "la poésie fantaisiste," might have equally well been used to illustrate the continuity of Verlaine or Laforgue. Indeed, when Duhamel reviewed Carco's *La Bohème et mon cœur,* he spoke of the "mélodie de Verlaine," and reporting on Derème's *Le Poème de la pipe et de l'escargot,* the same critic recalled the debt to Laforgue. The new generation appeared to find these references to the immediate past irksome. Content to be placed in the lineage of Villon, Marot, and La Fontaine, the "fantaisistes" refused to be called disciples of the symbolists, preferring the term "neoclassicism." The prewar years were filled with discussions concerning the need for discipline, clarity, and intelligence. From 1909, when J.-M. Bernard created the regional magazine *Les Guêpes* in Valence, to 1914, when *La Revue critique des idées et des livres* brought to a serious literary plane a double attack on romanticism and symbolism, the question of literary alliances could be deplored but could scarcely be avoided. Henri Clouard, who for some time had been storming against Verhaeren, casting pitying glances at Samain and Vielé-Griffin, and extolling the *Stances* of Moréas, expressed his viewpoint in a lecture given at the Vieux-Colombier on May 16, 1914. His title was "Les Poètes et le Néo-Classicisme." His purpose was to speak of certain poets who had retained an essential quality of the French national genius: subtle clarity in the expression of feeling. His choice of writers included P.-J. Toulet, Fagus, F.-P. Alibert, J.-M. Bernard, Carco, Francis Eon, Gustave Valmont, Maurice de Noisay, and Henri Martineau. He did not claim greatness for them. Nor did he wish to accept for them the name of neoclassicists. But these lyricists, who had his admiration, all remained, he felt, in the paths of authentic literary tradition.

Throughout Clouard's critical writing during the prewar years was visible a political allegiance prejudicial to fair discussion of literary matters. The whole group of the *Revue critique des idées et des livres* supported Charles Maurras and the *Action française*. The intrusion of ideas concerning nationalism and aristocracy of the intelligence confused his argument. Years later, in the introduction to his volume *La Poésie française moderne* (1924),

Clouard confessed that the idea of the opposition of classicism and romanticism was a youthful error he shared with Pierre Gilbert, J.-M. Bernard, and André Fresnois.[10]

In place of partisan arguments favoring particular literary tenets, a more objective and wider critical approach seemed called for. This was furnished to a certain degree by a series of three articles in *La Nouvelle Revue Française* in 1913. Written by Jacques Rivière, and entitled "Le Roman d'aventure," this tripartite essay was based on observation of cultivated tastes of the period rather than on personal promulgation of a doctrine. Rivière saw 1913 as the year when one could at last clearly discern the change that literature was undergoing. Symbolism, the era of poetry, was yielding to something else. Rivière suspected that the new epoch would be that of drama or the novel. The critic sought to analyze the elements in symbolism and romanticism that were displeasing to current tastes, and to discover what aspect of classicism was valid for the twentieth century.

In the first part of his study,[11] Rivière discussed the traits of the symbolists which were causing rejection of their poetic manner. They were overly self-conscious. Their emotions, the constant theme of their work, were not presented as immediate and dramatic, but as a diffused radiation after a long sojourn in the mind. In Rivière's opinion, this refinement of sentiment was unsuccessful because it was too vague and tenuous. The symbolist had exhausted the possibilities of emotional experience before he began to write. He expected the reader to imagine the processes of the mind that had preceded the composition of the poem. Each separate reader had to reconstruct the work according to a series of mysterious echoes and suggestions. But this demand, that the subjectivity of the author be interpreted by that of the reader, had become displeasing: "Nous sommes à l'égard du symbolisme cette génération seconde pour qui les œuvres sont déjà des étrangères, et qui ne sent à aucun moment, en les lisant, ni l'envie, ni le pouvoir de les avoir faites." [12]

Rivière was harsh when he spoke of romanticism, calling it not only an "art démodé" but an "art inférieur." Its absence of profundity, its grandiose effects, and its facility caused him to label it a monstrosity. He had called symbolism abnormal, but the appeal of the romanticist he condemned as crude and shallow. Intelligence, application, and clarity were necessary for future literary creation and in this sense classicism (particularly Descartes' *Méditations*) could be a guide.

Rivière, the keen and curious observer, was not blind to transformations

---

10. These three colleagues of Clouard in *La Revue critique des idées et des livres* all perished in World War I.

11. *Nouvelle Revue Française*, 9 (May 1913), 748–59.   12. P. 760.

that were taking place in arts other than the literary. He saw the advent of cubism as a presage of expressionism's doom; he expected music, as it sought some of the strength and form of Bach, to turn away from Debussy. What set Rivière's criticism apart from that of so many of his contemporaries was his method of analyzing current tastes, not for the purpose of imposing a point of view, but for offering an explanation of literary evolution.

In August 1914 discussion of poetic and literary theory was brought to an end. General mobilization to meet the German invasion, and the departure of so many writers for the front meant suspension of almost all publications. The imbroglio of "dramatisme," "paroxysme," and "néo-classicisme," as well as the unending dispute concerning free and regular prosody, was halted at a moment of great effervescence. The sudden silence among critics, the direction of thought toward the single theme of war, the ever-growing list of writers who perished in battle, created a discontinuity in the literary picture and for several years a sense of void. The conflict and conditions imposed by it retarded or accelerated literary reputations. Péguy's death in 1914 directed attention toward the *Tapisseries* and to *Eve*—that is, to the poetry which had appeared in *Les Cahiers de la quinzaine* between December 1912 and December 1913. Valéry's *La Jeune Parque,* published by the *Nouvelle Revue Française* in 1917, was a reentrance into the field of poetry that temporarily went unheralded. The temporal dislocation of literary matters was accentuated by the evolution in thought that took place in many minds during the war years. André Salmon, in a postscript to *Prikaz* (1919), announced that this was the first volume of the "seconde époque" of his poetic work. New voices, whether of those who had attained manhood during the hiatus of the conflict or of those who had been little heard before 1914, made a sudden change in the poetic tonality. Finally, a kind of perspective on the first years of the century became possible. What had once seemed important was often discarded, while new considerations took its place.

BETWEEN August 1914 and July 1918 poetry was dominated by the theme of war. Almost all periodicals were suspended during this period, and with increasing shortages of paper, the number of printed volumes was sharply reduced. A great number of poets were in uniform, either not writing or taking their subjects from the pity and the sacrifice of the conflict. One, Guillaume Apollinaire, found a continuous source of inspiration during his military service, losing none of his verve and fantasy and seemingly ever stimulated by brief meetings with and enforced separations from friends and the women he loved.

But the war, in spite of the noble themes of patriotism, courage, and sacrifice, did not produce great and lasting poetry. Verhaeren's *Les Ailes rouges de la guerre* (1916), Henri de Régnier's *1914-1916* (1918), and Romains' *Europe* (1916), to name but a few published collections, do not reveal their author's best work but rather the constraint on their talents.

Critics in the early 'twenties almost universally regarded the poetry of the war as an inevitable but regrettable hiatus in the currents of lyricism. In the postwar years, the memories of 1914-18 were best conserved in prose, by Duhamel, Barbusse, and Dorgelès, by collections of letters from soldiers, and by essays on the subject.

As the expected German retreat from the Marne became a reality, literature resumed its place. Several of the little periodicals which had survived (*Le Feu, La Vie,* and *Le Divan*) took on new life. The *Mercure de France* resumed publication in April 1915, was a monthly for the rest of that year, then took back its character as a fortnightly. *La Nouvelle Revue Française* did not emerge until May 1919. Martineau's *Le Divan* suffered little interruption, consecrating its successive issues to writers who had died for their country: Drouot, Despax, Fresnois, Péguy, Lionel des Rieux, Louis Codet, and Olivier Hourcade. *Le Double Bouquet* continued to publish numbers until March 1917. *Les Marges,* suspended since July 1914, was reborn in May 1918. The old and established periodicals, such as *La Revue des Deux Mondes,* were stable, but during the war contributed little to criticism or publication of poetry. Mme. de Noailles was their favorite lyricist, and she composed a great number of patriotic poems which are now forgotten. Paul Fort was most prolific, publishing in little pamphlets his *Poèmes de France* as a "bulletin lyrique de la guerre."[1]

---

1. Later printed as the nineteenth series of the *Ballades françaises.*

A new magazine, *Les Ecrits nouveaux,* organized by André Germain to continue and expand the defunct *Double Bouquet,* appeared in November 1917. In the first number were poems by Mme. de Noailles and Maurice Magre, and in subsequent issues Tristan Derème, Pierre Camo, Jean Pellerin, F.-P. Alibert, Léo Larguier, Paul Fort, Paul Valéry, and André Breton were among the contributors of verse. Such a group represented totally diverse lyric currents; *Les Ecrits nouveaux* would have been non-partisan if André Germain had not written a number of satirical imaginary conversations in which he savagely attacked Bourget's aristocratic snobbery and represented Jean Cocteau as the spoiled darling of literary salons.[2] An essay by René Gillouin reproached Claudel with building a theory of aesthetics on the word-play "naître" and "connaître," with lacking Christian prudence, humility, and charity, although according him literary genius.

One of the first critics to consider the postwar directions of poetry was the Swiss writer Paul Aeschimann. In May 1918 he contributed to *Les Marges* an essay entitled "Les Tendances de la jeune poésie française." [3] Looking back to 1914, he saw the poetic schools of that period as passing fads and bluntly stated that the last grouping to have importance in literary history was that of symbolism. From it emerged the masters of contemporary poetry. Those whose influence had been greatest, Aeschimann believed, were Verhaeren, Vielé-Griffin, and Fort; he chose these because modern verse had love of life, human tenderness, and especially fantasy. His contention was that these three qualities persisted in 1918 and that the war had not greatly modified individual talents. Regular and free verse held equal dominion; new periodicals and new names had not changed the picture.

Aeschimann mentioned two of the new periodicals, *Sic* and *Nord-Sud.* He named one of the new poets, Pierre Reverdy. Today we may wonder, complacently demanding that the critic be also a seer, how he could have serenely dismissed these phenomena as mere continuations of a tendency toward fantasy. At any rate Aeschimann accepted the newcomers' writing as a form of art. This was more than most of his contemporaries were willing to admit.

After Marinetti's futurism, after Apollinaire's typographical audacities in poetry and his ardent defence of Henri Rousseau's painting in *Les Soirées de Paris,* most critics were of the opinion that *Sic* and *Nord-Sud* were new manifestations of a not-very-funny literary joke. Pierre Albert-Birot's "Poèmes à parler et à danser," published in his magazine *Sic,* André

2. Germain's first satire was directed against the painter-writer J.-E. Blanche. Gide, who had contributed to the first number of the magazine was so disgusted by its tone that he asked that his name be stricken from the list of contributors.

3. *Les Marges,* No. 52 (May 15, 1918), pp. 199–206.

Breton's and Philippe Soupault's "Etudes" in *Nord-Sud* provoked only
hilarity. *Sic* first appeared in January 1916; Reverdy's *Nord-Sud* on March
15, 1917. The former must have seemed for some time to be the organ of
the verbal acrobatics of Albert-Birot, a writer who composed an entire poem
on the airplane with letters which endeavored to convey the sputtering of
an engine and the shriek of flight. *Nord-Sud* announced in its very first
number that it gave allegiance to Guillaume Apollinaire, the only poet who
had definitely brought new life into French letters. Paul Dermée's "Quand
le symbolisme fut mort" stated *Nord-Sud*'s literary position, while Reverdy
brought in a relationship with the fine arts by writing an essay on cubism.
Max Jacob, André Breton, Philippe Soupault, Jean Cocteau, and Tristan
Tzara were also contributors to *Nord-Sud* during 1917. While war-torn
France was little acquainted with the invention of Dada, in Zurich, on
February 8, 1916, or with *La Première Aventure de M. Antipyrine,* published in Switzerland that same year, these two little magazines which
sprang up in Paris conveyed clearly enough a demolition of the past, even
the immediate past, and hopeful projection into the future. Apollinaire's
final lines to "La Victoire," which appeared in the first number of *Nord-
Sud,* conveyed that hope:

> La Victoire avant tout sera
> De bien voir au loin
> De tout voir
> De près
> Et que tout ait un nom nouveau.

Apollinaire's death on November 9, 1918, the publication of "L'Esprit
nouveau et les poètes" in the December issue of the *Mercure de France,* a
memorial number of *Sic,* and the appearance of the poems of war and
peace, *Les Calligrammes* (1918), inaugurated a period when the author of
Alcools became a directing force, changing the whole picture in the poetic
world. Cendrars' *Dix-neuf Poèmes élastiques* and Soupault's *Rose des vents;*
the founding of the magazine *Littérature* in March 1919, by Aragon, Breton,
and Soupault; and a number of strange volumes from the Sirène and Sans
Pareil presses gave a new meaning to "avant-gardiste" literature.

Of course, the complete revelation of poetic change was not yet apparent.
Critics spoke of "littérature cubiste" and "mots en liberté" as a silly and
passing fad. Implications that young authors, intoxicated by reading the
works of Rimbaud, were passing through some sort of juvenile malady
were standard remarks. Magazines of the prewar period, on reappearing,
showed little inclination to change. In 1919 *Les Marges* was printing poems
by Aeschimann, Ernest Raynaud, Emile Sicard, Guy Lavaud, Tristan
Klingsor, Fagus, Julien Ochsé, and other young writers who stemmed from

either "fantaisiste" or romanist tradition. The *Nouvelle Revue Française,*
with F.-P. Alibert, Paul Claudel, Duhamel, L.-P. Fargue, Luc Durtain, Jules
Romains, and Paul Valéry, showed some sympathy for revolutionary
changes. If it opened its doors to André Salmon, a contributor to *Sic* and
Littérature, it was because his new manner appeared to be predicated on an
acceptable and serious doctrine: "substituant aux saisons du vieux lyrisme le
climat instable de l'inquiétude universelle." [4]

As always in difficult and stormy periods the voices of complete re-
actionaries were raised. A new periodical, which appeared three months
after the founding of *Littérature,* revealed absolute fidelity to a conservative tradition. *La Minerve française* warned in its first number (June 1,
1919) against "funestes fantaisies littéraires" and "un appétit immodéré
de la nouveauté." It also spoke patriotically against "l'inconsciente survivance
d'influences ennemies." The poets who contributed to successive issues of
the magazine (Louis le Cardonnel, Emile Henriot, Léo Larguier, Fernand
Séverin, Louis Pize, Charles Derennes) admirably represented the metrical
traditions of romanticism and the clarity of expression which the periodical
preached. Pierre Lasserre's series on "Les Chapelles littéraires," principally
aimed at adulators of Claudel, Jammes, and Péguy, also contained many
sharp reproofs for prose masquerading as poetry. The poetry critic for *La
Minerve française* was Marius André, an employee in the ministry of foreign
affairs, who had written Provençal poems in his youth and who was in 1919
past fifty years of age. A firm believer in rhyme, caesura, and carefully
counted poetic feet, he rarely spoke of poets who did not follow precise rules.
He even reproached the owner of the periodical, A.-P. Garnier, with not
counting a mute *e* in one of his lines. Duhamel's and Vildrac's "Constante
rythmique" excited his satirical talents and he demonstrated how one could
discover this phenomenon in the most banal prose. This stern attitude
precluded much discussion of new poets, yet on one occasion André chose
to speak his mind on Apollinaire, Cendrars, and Soupault.[5] He saw Apollinaire as a double personality, devoted to traditional sources on the one
hand, but indulging a taste for dry humor in the creation of typographical
and verbal nonsense. André explained such writers as Cendrars and Soupault
by saying that they had stupidly taken Apollinaire's joke seriously. He was
outraged at seeing the name of Paul Valéry associated with the Dadaists.

La Minerve française, in its severe conservatism, seemed closed to any
poetic innovation. Pierre Lasserre's attacks on "Les Chapelles littéraires"
allied the periodical with the prewar viewpoint of *La Revue critique des
idées et des livres,* with the ideas of intelligence and clarity, of order and

4. A. Salmon, preface to *Prikaz* (1919).
5. *La Minerve française,* 3 (Dec. 15, 1919), 536–40.

discipline, and with the notion that the nineteenth century had been a terrible force for the destruction of these virtues. The extremes of poetic aesthetic, represented by *La Minerve* on the one hand and by *Sic* and *Nord-Sud* on the other, seemingly needed a literary organ of broader tendencies. The *Mercure de France,* rooted in the traditions of symbolism, but with Georges Duhamel again on its staff, and currently publishing the works of its erstwhile collaborator Guillaume Apollinaire (*Vitam Impendere Amori,* 1917; *Calligrammes,* 1918), seemed the most logical organ for the expression of an eclectic attitude. The death of Remy de Gourmont in 1915 removed an authoritative voice which had often dictated the policies of Alfred Vallette. Duhamel having decided against continuing in his post of poetry critic, the magazine could embark on new paths.

Vallette asked André Fontainas to undertake the task of reviewing current poetry. Fontainas, who was born in 1865, and whose first volume of verse dated from 1889, had a long association with the *Mercure,* to which he regularly contributed reports on modern art (1896–1902) and on the drama (1908–11). He had written both free and regular verse, and was generally regarded as a disciple of Mallarmé, both because of his lofty conception of poetic art and his kindly urbanity in human relations.

In Fontainas, Vallette chose the poet who had remained most faithful to the ideas of 1885, to music and suggestive imagery, and to the notion of the poem as an expression of universal beauty demanding sacrifice and labor. Fontainas' loyalties and sympathies went chiefly to those friends of his youth, the symbolists. In his first article on poetry, in July 1919, just after he had accepted Vallette's offer, he proclaimed his admiration for Verhaeren, Henri de Régnier, Paul Fort, Kahn, and Vielé-Griffin. Thirty years later, in his last essay in the *Mercure* (January 1, 1949), his concluding paragraphs celebrated his youthful friendship with the group of *La Pléiade* (Mikhaël, Merrill, and Quillard), and with the French and Belgian symbolists.

The appointment of the fifty-four-year-old poet to the post on the *Mercure* might have been of only slight importance. But the fact that Fontainas became such a permanent feature of the magazine, outliving Vallette and indeed all friends of his youth except Mockel, still writing his reviews of poetic collections at the age of eighty-three, was of tremendous importance for the policies of the magazine. Fontainas, with the best intentions in the world, was incapable of understanding or appreciating some of the directions taken by poetic art after 1920. Instead of revealing the contemporary, he returned constantly to the past. One has only to read his *Poésie française d'aujourd'hui* (1931) to comprehend his understanding of the general currents of the early part of the century (continuation of symbolism and romanticism, return to classicism) and his utter confusion when he was confronted with younger poets such as Reverdy, Eluard, Aragon, René Char, and André Breton. More accessible to his critical judgment were Blaise Cendrars, Jean Cocteau, and Alibert. His real interest was in the "symbolistes les plus authentiques parmi les jeunes," [6] as he confessed in 1930. Raoul Boggio, G.-C. Cros, Guy Lavaud, Marcel Ormoy, Philippe Chabaneix, and Henry Charpentier are those he chose for special study from the decade 1920–30. Within certain limits, Fontainas showed considerable eclecticism. He accepted as genuine poets those who, far from being symbolists, represented a return to romanticism or classicism: Marie Dauguet, A.-P. Garnier, André Payer, Jean-Marie Guislain, François-Paul Alibert, and André Mary. He constantly expressed his high regard for the form as well as the content of Paul Valéry's verse. Finally, in Fontainas' favor, it must be said that he was most conscientious, reviewing hundreds of volumes each year. His very scrupulousness was a source of danger: he spoke of many insignificant volumes, seemingly well aware of their small worth, but ever intent on being courteous. The *Mercure* remained cautious and even suspicious in the face of too great poetic originality.

Jacques Rivière, the director of *La Nouvelle Revue Française,* represented a much more generous attitude toward innovations in poetry and art than other editors of established periodicals. During the last half of 1920 André Breton's "Pour Dada," André Salmon's "Vie de Guillaume Apollinaire," and Rivière's "Reconnaissance à Dada," as well as a collection of "Haï-Kaïs" assembled by Jean Paulhan, were printed in *La Nouvelle Revue Française.* Among the contributors of the hai-kais were Pierre Albert-Birot, the ex-director of *Sic,* and Paul Eluard, the founder of *Proverbe,* two names which at that time represented the lunatic frontier of poetic art. Jacques Rivière's interest in Dada did not extend to admiration for Tzara's or Picabia's poems; he was concerned mainly with some of the concepts and ideas of a group who tried to seize the incoherence of existence before the mind began its ruthless work of opposition, differentiation, and evaluation. The negation of literature, proposed by the adherents of Dada, appeared to Rivière the logical consequence of subjective tendencies which had begun with romanticism, become intensified with symbolism, and changed to a form of auto-expulsion with literary cubism. Writers, intent on plunging deeper and deeper into the realm of the subconscious, had reached a point where they no longer understood themselves. Mallarmé and Rimbaud, whom Rivière admired intensely, contributed to the debacle by giving words so personal a sense that, carried to its ultimate conclusion, this subjective vocabulary can mean anything. Rivière had but one answer to Dada's

6. Fontainas, A., *Dans la lignée de Baudelaire* (Nouvelle Revue Critique, 1930), p. 231.

nihilism: art also is a human fact and no amount of demonstration that art is impossible will erase its presence. Dada having shown where the reigning principles were leading, the writer must find new principles: "Il faut que nous renoncions au subjectivisme, à l'effusion, à la création pure, à la transmigration du moi, et à cette constante prétérition de l'objet qui nous a précipités dans le vide. Il faut qu'un mouvement subtil de notre esprit l'amène à se dédoubler de nouveau; il faut qu'il reprenne foi en une réalité distincte de sa puissance, qu'il arrive à distinguer à nouveau en lui un instrument et une matière." [7]

Taken out of context, Rivière's words sound like a manifesto, but read with his entire essay, they seem more like an appeal to writers to find a true reason for the creations of their spirits. The ironic name of Breton's, Aragon's, and Soupault's magazine, and its equally ironic question "Why do you write?"; the manifestation of the Dada spirit of insulting challenge; the provocations of which Arthur Craven had been a forerunner in New York; Picabia's two numbers of *Cannibale* (April–May 1920) and his irregular issues of *391* all provided the background of Rivière's doubts and attempted resolution. The arrival of Tzara from Switzerland in 1919; the newspaper clipping he read with an accompaniment of bells and rattles on January 23, 1920, and which he called a poem; the signatures of Picabia, Aragon, Breton, Eluard, Ribemont-Dessaignes, and Dermée on the February Dada bulletin; the riotous meetings in the Salle des indépendants and the Salle Gaveau marked a turning point in literary history and particularly in the history of poetry. A year later Breton and most of his friends had broken with Tzara, but Breton gave credit to Dada for having left him and his fellows in a receptive state until they could work out their own paths of action.

The destructive and violent actions of 1920 established divisions which had hitherto been confused. During 1919, in *Littérature,* the names of Valéry, L.-P. Fargue, André Salmon, and André Gide had been associated with those of Breton, Reverdy, Cendrars, and Aragon. The place given to Rimbaud, Apollinaire, and Lautréamont, as well as the respect accorded Mallarmé by *Littérature,* created an impression of cohesion, of an association of writers, each of whom was "pressé de trouver le lieu et la formule." Dada, as Breton explained in *Les Pas perdus,* was a state of mind, "la libre pensée artistique." [8] But the destructive, antiliterary aspect of this state of mind alienated a number of the contributors to *Littérature.* The issue which made the cleavage was the thirteenth, that of May 1920, in which were printed twenty-three manifestoes of the Dada movement. In December 1920 *Littérature* was devoted to a "Procès-verbal." Among the inter-

7. *N.R.F., 15* (Aug. 1, 1920), 236.   8. P. 70.

locutors were Aragon, Breton, Drieu La Rochelle, Eluard, and Jacques Rigaut. The conversation recorded concerned future directives for the magazine. It was decided not to waste much time in talking about living or dead authors, not to include philosophical articles, and not to make criticism an important element. On the question whether poetry would be accorded a place, opinion was divided, but only two voted for it. The title *Littérature* had now assumed its full irony. The group then proceeded, with the help of Tzara, Péret, and Soupault, to engage in a joyous game not entirely without serious implications. It was a question of making numerical evaluations on the literary artistic worth of such names as came to the minds of the participants.

Breton received the high mark of 16.85 out of a possible 20. Then came Soupault, Charlie Chaplin, Rimbaud, Eluard, and Lautréamont, the last receiving 14.27. At the other end of the scale were many symbolist poets: Henri de Régnier (—22.90), Paul Fort (—16.54), Verlaine (—11.90), and Moréas (—7.82). Valéry received a positive marking of 1.09, and Baudelaire a relatively high one of 9.00. This "Liquidation," as the enterprise was called, also revealed some admiration for Jarry, Apollinaire, and the Marquis de Sade.

This year, 1920, so important as a chaotic preview of surrealism, is also the moment of a determined effort in an opposite direction, one calling for respect for tradition, order, and the rule of intelligence. Before the war, the cult of Moréas, the literary concepts of Charles Maurras in *L'Action française,* and the poetry criticism of Henri Clouard in the *Revue critique des idées et des livres* had been outstanding expressions of this tendency. In 1920, on the tenth anniversary of Moréas' death, there was a new manifestation of fidelity to his art. *La Renaissance* of March 20, 1920 carried a long panegyric by Raymond de la Tailhède as well as some unpublished letters to Moréas from Mallarmé and Banville. *La Revue critique des idées et des livres* (March 25, 1920) devoted an entire issue to an "Hommage à Moréas," with essays by Maurice Barrès, André Thérive, Albert Thibaudet, Emile Henriot, Jean Longnon, and Eugène Marsan. Meanwhile, two poets from southern France, Xavier de Magallon and Joachim Gasquet, were urging Charles Maurras to permit publication of his verse. Their prayers did not go unheeded, and Maurras' *Inscriptions* appeared in 1921. The declamatory, didactic, and cold tone of these poems displeased most critics, but in 1920 the name of Maurras was, by some, associated with the lofty ideas of perfection and meditation which were suggested by the reticence of Mallarmé or the silence of Valéry. In the volume *La Pléiade* (1921), the collective anthology of Mme. de Noailles, Pierre Camo, Charles Derennes, Joachim Gasquet, Xavier de Magallon, Fernand Mazade, and Paul Valéry, the introduction stated: "Charles Maurras, poëte et grand poëte parmi les grands, n'édifie les strophes de la *Bataille de la Marne* ou du *Colloque des Morts* que dans les brûlants loisirs d'une obstinée action. D'autant plus rares et sur eux-mêmes ramassés, ses vers n'en sont que plus denses et plus féconds" (p. 6).

The essay in which these words occurred also contained an expression of praise for Raymond de la Tailhède. He had proved "de quelle amplitude inattendue pouvaient résonner sous des mains savants les cordes de l'alexandrin" (p. 15). The spirit of the "Pléiade" thus appeared in close sympathy with the Ecole romane, especially since poetic activity after 1870 was summed up by the passage: "Chez les meilleurs, le vers après avoir voulu s'incorporer la philosophie et l'histoire, tente de ne plus se nourrir que de sa propre substance, de ne plus briller que de son intime cristal, de ne plus exprimer, d'isoler la poësie, a écrit l'un de nous, de toute autre essence qu'elle-même. Dans cet effort du Symbolisme, l'excès du raffinement aboutit à l'évanescence" (pp. 4–5).

The "l'un de nous" was Paul Valéry. In the preface to Lucien Fabre's *Connaissance de la déesse* (1920) Valéry had written a long meditation on the poetic movement of his youth, considering its fervor, its aims, and its defeat. From this preface posterity has largely retained Valéry's paraphrase of Mallarmé: "reprendre à la Musique, leur bien," and the conjecture that the symbolist ideal led to an almost inhuman state. In this introduction, written for a book of poems composed by an engineer and mathematician, Valéry stressed the role of intelligence, controlling and dominating the poet's emotion. What he said in presenting Fabre's book was echoed to a certain degree in the collective essay of *La Pléiade* but with decidedly more emphasis on the return to the inspiration of Ronsard and Chénier.

It must have been difficult for the 1920 reader to identify Valéry's poetry and aesthetics. During 1919–20 the appearance of "Palme," "Abeille," and "Le Cimetière marin" in the *Nouvelle Revue Française,* and, in 1920–21, the publication, from the presses of that periodical, of the *Odes* ("Aurore," "La Pythie," "Palme"), of the *Album des vers anciens,* of *La Soirée avec M. Teste,* of *Le Serpent,* and *L'Ame et la Danse,* certainly associated his name with Rivière's periodical. But how was one to reconcile the publication of "Ode secrète" in the audacious February 1920 [9] issue of *Littérature* with the conservative "Pléiade" grouping? By the end of 1920 the question was partly answered. Valéry was on the side of order and discipline; his poetic mystery was not that of the authors of "Les Champs magnétiques." Two years later, when Valéry's verse had been composed in its entirety, his was

9. Picabia, Jacob, Aragon, Breton, Tzara, and Soupault were other contributors to this number of *Littérature.*

a truly important name. This can be seen in an impressive list of "Hommages" published in the May 1922 issue of *Le Divan*. There, among the contributors, the names of the symbolists (Fontainas, Mockel, Régnier, and Vielé-Griffin) recalled Valéry's debt to Mallarmé while the neoclassic discipline was suggested by Noailles, Mauriac, Dubech, and Vaudoyer. Joachim Gasquet, shortly before his death in 1921, had attempted to place Valéry in a poetic lineage and had emerged with the spiritual genealogy: Vigny-Baudelaire-Mallarmé-Valéry. In 1922, in the "Hommage" issue of *Le Divan,* Fernand Alary subscribed to and elucidated this association of names.[10]

Paul Léautaud maliciously suggested [11] that Valéry's sudden rise to poetic eminence was aided by recitations of his verse in Adrienne Monnier's bookstore. An article of 1920 by Daniel Halévy [12] described the enchantment of hearing André Gide read "La Pythie" and Adrienne Monnier recite "Le Cantique des colonnes" in the shop which bore the name "Les Amis des Livres." There were, however, other and more important reasons for Valéry's ascendency besides the intrinsic beauty of the lines of verse. Valéry represented order and tradition at a moment of literary anarchy when the conservatives felt menaced by "Les Novateurs." The definition of Valéry by J.-L. Vaudoyer in 1920: "un poète qui a reçu et qui fait fructifier de grands héritages, l'un de ceux qui plongent les racines de leur art dans le cœur même de notre terre . . . ," [13] was paraphrased by many critics. Some indeed, among them Guy Lavaud, found the prosody of the "Odes" too near that of J.-B. Rousseau, but their voices were lost in a chorus of praise.[14]

The cult of Valéry's poetry in 1922 was also visible in the answers to an inquiry on "Les Maîtres de la jeune littérature," which appeared in *La Revue hebdomadaire* from September to December. "Le symbolisme, enfin, met une marque éclatante sur notre époque avec l'œuvre de Valéry," wrote Pierre Camo. "Valéry commence à être suivi," asserted Lucien Fabre. "Voici les poètes à qui je dois le plus de plaisir: Racine, Moréas, Charles Maurras, Paul Valéry, Louis le Cardonnel," said René Fernandet. Benjamin Crémieux

10. The placing of Valéry among the great poets did meet with resistance. For instance, in *Fortunio* (Oct. 1921) one reads: "Quant à M. Paul Valéry—doit-on réclamer chez lui quelque lumière surnaturelle ou s'ingénier à déchiffrer ses inscriptions lyriques, dont il fait volontiers de plaisants rébus?" (p. 270).

11. In his "Notice" on Valéry in *Poètes d'aujourd'hui.*

12. *Revue universelle, 1* (May 1920), 280–8.   13. *1* (July 1920), 84–5.

14. Valéry's fame continued to evoke occasional dissenting opinions. Pierre Lasserre, in the *Nouvelles littéraires* (Dec. 29, 1923), was among the most outspoken: "Valéry est porté dans les lettres par un mouvement si insolent que l'on a le droit de se déchaîner contre lui, je dirai même, le devoir, car je considère la place que certains s'efforcent d'attribuer à Valéry, poète, comme une erreur publique."

praised Valéry, together with Verlaine and Mallarmé, for having obtained new and individual effects from regular verse patterns.[15] The traditional form of Valéry's poetry, as well as the intellectual preoccupations of the author, were eagerly seized upon by the neoclassicists, particularly by those who felt that Jean Moréas had shown the twentieth century the paths it should follow. André Thérive, a staunch believer in the Ecole romane, although somewhat embarrassed by the hermetic qualities of Valéry's verse, opined that the poet would become more and more "roman," less and less "mallarmiste." [16]

Postwar critics of poetry who were interested in the new lyric manifestations often built their remarks around this problem of hermeticism. There were many difficult poets, either in the *Feuilles libres* where Salmon, Jacob, Soupault, Ribemont-Dessaignes, Cendrars, Pascal Pia, and Eluard formed an audacious group, or in *Les Ecrits nouveaux*, of eclectic tendencies, in which had appeared Valéry's "La Pythie," Jacob's "Le Christ à Montparnasse," fragments of Salmon's "Prikaz," the numerous quotations of poems in André Billy's "Apollinaire vivant," and Paul Morand's modernistic lyrics in free verse. The severe control of a Valéry and the liberty of an Aragon, who asserted that he had felt the influence of a single individual, Jacques Vaché, both led to the theme of difficult verse. Soupault, confessing in 1922 that the two profound influences on his poetry were Rimbaud and Lautréamont, also offered the reader perplexing problems of interpretation.

One of the early attempts to deal with this tendency was an article by R. Aron, "Introduction à la littérature d'avant-garde." [17] Aron found as a basis for modern hermeticism a poetic preoccupation which had existed in incipient form during the romantic era and which had become of vital concern during the symbolist period. He called this the "angoisse de l'inexprimable" and insisted that the Dadaists had intensified to the point of insanity the symbolist state of mind. But from the ashes of Dada he expected the modernists to evolve a poetic expression which would be unadorned and simple in contrast to the difficulty of the ideas. This was the theme which he had been expanding for some two years, and which partly explained why Valéry was placed among the neoclassicists. Critics pointed out the purity of Valéry's vocabulary and the correctness of his syntax, often contrasting the ornament of his early verse with the directness of his later

15. The results of the inquiry made by Pierre Varillon and Henri Rambaud were reprinted in *Enquête sur les maîtres de la jeune littérature* (Bloud and Gay, 1923). It was not a very good sampling of the contemporary literary scene, since too few of the younger writers were represented and too many of those consulted were either from the groups of *La Revue critique des idées et des livres, Le Divan,* or *Les Marges.*

16. *L'Opinion*, Sept. 29, 1922.　　　17. In *Revue de la semaine*, July 28, 1922.

compositions. Although some accused Valéry's lines of coldness, it was generally agreed that they presented difficulty in their thought rather than in their expression.

The postwar period witnessed the consecration of a type of poetry, prevalent since 1910, which had been chiefly found in the pages of *Le Divan* and *Les Guêpes*. It has come to be known as "la poésie fantaisiste," but its frontiers are vague and the list of its authors varies from critic to critic. Francis Carco, when he presented an anthology of such poetry in the October–December 1913 issue of *Vers et Prose,* indicated as its ancestors Corbière, Laforgue, and Rimbaud. Others have felt the importance of Verlaine as an influence. Carco's own title, *Chansons aigres-douces* (1912), indicated an important element in this verse where the ironic, the humorous, and the satirical opposed emotional seriousness. Tristan Klingsor, whose first published volume of verse dated from 1895, had maintained this tradition of mocking seriousness through the first decade of the twentieth century, alternating little collections of poems with his art studies. Henri Martineau's *Divan* then became a kind of treasury of "fantaisiste" poets with contributions not only by Klingsor but also by Derème, Vérane, Pellerin, and especially P.-J. Toulet.

There are two reasons why the "fantaisistes" assumed importance in critical articles after the war. Two of them, J.-M. Bernard and Louis Codet, perished in the conflict. Death claimed two others, P.-J. Toulet and Jean Pellerin, soon after. Commemoration played its part. *Le Divan* set about publishing the works of J.-M. Bernard and the *Contrerimes* of Toulet. The *Nouvelle Revue Française* was largely responsible for the posthumous divulgation of the work of Louis Codet and Jean Pellerin.

The large number of volumes appearing during 1921 and 1922 and containing this type of half-serious, half-comic verse also contributed to the current use of the term "fantaisiste." Among them were Tristan Derème's *La Verdure dorée* (1922), P.-J. Toulet's *Les Contrerimes* (1921), Jean Pellerin's *La Romance du retour* (1921), Francis Carco's augmented edition of *La Bohème et mon cœur* (1922), Tristan Klingsor's *Humoresques* (1921), and Léon Vérane's *Images au jardin* (1922). Roger Allard's *Poésies légères,* although not collected in a volume until 1928, were appearing in many periodicals during the early postwar years. In 1913 Carco had included Apollinaire and Salmon among his "fantaisiste" poets, and these two names remained loosely linked with the group.

The modest aims and lack of complete seriousness of these poets precluded their attaining a place of first rank. They were frankly recognized as *pœtae minores,* but they were often praised for their self-imposed limitations. They offered sharp contrast to the pretensions of the prewar programs of Barzun and Beauduin, and to the contemporary rebirth of Ghil's scientific and evolutionary poetry which was being supported by Paul and Georges Jamati in *Rythme et Synthèse*.

The old group of the Abbaye de Créteil, although refusing to accept any collective name, was still important in the poetic world. They were soon to gain greater fame in the novel, the essay, and the theater, but their poetic activity was pronounced in the early 1920's. When Fernand Vandérem made up his first anthology of unpublished poems for the *Revue de Paris* in 1919,[18] Romains, Duhamel, Durtain, Arcos, and Chennevière were among his writers. During the following two years, the Abbaye poets were the authors of several volumes of poetry: Chennevière, *Poèmes 1911–1918;* Duhamel, *Elégies;* Romains, *Le Voyage des amants* and *Amour couleur de Paris;* Durtain, *Le Retour des hommes;* Vildrac, *Les Chants du désespéré.* The fact that all these poets continued to make their personal experience subservient to mankind's collective emotions and anguish tended to make critics group them under the standard of *La Vie unanime.* The Créteil group had written and continued to write about one another's work.[19] Romains and Chennevière were collaborating on a *Petit Traité de versification.*[20] All these poets continued to defy those who called them a school, but their close friendship made disassociation of their names difficult.

The "fantaisistes," the Créteil group, and the neoclassicists formed a valid part of the poetic picture after the war, but only a part of it. They had been more or less established patterns by 1914, but nearly five years of channeled poetic activity on the theme of war had meant unpublished writings by a younger generation, not yet recognized, but soon to determine new orientations.

18. Vandérem apparently intended to create a series of examples of modern poetry in the *Revue de Paris*. Only one issue (Sept. 15, 1919) carried this innovation. Soon Vandérem joined the staff of the newly founded *Revue de France*. The *Revue de Paris*, save for verse of Mme. de Noailles and Fernand Gregh, remained unimportant for the publication of poetry.

19. Luc Durtain's *Georges Duhamel* appeared in 1920; Jules Romains wrote on Charles Vildrac in *L'Art libre*, March 1921.

20. The *Petit Traité* appeared in 1923, but the collaboration of Romains and Chennevière was known in 1921. See Romains' "Petite introduction à un cours de technique poétique" (*N.R.F.*, July 1921) and Chennevière's "De la nécessité d'un discipline poétique" (*Mercure de France*, Oct. 1, 1921).

CHAPTER 13. Retrospect and Prospect

PIERRE CAMO, the poet of *Le Jardin de la Sagesse* (1906), of *Les Beaux Jours* (1913), and of *Le Livre des regrets* (1920), wrote in 1922:

J'appartiens à une génération qui semble avoir voulu, avant toute autre chose, échapper à l'emprise du symbolisme, et qui n'y a guère réussi qu'en retombant sous l'influence encore vive, à la fin du siècle dernier, des grands poètes romantiques et de ceux qu'on appela les parnassiens. J'incline à croire qu'elle y a perdu, quand je compare à la plupart des œuvres qu'elle a fournies, celle d'un Paul Valéry par exemple; je ne pense pas, en tout cas, qu'elle y ait gagné ce qu'elle a de meilleur.[1]

This opinion, penned by a man born in 1877, is not unworthy of meditation. Camo, a colonial magistrate whose great admiration for du Bellay and Ronsard had determined the technical form of his poems, spoke frankly of an experience which was shared by many of his contemporaries. Baudelaire was Camo's favorite nineteenth-century poet; Henri de Régnier and Moréas were the great later influences. A conservative, Camo was yet mindful of the originality of the "fantaisistes," of the validity of free verse, and of the postwar influence of Apollinaire. What is chiefly noteworthy is his sense of the failure of the postsymbolist generation in its efforts to escape the "emprise symboliste."

The return to the romanticists and to the Parnassians, indicated by Camo, was an interesting phenomenon of the early years of the twentieth century. Fernand Gregh and Léo Larguier showed fidelity to Hugo and to Lamartine in *La Beauté de vivre* (1900) and *La Maison du poète* (1903). Critics were quick to find the tradition of Vigny in the work of Charles Guérin. Mme. de Noailles and numerous women poets of her time were labeled neoromanticists. Most of the provincial poets, particularly those of Bocquet's *Le Beffroi*,[2] were not far from a romantic pattern in which descriptions of nature and detailed elaborations of emotional life were the themes. Two naturist poets, Bouhélier and Albert Fleury, were of Camo's generation. Expression was often tempered by the example of Baudelaire, of Verlaine, and of Samain, but the first decade of the twentieth century bore distinct marks of a lyricism which had flourished seventy years before.

1. Varillon et Rambaud, *Enquête sur les maîtres de la jeune littérature,* p. 148.

2. Among these one could name Francis Eon, Léon Deubel, and Théo Varlet. Charles Vildrac, in his youth, was also of the group.

Equally strong were Parnassian currents, not so much the influence of Leconte de Lisle as of Sully-Prudhomme and Heredia. The volumes of *La Revue des poètes* bear witness to the number of poets who subscribed to severe prosody and to a clear, almost didactic, poetic expression. Camo's contemporaries, if poets born between 1875 and 1880 are selected to represent his generation, were remarkably docile in matters of technique. Bocquet, Bouhélier, G.-C. Cros, Deubel, Droin, Erlande, Eon, Lafargue, Larguier, André Mary, Magre, Muselli, Noailles, Porché, Sicard, Thaly, and Renée Vivien all represented this respect for rhyme and for syllabic count.

Camo's generation offered a few less tractable, more original poets. Almost without exception, their literary reputations were established after the first World War, and these atypical lyricists remained of minor importance during the first fifteen years of the century. Max Jacob was born in 1876, O. W. de Lubicz-Milosz in 1877, Léon-Paul Fargue in 1878, Guillaume Apollinaire in 1880, and André Salmon in 1881. *Le Cornet à Dés* (1917) and *Le Laboratoire central* (1921) established the reputation of Jacob in the prose-poem and in verse. Milosz, after some years devoted to mathematics and philosophy, emerged in 1920 with the *Confession de Lemuel* where the free verse and the "versets" of the "Cantique de la Connaissance" provoked comment. Fargue, after the *Nouvelle Revue Française* had published a collection of his prose-poems in 1912 and a slender volume of poetry in 1914,[3] reached a wider public with the reprinting of these works in 1919. Apollinaire's *Alcools* had been printed by the *Mercure de France* in 1913, and his *Calligrammes* in 1918. A new edition of *Alcools,* by the *Nouvelle Revue Française* in 1920, greatly increased his posthumous fame. The youngest of this group, Salmon, thanks in part to his association with *Vers et Prose,* but also to his fecundity, was well known after 1905, the date of his *Poèmes.* His production of poetry, art criticism, and fiction, his abundant contribution to periodicals, his very unpredictability in aesthetic outlook kept him continually in the public eye. Salmon's work defied classification: with Apollinaire, he was the defender of cubism; with Paul Fort, he was a champion of neosymbolism. His poetry took multiple forms: regular, free, and blank verse; his temperament was variable. Salmon's tonality, like Apollinaire's, ranged from sentimentality to irony and burlesque.

In this generation born between 1875 and 1880 was also F.-T. Marinetti, the international exponent of futurism whose chief centers of activity were Milan and Paris. His founding of *Poesia* in 1905, to which many of the symbolists were contributors, marked the beginning of a militant campaign for free verse in Italy. His February 20, 1909 manifesto in *Le Figaro* proclaimed the tenets of futurism, the doctrine of energy, fearlessness, and love

3. *Poèmes* and *Pour la musique.*

of danger, of modernism, of speed, and of conquest. Marinetti's impact on French poetry cannot be well measured in terms of disciples of his theories. Though Lamartine's grandniece, Valentine de Saint-Point, expounded her theories of "la femme futuriste" in 1912, and Guillaume Apollinaire wrote his *Antitradition futuriste* for Marinetti in 1914,[4] Marinetti's bombast and megalomania alienated even modernists from his movement.[5] But the incursion of a twentieth-century vocabulary into poetry, that of airplanes, automobiles, and machinery, and even such concepts as "Dynamisme" and "Intensisme," was akin to certain aspects of futurism.

The desire to reassess the purpose of poetry, its themes and its forms of expression, was a distinctive mark of the first generation of twentieth-century poets, those who reached their twentieth year between 1901 and 1906. Most striking was the effort to embrace group consciousness rather than individual feeling. Consciousness of this direction was augmented by the creation of L'Abbaye de Créteil, by Romains' articles on "les sentiments unanimes," by Duhamel's and Vildrac's defense of free verse, and by the friendships of the poets just mentioned with Arcos, Barzun, Durtain, Mercereau, and Chennevière. Sometimes these poets were referred to as "modernistes," both because of their liberties in versification and their intense desire to probe the mentality of twentieth-century man.

Some contemporaries of these poets of social consciousness had a completely opposite view of lyrical art. Their verse was gay, spontaneous, and even humorous; their sentimentality was often colored by irony. Above all, their verse was expressive of the individual, not the group. They noted, in short poems, their thought and emotions. In the generation of 1881–86, J.-M. Bernard, Francis Carco, Fernand Fleuret, and Jean Pellerin represented this form of art. Search for their literary ancestry could well evoke the name of Jules Laforgue, but also those of Villon, Saint-Amant, or Verlaine. Tristan Klingsor and P.-J. Toulet, born in 1874 and 1867 respectively, were not dissimilar to Bernard and Pellerin in their poetic aims. After 1910, Montfort's *Marges* and Martineau's *Divan* printed many of these little poems in which whimsy or irony set the tone. Gradually the name of "fantaisiste" became current, particularly after Tristan Derème, born in 1889, used the term in 1912. Derème, whose very titles (*Les Ironies sentimentales* of 1909 and *Petits Poèmes* of 1910) suggest the tonality and the unpretentious goal of his verse, did not reach a wide public until his little pamphlets of verse were gathered in *La Verdure dorée* in 1922. Pellerin's, Toulet's, and Bernard's writings were better known in 1925, after all three

4. Published in Milan.
5. Ricciotto Canudo (1879–1923) is often cited as a disciple of futurism, largely because of his *Poème du Vardar* (1923).

authors were dead, than during their lifetimes. But the poetic direction, which
came to be called "fantaisiste," was discernible several years before World
War I, especially in the provincial periodicals such as Touny Lérys' *Poésie,*
Bernard's *Les Guêpes,* Vérane's *Les Facettes,* and Martineau's *Le Divan.*
Derème himself had endeavored to found a periodical, *L'Oliphant,* in 1908.
This he later described as a "revue de littérature, décédée dans le deuxième
fascicule de son âge."

High seriousness on the part of the group of Créteil and a spirit of
mockery or irony among many of their contemporaries represented two
extremes of poetic purpose. But the years 1881–86 also contain the birth-
dates of poets who commend themselves to our attention for other reasons.
Roger Allard was born in 1885, Louis de Gonzague-Frick in 1883, Valery
Larbaud in 1881, Guy Lavaud in 1883, Jacques Supervielle in 1884, François
Mauriac in 1885. Allard's gently ironic treatment of romantic themes,
Frick's preciosity of language, the modernity of Larbaud's Barnabooth, the
water imagery in Lavaud's verse, the imaginative transposition of reality
accomplished by Supervielle, and the pious simplicity of Mauriac's poems
were some aspects of literary art which bespoke individuality rather than
group endeavor. True, one can find "fantaisiste" elements in Allard's work,
one can discuss Mauriac in relation to Catholic verse, and Guy Lavaud can
be defined as an "élégiaque," but the reader's impression of their work is
chiefly that of individual talents, each seeking his own means of expression.[6] This impression is accentuated when one adds poets who
were only slightly younger. Blaise Cendrars, Jean Cocteau, Tristan Derème,
Henri Franck, P.-J. Jouve, Saint-John Perse, Pierre Reverdy, and Paul
Morand were all born between 1887 and 1889. Of these, Derème can be
placed in the "fantaisiste" tradition and Franck, who died in 1912, can be
judged only by his one volume, *La Danse devant l'arche.* The others, however, were all poets whose personalities rebelled against imitation of the
past and who sought new themes, new techniques, and new imagery.
Their careers often showed change. The Jouve who was associated with the
Créteil group emerged as a different poet with the publication of *Parler*
(1913). Cocteau's poetic career touched on the realms of "fantaisistes," then
was affiliated with the adherents of free-verse, finally in 1922 finding
equilibrium in the regular meters of *Plain-Chant.* The unity in Cendrars'
work, his passion to hold within the poem not one place but the whole
world, was contradicted by successive attachments to cubism, to Dada, and
especially by his mutable temperament, always alert to find the new.

6. The great diversity of these poets can be appreciated by perusal of the following volumes:
La Floraison des eaux (1907), *Poèmes par un riche amateur* (1908), *Les Mains jointes* (1909),
Comme des voiliers (1910), *Le Bocage amoureux* (1911), and *Trèfles à quatre feuilles* (1915).

What immediately stamps these poets as modernists is the imagery in their verse, whether the form be that of "verset" of Saint-John Perse, or the free verse patterns of Reverdy, Morand, or Cendrars. The image tends to become isolated, the series of images, unrelated. The demand on the reader's imagination is greatly increased, for it is no longer a question of a selection of related notations, but rather juxtapositions created by the poetic mind, drawn from varied times and places in the writers' mental or physical experience. Critics were led to make comparisons with moving-picture techniques, or even a series of camera "shots." The *Illuminations* of Rimbaud and the work of Claudel offered examples not unlike the modern usage of the isolated image. The atypical poets of the early part of the twentieth century, Apollinaire, Salmon, and even Valery Larbaud assumed new importance as directive forces of the new age. Beyond these more recent figures loomed Baudelaire, the inventor of surprising and original imagery.[7]

Such imagery assumed major importance in poetry in the period immediately following the first World War. Its real importance, even at that late date, was clouded by the incursion of Dada, but the youngest talents were accepting this illogical sequence of flashes. Eluard, Soupault, Breton, and Aragon were entering the literary world. The first fifteen years of the century, the age of Paul Fort and Moréas at the Closerie des Lilas, of Royère's *Phalange,* of Henri de Régnier at the weekly receptions of the *Mercure de France,* of the brief fame of Charles Guérin, became strangely remote.

That period was not without indications of the directions that postwar poetry would take. From 1902 to 1908, Valery Larbaud was composing the poems and prose that were to become the complete works of "A. O. Barnabooth." Published at Larbaud's expense in 1908, the *Poèmes par un riche amateur* attracted little attention, save from Francis Jammes, Charles-Louis Philippe, and André Gide. In 1913, a new edition in which the author had suppressed many of the poems was published by the *Nouvelle Revue Française.* This is the standard text we know today, in which is still recognizable the will to create a poetic successor for Laforgue, Rimbaud, and Walt Whitman:

> Je chante L'Europe, ses chemins de fer et ses théâtres
> Et ses constellations de cités, et cependant
> J'apporte dans mes vers les dépouilles d'un nouveau monde . . .[8]

The modern quality of Valery Larbaud's poems of 1908, their cosmopolitanism, their mingling of reality and dream, their background of literary

7. "Glorifier le culte des images (ma grande, mon unique, ma primitive passion)." *Mon Cœur mis à nu,* LXIX.

8. Valery Larbaud, *Œuvres complètes, 4,* 87.

references not unlike that of T. S. Eliot, and even their straightforward utterance had to await the postwar years to be appreciated. Cendrars bitterly complained that in 1912–14 French periodicals of all kinds refused his poetry. "C'est qu'à ce moment-là, il ne faisait pas bon, en France, d'être un jeune authentique parmi les jeunes." [9] Finally, in 1914, Apollinaire's *Soirées de Paris* printed "Journal," "Aux 5 coins," "Fantôme," "Titres," and "Mee Too Buggi," while Ricciotto Canudo's *Montjoie!* accepted "Ma Danse," "Hamac," and "Mardi-gras." Other poems of the *Dix-neuf Poèmes élastiques* first appeared in little magazines in Germany, Switzerland, Italy, and Holland.

In the field of poetic discussion, the prewar years of which Cendrars spoke were chiefly remarkable for the activities of neoclassicism versus unanimism, dramatism, and dynamism. Clouard was waging a campaign in *La Revue critique des idées et des livres*. Vildrac delivered a lecture in London in November 1912, limiting his selection of "Poètes nouveaux" to Arcos, Chennevière, Duhamel, Jouve, Romains, and Spire. Barzun was promulgating his theories in "L'Esthétique dramatique" and in his periodical *Poème et Drame*. Beauduin's *La Vie des lettres* succeeded *Les Rubriques nouvelles* and advocated "l'esthétique paroxysiste." These were considered the advanced ideas of the times; Apollinaire's defense of cubism and certain of the poems in *Alcools* (1913) were the extreme limits of aesthetic innovation. Small wonder that Cendrars found no ready reception for his poetry.

This state of affairs, in which the post-symbolist activities of *Vers et Prose, La Phalange,* and the *Mercure de France* played a less noisy but not unimportant role, was suddenly interrupted in 1914. The four years that followed can best be considered a hiatus rather than a development. But these years were silently preparing a new era.

Paul Aeschimann's contention of 1918 that the war had not changed the currents of poetry seemed definitely disproven by 1922. The rise to fame of Paul Valéry, of whom Crémieux wrote in 1921: ". . . un Paul Valéry concentre en lui, en le vivifiant, tout le legs de notre passé poétique, de Villon à Mallarmé"; [10] the rising stars of younger writers such as Eluard, Aragon, and Soupault; the tardy ascendency of poets in their middle thirties: Cendrars, Supervielle, and Saint-John Perse; the new poetic manner of André Salmon; and the fecundity of Max Jacob were important elements of new poetic currents. The efforts of Apollinaire and his friends before the war, confined to a small circle and a none-too-receptive public, were bearing fruit, not only in the advanced group stemming from *Sic, Nord-Sud,* and *Littéra-*

---

9. Blaise Cendrars, *Dix-neuf Poèmes élastiques* (1919), "Notule d'histoire littéraire." (No pagination.)

10. *N.R.F., 16* (May 1921), 619.

ture, but also among the "fantaisistes." There were equally strong forces combating the "esprit moderne" of Apollinaire. Chief among these were the neoclassicists, but equally important were Jules Romains and later André Breton.[11] In the July 1921 number of *Feuilles libres,* the author of *La Vie unanime* contended that Apollinaire had remained faithful to symbolism when its tenets had been abandoned even by its founders. Romains called Apollinaire a Noah's ark of symbolism, holding shut within himself its preciosity, obscurity, and "déliquescence." The "new spirit" of Apollinaire, Romains contended, was but the release of these superannuated poetic faults. A gullible public accepted them as new.

To deny the originality of Apollinaire's ideas was one thing, but to gainsay his influence was another. Romains did not attempt to do this; he would not have written his article had Apollinaire's work not been a potent force in current poetry. The very range of Apollinaire's verse, from delicate, regular lyrics in *Alcools* to the acrobatics of *Calligrammes* and the "Quelconqueries" so avidly seized by the adherents of Dada, partly explains the breadth of his prestige. But this, the dual influence of the poet of "Le Pont Mirabeau" and of "Zone," Romains did not discuss.

Apollinaire's place in the esteem of a considerable body of young poets was secure. Another writer belonging to the symbolist period, but in 1922 rarely referred to as a symbolist, enjoyed new prestige among contemporary poets. This was Arthur Rimbaud. He assumed after the war a meaning different from that given him by Paterne Berrichon or even by the Claudel preface of 1912.[12] Drieu La Rochelle wrote in 1922: "Rimbaud m'a donné tout ce que les autres Français ne m'avaient pas donné: ce sens de la Nature qui est la haute sensualité des Anglais, plutôt que notre goût de la vie cet amour déchirant de l'humain qu'on trouve chez les Russes, et enfin cette continuelle échappée vers la connaissance mystique que seul Pascal, de tous les écrivains religieux qui pourtant ont abondé en France, a su révéler au monde." [13]

André Breton, in a lecture given in Barcelona on November 17, 1922, defined Rimbaud's work as follows: "A cet égard il convient de faire observer que Rimbaud n'a fait qu'exprimer, avec une vigueur surprenante, un trouble que sans doute des milliers de générations n'avaient pas évité, et lui donner cette voix qui résonne encore à notre oreille." [14] André Salmon,

11. Breton had admired Apollinaire's poems, had indeed written enthusiastically about them in 1917, but he was disgusted by what he called the "néant" and the "inutilité" of the "Esprit moderne."

12. One should not underestimate, however, the importance of the *Œuvres complètes* of Rimbaud in 1912, or indeed the astonishing preface by Claudel. Rimbaud's work was at last accessible to a large number of readers.

13. Varillon et Rambaud, *Les Maîtres de la jeune littérature,* p. 66,

14. Printed in *Pas perdus,* p. 186,

answering the questionnaire conducted by *La Revue hebdomadaire* that same year, told how his literary and intellectual life was dominated by Rimbaud after his reading of the poet in 1900. During the 1920's the critical literature on Rimbaud was to assume great proportions, in contrast to those isolated examples such as Rivière's essay of 1914, that were to be found before the war.

While Rimbaud's work and example were gaining in authority, apathy was beginning to cast a long shadow over Verlaine's work. Although few would have subscribed to Breton's pronouncement: "Verlaine que nous abandonnons avec Samain aux petites filles de province," it was all too clear that the postwar generation found little nourishment in Verlaine's style or themes. The contrast is all the greater because in the first fifteen years of the century many poets had apparently found in Verlaine a genuine guide and inspiration. Charles Guérin, G.-C. Cros, Toulet, Charles de Saint-Cyr, and Fagus were noteworthy among these, but the pattern Verlaine had set for poetry of intimate confession extended to many others, including the group of women poets. His influence touched Apollinaire. The reaction against Verlaine and Samain was strong enough to appear unjust: a special number of *Belles-Lettres* (January 1921) was devoted to the poet of *Romances sans paroles* and *Sagesse;* the same periodical prepared a commemorative issue on Samain in July 1922.

The new generation, except for the so-called neoclassicists, was remarkably uninterested in emulation of masters. It was the moment when Supervielle's *Débarcadères* (1922), Milosz' *La Confession de Lémuel* (1920), Eluard's *Les Animaux et leurs hommes* (1920), Max Jacob's *Le Laboratoire central* (1921), and Pierre Reverdy's *Etoiles peintes* (1921) were published. It was also the time when *Charmes* (1922) gave definite consecration to Valéry's poetic fame. The diversity of temperaments, form, and style, the originality of each author were such that comparisons with past and even with contemporary writers were obviated. The era of individualism, of a break with the past appeared to be taking form, although Jean Cocteau slyly observed in 1922:

Ceux que le journalisme appelle: les jeunes d'avant-garde, vivent encore sous le joug du péché original d'Adam-Rimbaud et d'Eve-Mallarmé. La pomme est de Cézanne.

Ils ne se rendent pas compte que des vieilles audaces maudites sont devenues à la mode, ce qui les prolonge, et que comme il y aura toujours malédictions sur le nouveau, l'œuvre maudite actuelle est l'œuvre maudite par eux.[15]

The journalists of whom Cocteau spoke, and indeed many critics, still tried to classify the diverse currents in poetry. They emerged with three

15. Varillon et Rambaud, *Les Maîtres de la jeune littérature*, p. 161.

groupings: the neoclassicists, the "fantaisistes," or simply the "novateurs." The friends of Jules Romains had so long protested against the so-called "unanimistes" that finally critics were content to treat them as individuals rather than a group. Still, when Gilbert Charles conducted an inquiry in 1922 on "Les Tendances de la jeune poésie française," [16] the answers revealed that Romains was considered the leader of a school comprising Arcos, Duhamel, Chennevière, Vildrac, Castiaux, and Jouve.

In this same inquiry, where the voices of tradition predominated, were heard those who demanded obliteration of the past: Soupault, Picabia, Breton, and Vitrac. Soupault was especially vehement, calling the neoclassicists dangerous versifiers, asking how anyone could take the "fantaisistes" seriously, and attacking sentimentality in poetry. His only praise went to the Dada movement, "dont une des plus grandes forces est la poésie absolue, totale et magnifique."

This was an important moment for inquiries concerning poetry.[17] After that of Gilbert Charles in Le Figaro, came another, during 1923 and 1924. The sponsor was La Muse française, founded in 1921 by the same group who had created the Minerve française. This meant that answers to the question "Comment définir la poésie" were often from partisans of traditional prosody, yet the 116 responses represented a fairly wide range of contemporary poets. For the first time in an expression of group opinion concerning poetic art in the twentieth century, such words as "Parnassian" and "symbolist" were notably absent. The poets of the past were mentioned as individuals and not as part of a literary movement.[18] The oft-repeated statement, "Il n'y a plus d'écoles," seemed at last a reality. Naturally no answer to the question proposed could prove satisfactory, but the inquiry at least brought out the fact that the individual's mind and talent, not his affiliations with a group, were important. During the following year, La Muse française sponsored another questionnaire on a subject dear to the hearts of its editors, the question of free verse. Again no conclusion was reached; the poets of the periodical spoke in favor of traditional meters, and others, such as Soupault,

16. Replies were published in the Supplément littéraire du Figaro during April, May, and June 1922.

17. These inquiries, serious in nature, were seemingly reactions in part to more facetious questionnaires during 1920 and 1921. The second number of l'Esprit nouveau (Nov. 1920) proposed the question "Doit-on brûler le Louvre?" The first number of L'Œuf dur (about Feb. 1921) asked, "Quel est le plus pompier des littérateurs actuels?" Marcello Fabri's Revue de l'Epoque (April–May 1921) published replies to the question: "Faut-il fusiller les dadaïstes?"

18. Charles Derennes, who had instigated the inquiry, had indicated the need for defining poetry. He cited the examples of Gasquet's hostility toward the work of Edmond Rostand, André Thérive's invective against that of Sully-Prudhomme, and his own definition of Samain as a "poète pour sous-préfètes." These names might have provoked remarks on neoromanticism, on Parnassianism, and on symbolism, but such was not the case.

suggested that only free verse was admissible. Again utter individuality was the keynote, and this in the most reactionary of periodicals.

In the 1920's, at long last, militant activity ceased in favor of symbolism as a guide for modern poetry. If Mallarmé's name was associated with that of Valéry, and Rimbaud's with the diverse currents of Claudelian art and surrealist vision, it was not with the intention of linking them with the literary movement they had helped to inspire. Even if the *Mercure de France,* faithful in great measure to its literary origins, continued to print essays on poets of the late nineteenth century, it was in a spirit of retrospective consideration rather than contemporary defense. Thus in 1921 studies of Paul Verlaine by Gustave Kahn, of Ernest Raynaud and Albert Aurier by Marcel Coulon, and chapters that were to form Edouard Dujardin's *Les Premiers Poètes du vers libre* appeared in issues of the *Mercure.* Poems by André Fontainas, Vielé-Griffin, Porché, Claudel, and André Spire indicated the magazine's tendency to present chiefly "poètes classés," but scarcely a loyalty to symbolist aesthetic.

Symbolism had cast a false shadow over poetry in the early years of the century. Even Paul Fort's *Vers et Prose,* the prewar quarterly which had printed more poems by the symbolists than any other periodical of the time, was important not so much for its continuation of the past as its revelation of new directions. According to Salmon, the managing editor, this double wish existed in Fort's mind,[19] but it is revealing to note the terms in which Salmon spoke of the older generation favored by Fort:

Paul Fort voulait donc donner une chance nouvelle—la "dernière chance"? —aux écrivains de la première et de la seconde vagues symbolistes à qui la médiocrité de leurs tirages n'avait pu accorder le bénéfice d'un public suffisant. Par exemple Paul Claudel dont, entre autres ouvrages capitaux, *Connaissance de l'Est* [20] n'avait encore été publié qu'à quelques exemplaires par les soins de la veuve Rosaris, à Fou-Tchéou. Et, moins haut, Albert Mockel, Qui connaissait ce poète liégeois? [21]

They were indeed given "une chance nouvelle" in *Vers et Prose* between 1905 and 1914; not only Claudel and Mockel, but Vielé-Griffin, Régnier, Souza, Merrill, Moréas, Saint-Pol-Roux, Jammes, Louis le Cardonnel, Fontainas, Raymond de la Tailhède, Verhaeren, Van Lerberghe, Retté, Kahn, Herold, Maurice du Plessys, Jarry, and Albert Saint-Paul. There were numerous contributions by Paul Fort. The symbolists, and their contemporaries the romanists, dominated the magazine.

19. André Salmon, *Souvenirs sans fin, 1,* 191.

20. Was Salmon thinking of *Connaissance des temps?* The *Connaissance de l'est* had been published by the *Mercure de France* in 1900.

21. André Salmon, *Souvenirs sans fin* (Gallimard, 1955), *1,* 191.

Vers et Prose had however on its staff a young man, André Salmon, who had no intention of imitating the symbolists. Paul Fort himself was a champion of free verse, and according to those who knew him, far from narrow in his poetic opinions. Thus Salmon, Apollinaire, Suarès, Milosz, Spire, Romains, Lavaud, Vildrac, Arcos, and Duhamel were all represented in the magazine during the first five years of its existence. The periodical was not closed to innovation.

The purpose served by *Vers et Prose* before the war was of equal urgency in 1920. A new generation was clamoring for expression. The antics of Dada were only a part of this foment; his destructive literary ideas were also in the air. In March 1920 appeared a little magazine called *Action*. In the first issues, Allard, Cocteau, Jacob, Suarès, and André Thérive were among the contributors. Later numbers of the periodical offered poems by Radiguet and Paul Eluard. A little earlier Paul Dermée's *L'Esprit nouveau,* a "revue d'esthétique," made its appearance.[22] During 1919, a weekly sheet called *La Rose rouge* printed Cendrars' poems of *Les Pâques à New York*. In 1920 Marinetti's *Poésie* resumed publication in Milan, and several young French poets, including Reverdy, were contributors. In the fall of 1921, Aragon, Crevel, Roger Vitrac, and Jacques Baron organized a new and extremely modern periodical, *Aventure*.

Monetary difficulties, rather than waning enthusiasm, quickly forced suspension of these little magazines. The more audacious of the young poets were encountering the same difficulties that had faced an equally enterprising generation in the 1880's. Fortunately for them, a publishing house, René Helsum's Au Sans Pareil press, undertook to publish some of their poetry. Even more significant for the future was the broad eclectic policy of Jacques Rivière's *Nouvelle Revue Française* and that associated institution, Gaston Gallimard's press.

A glance at the bibliography and the names of the writers in the *Anthologie des poètes de la N.R.F.* of 1938 is sufficient to reveal the postwar role of the magazine and its publishing house. The periodical, in which Gide, Proust, and Thibaudet were the great names in the early 1920's, was also a force for the acceptance of new forms of lyric art. The policy was not one of excluding the past; the value of the magazine was in the mingling of diverse forms of poetic expression. During 1920, for instance, the magazine offered Paul Claudel's "Saint Louis" and "Saint Martin," Valéry's "Le Cimetière marin," fragments of Henri Ghéon's "Les Trois Miracles de Sainte Cécile," Apollinaire's "Couleur du temps," an "Ode" by Jules Romains, and some portions of Jean Pellerin's "La Romance du retour." Dur-

22. Dermée's poems, employing typographical artifices similar to these in Apollinaire's *Calligrammes,* are collected in *Beautés de 1918* and *Films,* both published in 1919.

ing the same year, a series of poems by Paul Morand (qualified in the periodical report of the *Mercure de France* as "bizarres"), and others by Jules Supervielle, appeared in the *Nouvelle Revue Française*. In 1921, along with selections by Jammes, Alibert, Claudel, and Valéry, the periodical printed poems by Raymond Radiguet, Philippe Soupault, and Morand. Supervielle, Salmon, and Luc Durtain were among the poets featured in 1923; Saint-John Perse, Pierre Reverdy, and Pascal Pia in 1924. A comparable eclecticism was adopted in reviews of books of poetry. Roger Allard and Paul Fierens, both of whom were poets, wrote quite a few of the poetry reviews. On occasion, the critic was chosen because of his special literary interests. André Breton wrote on the Sirène edition of *Les Chants de Maldoror;* Georges Duhamel on Romains' *Europe;* François Mauriac on *Le Premier Livre des quatrains* by Jammes; Jean Paulhan on Breton's *Clair de terre.*

The variety in points of view, the comments written by young writers in *La Nouvelle Revue Française* offered contrast to the polite but monotonous criticisms by Fontainas in the *Mercure de France*. Vallette's periodical gave far greater coverage to poetry, but Rivière's magazine, much more selective, was stimulating and alive to current changes. The *N.R.F.* had no intention of becoming an "avant-garde" magazine; neither did it exhibit incomprehension and scorn before new manifestations in literature. A little later *Les Cahiers du Sud* adopted a comparable attitude.

Somewhat the same policy, combined with considerable business astuteness, characterized the publishing activities of Gallimard. The 1920 re-edition of *Alcools,* first published by the *Mercure de France* in 1913, was an example of Gallimard's careful following of the rise of literary reputations. Publication of Eluard's *Mourir ne pas mourir* and of Reverdy's *Les Epaves du ciel* in 1924, of Supervielle's *Gravitations* in 1925 would seem part of the Gallimard policy of welcoming the new if the risk was not too great. Meanwhile, the publishing firms of La Sirène and Au Sans Pareil were much more audacious.

The year 1924, with the founding of surrealism, best marks the cleavage with the past. The "époque des sommeils" of 1922 and 1923, coinciding with Breton's break with dadaism, culminated in noisy publicity. The surrealist adventure has little to do with the 1900–14 period. In poetry its effect was mainly to negate questions which had seemed important before the war. Its impact was powerful enough to engage the names, if not the allegiance, of the most talented poets of future years. When the third and last volume of Ernest Raynaud's *La Mêlée symboliste* was published in 1923, the age of symbolism had ceased to have contemporary value. It was history.

CHAPTER 14. Conclusion

POETRY and poetic criticism in the early years of our century scarcely leave us with a sense of admiration or of positive accomplishment. How are we to judge, other than harshly, a period which granted so much posthumous praise, first to Albert Samain, then to Charles Guérin, and finally to Jean Moréas, and yet accorded only scattered words of commendation to Apollinaire, Claudel, or Milosz? The most discussed of the would-be innovators no longer have significance for us. Lacuzon, Barzun, and Beauduin have been erased from our memories, and even the authors of the Abbaye have assumed meanings other than poetic. Romains, Duhamel, and Vildrac now represent the drama, the novel, or the essay, rather than poetry.

Yet it would be difficult to discover a period in which a greater variety of lyric expression was attempted, or one in which more questions concerning the ultimate purpose of poetry, the relation between poet and public, and the matters of poetic technique were aired. The nineteenth century had left a legacy of variety in poetic utterance such as had never been known. Not only the unresolved problem of regular as opposed to free verse or rhythmic prose, but the equally essential ones of theme and tonality, of clarity and mystery could and did serve as premises for lyric art. Long-established tradition or the precedent of recent invention were the points of departure for many poets; the neoclassicism of Moréas, the neoromanticism of Mme. de Noailles or of Charles Derennes, the neosymbolism of Jean Royère and his friends of *La Phalange* are clear examples. But it is easier, and in many cases more accurate, to define the basis of inspiration for poets by naming their predecessors.

Verlaine was by far the favorite. His direct and confidential tone, particularly in the poems relating the struggle between the flesh and the spirit, was transmitted to Léon Deubel and, in spite of turns of expression closer to the romanticists, to Charles Guérin. Other poems by Verlaine had offered the example of a half-serious, artless style and this tonality served as a model for the majority of the "poètes fantaisistes," although Villon, Corbière, and Laforgue were suggested in passages where the humor became more ironic, more bitter, and more profound. Verlaine had also left a legacy of mannerisms, such as the repetition of words or phrases, or the interrogative form which leaves the thought suspended and the poem unresolved. Here the field, insofar as emulation is concerned, was wide. As illustration, one might offer lines from two poems in Maurice de Noisay's *L'Ame en route* (1905):

> Les yeux de mon amie
> Font songer à la mer,
> A la mer d'accalmie
> Où mon rêve se perd.
> ("Berceuse")

> Reconnais-tu pas, ô mon âme,
> Le soir tombant, baigné de pleurs,
> Qui projeta toute ta trame
> Dans ton miroir intérieur?
> ("Le Soir tombe sur la lagune")

Finally, in the tradition of Verlaine, were the fragile little songs in which was accomplished the fusion of a landscape and a mood. Of his work, these were the most quoted, the best loved pieces, and they apparently served as models for a number of writers. Francis Carco, in *La Bohème et mon cœur* wrote:

> C'est la pluie qui sanglote, c'est
> Le vent qui pleure, je t'assure.
> Je meurs d'une exquise blessure
> Et tu ne sais pas ce que c'est.
> ("Impressions")

Jean Royère, in *Eurythmies,* despite the dominant inspiration of Mallarmé, took something from Verlaine:

> Je regarde les yeux si pâles,
> Si pâles, dans les blancs rameaux,
> Aubes et langueurs vespérales
> De mon cœur les frères jumeaux.
> ("Je regarde les yeux . . .")

The emulation of talented predecessors, discernible in phrases and stanzas, did not of course mean utter absence of originality in the new poets. But the servility of the majority to literary styles, whether of Lamartine, Hugo, Sully-Prudhomme, Baudelaire, or Verlaine, was paradoxically characteristic of this period when more poetic manifestoes were issued than at any time in the history of French poetry. As we have seen, most of these credos have passed into oblivion. Most, but not all. Not the painstaking elaboration of theory, but the theory in action, the poetic expression of the individual mind, has survived. Claudel's lines:

> Que mon vers ne soit rien d'esclave! mais tel que
> l'aigle marin qui s'est jeté sur un grand poisson,

> Et l'on ne voit rien qu'un éclatant tourbillon d'ailes et
> l'éclaboussement de l'écume . . .
>   ("Les Muses")

or Apollinaire's message:

> Nous voulons nous donner de vastes et d'étranges domaines
> Où le mystère en fleurs s'offre à qui veut le cueillir
>   ("La Jolie Rousse")

have greater meaning for us than the pages in which Lacuzon, Barzun, or
Beauduin strove to legislate on verse. But in our recognition of talent and
our rejection of its lack, it were well not to disparage utterly a measure of
accomplishment among theoreticians. The poets of the Abbaye de Créteil,
while admitting technical reforms effected during the symbolist period,
were resisting a characteristic of that era which they judged invidious. This
was the tendency to imprison poetic expression in the experience and
thought of the individual writer, to speak *of* oneself rather than *to* others.
At the beginning of the century Samain and Guérin exemplified this manner; it was their personal emotion and anguish and that alone which they
expounded. The Créteil group, intent on addressing not a chosen few, but
on bringing humanity within the orbit of their discourse, aided in accomplishing a stylistic transformation which has found increasing favor with
the years. The simplicity of utterance, the direct expression, the restraint of
adornment that they gave their verse in the first decade of the century have
become qualities in modern verse. Jules Romains, in *Odes et Prières* (1913),
demonstrated this simple directness. In the "Ode" which ends:

> Mais ne venais-tu pas
> De sentir disparaître
> Un effroi merveilleux
> Qui te suivait partout?

or in another "Ode" of which the final lines read:

> Car je suis comme un voyageur
> Assis au soir devant l'auberge;
> Il sourit mais songe quand même
> Que ce n'est pas là sa patrie.

are the stylistic elements which have now become commonplace in contemporary poetry and which are so dissimilar to usual romantic, Parnassian,
and symbolist manners. Vildrac, Romains, Duhamel, and Arcos are thus
probable directive forces for the poetry of Maurice Fombeure, Lucien Becker,
Robert Desnos, Michel Manoll, and André Frénaud. In a broader sense they
are also precursors of contemporary poets who seek to communicate with

man on the human, everyday level: Robert Sabatier, Benjamin Fondane, or Toursky.

There is even a significant value, not in specific aspects but in general directions, in the efforts of less gifted theoreticians. An example might be Nicolas Beauduin. The poet of *Les Triomphes* (1909), *La Divine Folie* (1910), *Les Deux Règnes* (1911), and *Les Cités du Verbe* (1911), despite much banality in expression and carelessness in style, was fighting against the stifling subjectivity of personal emotions, toward the vast and the cosmic. His solution was the adoption of an eloquent and sonorous style which suggests the inspiration of Victor Hugo, and in less degree, Verhaeren. The amplifications, verbiage, and triteness of his lines cannot completely hide the positive values of enthusiasm, vigor, and power which he felt should belong to poetic creation. Present taste understands the word "intensity" in a way that was totally foreign to Beauduin, but he and others of his generation who sought to inject strength and breadth into poetry were combating a tone of vague lassitude and despair which had flourished among the symbolists and been continued by such poets as Guérin and Deubel. Even Beauduin's personal lamentations reveal this aim at a more affirmative verse:

> Eternel, Dieu des cœurs robustes, fixe-moi,
> Contemple mes tourments, ma crainte et mon émoi,
> Ma douleur, et ma paix à jamais endormie.
> Je fus vaincu, mais vois quelle était l'ennemie
> Qui s'attachait sans cesse à chacun de mes pas.[1]

The reader of Pierre Emmanuel's *Combats avec tes défenseurs,* of Jean Cayrol's *Les Phenomènes célestes,* or Luc Estang's *Le Passage du Seigneur,* despite the greater originality of expression, is likely to see the kinship with the goals of Beauduin as well as an antithesis to the spirit of Guérin's *L'Homme intérieur* or Deubel's *Régner.*

The effort to communicate to fellow men and the desire to give poetry force and breadth were accompanied by a divergent direction in the first decades of the century. This third tendency, the "fantaisiste," seems at first glance to have perished in an era which has undergone two world wars and is still living in anguished tension. Pellerin's, Toulet's and Derème's work seem to be period pieces rather than permanent forces. Even Noël Ruet, born in 1898, and Philippe Dumaine, three years younger, who in their early works appeared to offer continuation of humorously ironic, unpretentious verse, changed to a serious, more thoughtful, and more bitter expression. Surrealism's "humour noir" and the tragic sense of contemporary history have produced barbed wit that is more serious than farcical. But the "fan-

---

1. These are the opening lines of "L'Ennemie" in *La Divine Folie.*

taisiste" vein is not altogether nonexistent. We have it in Jean Follain (1903–), Maurice Fombeure (1907–), and Roger Lannes (1909–). When we read, under the title "Métempsychose," Fombeure's choice of desired existences ("un coquemard," "un solfège, une pluie de roses," "un caparaçon de homard"), we are able to telegraph "esprit fantaisiste pas mort," although we should probably add comment on its rarity.

These years before the first World War might well be characterized by Apollinaire's expression, "cette longue querelle de la tradition et de l'invention." Unanimism, dramatism, the Claudelian "verset," the pirouettes of the "fantaisistes" are all manifestations of inventive intention. But the period was not one of triumph for originality; tradition held the advantage. The most inventive poets were not the universally acclaimed. Whenever a magazine, formulating as part of its program the presentation of poetry, was founded, two poets were almost sure to be sought as contributors. They were cornerstones of poetic art, representing sure reputations and acquired fame; their names were Henri de Régnier and Emile Verhaeren.

Régnier, from *Les Médailles d'argile* (1900) through *La Cité des eaux* (1910), retained a temperate conservatism which probably was not prejudicial to his election in 1911 to the Academy. Meter, rhyme, a measured dosage of imagery, a judicious amount of classical allusion, a discreet and often moralizing tone made this poet the opposite of an adventurous spirit. His talent, his musical cadence justly gained him universal respect. But he was scarcely exciting, and rarely took the reader by surprise. His thought and his metaphor both proceeded in an orderly fashion. The reader and the critic could find little to criticize in this able technician, but they received little stimulus for comment. This manner was permanent with Régnier. Even in 1921, a year so full of emerging poetic revolution, his *Vestigia flammae* was continuing the reasonable, established cadence of:

> Si tu veux être heureux, ne cueille pas la rose
> Qui te frôle au passage et qui s'offre à ta main;
> La fleur est déjà morte à peine est-elle éclose
> Même lorsque sa chair révèle un sang divin.
>
> ("Le Bonheur")

That other established pillar of French poetry, the Belgian Emile Verhaeren, was certainly less conservative than Régnier. Bold in imagery, fond of combining meters for great variety in a poem, prone to give free rein to his imagination, enthusiastic in utterance, he offers contrast to Régnier's control. His vision was broad; his very titles—*Les Forces tumultueuses* (1902), *La Multiple Splendeur* (1906), *Les Visages de la vie* (1908), and *Les*

Rythmes souverains (1910)—testify to the broad reach of his thought. Extremely prolific, he was also composing volumes celebrating his native Flanders, and other, more intimate, collections inspired by the day's divisions: morning, high noon, evening.

But Verhaeren nevertheless represented a spirit of order. A historical name, an event, a place, an abstract quality gave him a poetic theme, and he accorded this theme a logical development. Description played almost as great a role as it had with the romanticists. Narration, in tune with the epic tonality in which he excelled, also had its place. In *Les Rythmes souverains,* for instance, choosing Hercules, Perseus, St. John, Martin Luther, and Michelangelo as examples for celebration, not only did he treat their significance for mankind but he told their story. The opening lines of "Saint Jean" read:

> Lorsque Joseph d'Arimathie
> Eut descendu le Christ raide, livide et froid,
> Du sommet de la croix
> Et que la garde et que la foule étaient parties
> Et que les monts et que les cieux,
> Et que les eaux et que la terre,
> Un instant remués par les vents et les feux,
> Etaient redevenus silencieux
> Et solitaires,
> O le baiser de Jean sur le cœur de son Dieu!

While the form and tone of this quotation characterize a portion of Verhaeren's poetry, the Belgian writer was so versatile in style and theme that many examples would be required to give an adequate idea of his scope. Perhaps no lyricist in the French language, except Victor Hugo, sought more resolutely for variety. But this variety had imposed limits which made it conventional rather than revolutionary. The orderly progression of ideas, in contrast with some of his youthful poems, and the respect for metrical rules, showed the mature Verhaeren as an original but not an adventurous spirit.

From the standpoint of subsequent poetic direction, the element which was lacking in both Régnier and Verhaeren was Apollinaire's "surprise." Little demand was made on the reader; the two poets expounded fully their emotion and their thought. In this sense they had moved farther away from the symbolist aesthetic of mystery than many of their contemporaries. Claudel's imagery and Valéry's subtlety provided unexpected projections not to be found in either Régnier or Verhaeren. Modern taste has embraced this quality of the unforseen, giving values to *Les Sept Solitudes* (1906) and *La Confession de Lemuel* (1920) of Milosz, to *Les Œuvres burlesques et mystiques de Frère Matorel* of Max Jacob that were not appreciated at the time of publication.

Thus Apollinaire's "esprit nouveau," with its elements of invention, surprise, and adventure had prophetic validity for poetic evolution. That he, Salmon, and Jacob were all intensely interested in a transformation that was occurring after 1908 in another creative art deserves some comment. The appellation "poètes cubistes" can, if applied too literally, become inaccurate. Apollinaire, the champion of Picasso and his followers, made rigorous distinction between painting on the one hand and music and literature on the other. Whereas the eye can wander at will over the surface of a picture, returning to focus attention on some spot of color or form, music and literature are a succession, a progression which is deprived of such liberty.[2] But the possibility of regrouping elements of reality, of creating an artistic fourth dimension of innovation pervades his championship of painting and poetry alike.[3] The nature of artistic creation, as discoverable in Apollinaire's *Les Peintres cubistes* (1913), Salmon's *La jeune peinture française* (1912), and in the aesthetic pronouncements of Jacob's *Cornet à dés* (1917) and *L'Art poétique* (1922), is allied with disdain for tradition, with independence of vision and strength of will. The three poets did not see alike the problem of reality in relation to the work of art, but they recognized invention as the duty of the creator. The common ground of their belief is contained in two sentences of Max Jacob's *Conseils à un jeune poète:* "Or ce qui est original plaît et non ce qui est déjà vu" and "Il n'y a création que là où il y a invention."[4] Written in 1941, and addressed to "J.E.," an eighteen-year-old youth, these pieces of advice reject imitation: "Rimbaud, Lautréamont, Laforgue, Verlaine, Corbière très bien, il y a cinquante ans; J'attends J.E."[5]

The warning against servility to models was timely. Jacob even went so far as to compose "Pastiches" in order to avoid, by this exercise, involuntary imitation. His prose-poems "dans un goût qui n'est pas le mien," a number of poems in *Le Laboratoire central* (1920) were written in this disciplinary spirit. The general example of his contemporaries probably provoked this reaction in him, for dependence on example was all too prevalent.

To illustrate the dangers of involuntary parody one might cite a second-rate but rather well-known poet, Emile Henriot. His allegiance went to no single poet, but he usually appeared to be imitating one of them. He composed "Omphale," a sonnet all of which, but especially the final tercet:

2. See *Il y a,* p. 188.

3. For extensive discussion of cubism in painting and its relation to poetry see *From Cubism to Surrealism in French Poetry* by Georges Lemaître, *Cubist Aesthetic Theories* by Christopher Grey, and *Guillaume Apollinaire* by Emmanuel Aegerter and Pierre Labracherie.

4. Pp. 19, 16.   5. Ibid., p. 55.

> Car tout à son vainqueur débile, le Héros
> Ne bondit pas au rire insultant du Centaure
> Content d'être vengé par un monstre si beau![6]

suggests the presence of Heredia. In another poem, "Les Amants," a weak imitation of a Baudelairian style and theme destroys any impression of originality. The opening stanzas read:

> Dans le grand lit témoin de leurs ébats nocturnes,
> Côte à côte allongés ainsi que des vaincus,
> Comme elle abandonnait aux rêves taciturnes
> Son esprit exilé et ses membres fourbus,
>
> Lui, plein du souvenir de leurs premières joies
> Lucide et déchiré, tant gonflé de soupirs,
> Penché sur sa maîtresse, à ses regrets en proie,
> Mais sans la retrouver, la regardait dormir . . .[7]

This impression of imitation was not confined to a few poets. The reader may well be irritated by Royère's dependence on Mallarmé's style:

> Fantôme du seul vœu de t'apparaître nue
> Et qui frôles, oiseau livide, le flot pers
> Des ramures au ciel chantantes de mes vers . . . ,[8]

by Gaston Syffert's echoes of Baudelaire in such poems as "Spleen" or "Soirs mystiques," in *Les Brumes de la vie* (1907), by the stale romanticism of Fernand Dauphin's *Odes à voix basse* (1907), by Paul Castiaux' close following of two manners, those of Verhaeren and Vielé-Griffin, in *La Joie vagabonde* (1909). In the Baudelairian inheritance, another of the obvious thematic influences is that of the "paradis artificiels." The later poetry of Maurice Magre (*Les Belles de nuit,* 1913; *La Montée aux enfers,* 1918; *Les Soirs d'opium,* 1921) furnishes many examples similar to the following from *Les Belles de nuit:*

> Sur le divan étroit, mais grand comme l'espace,
> Dépouille notre orgueil, brûle notre pitié,
> Ote de notre chair la volupté vorace,
> Seigneur, délivre-nous de l'horreur du foyer!
>
> ("L'Opium")

Magre, in his youth so much nearer the romanticists in his poems of confession or of humanitarianism, seemed to draw ever closer to the author of *Les Fleurs du mal.* The fascination and temptation of Paris, as well as a pronounced taste for discovery of beauty in horror or evil, earned his mature

6. The poem is in Henriot's *Divinités nues et quelques autres* (1920).
7. "Les Amants" is from *La Flamme et les Cendres* (1914).
8. From "Thrène du couchant" in *Par la lumière peinte* (1919).

poetry the epithets of "bizarre" and "étrange" which had been so often applied to the volume of 1857. Magre lacked the magic gifts of a sure ear for music and of evocative power. At times the crudity of his effects suggests rather a Maurice Rollinat than a Charles Baudelaire. Here, taken from *La Montée aux enfers,* are two quatrains describing the issue of a mortal combat between two hussies for a lover:

> Celle qui demeurait vainqueur de la rafale
> Des poings épais et du couteau la tailladant,
> Geignit d'amour sous le baiser des lèvres mâles
> Qui buvaient sa salive et qui mordaient ses dents.

> L'autre, selon la loi du faible, n'eut pour couche
> Que le plancher pourri maculé de son sang
> Et n'eut pour seul baiser que celui d'une mouche
> Bleue et verte, qui vint sur elle en bourdonnant . . .
>
> ("Combat de femmes")

Magre is of course an extreme example. The possibilities of language revealed by Baudelaire, the marriage of sound and connotation, were a subtler and more salutary heritage. With some poets it was easily discernible, as in the case of Fagus or Jean Royère; more often it was an occasional phrase, and as such scarcely merited the accusation of imitation. In another literary form, that of the prose-poem, the authority of Baudelaire as ancestor is ubiquitous. Even Max Jacob, who was openly attempting something different, built his ideas with reference to the work of Baudelaire, Mallarmé, and Rimbaud. Fortunately, among more gifted poets, admiration did not mean imitation. Rimbaud's message of a supernatural world, Baudelaire's comprehension of the subconscious, and Mallarmé's realization of the musical resources of language nourished but did not enslave a Claudel, a Jouve, a Valéry.

Perhaps the public of 1920 saw chiefly in "l'esprit nouveau" the elements enumerated by Jacob in *L'Art poétique* (1922): names of streets and advertizing signs, memories of readings, conversational slang, and especially unexpected deviations of thought and unforeseen conclusions. But Jacob included in that same volume a more meaningful and prophetic sentence which can be read as an indictment of the past two decades: "La poésie moderne saute toutes les explications." [9] It would seem that poetry had been tending in this direction for a long time. Baudelaire, in contrast to the romanticists and the Parnassians, had represented concision. The symbolists had, either through ellipsis, through metaphysical imagery, or through impressionistic suggestion often sought to avoid amplification. A contrary tendency appeared to triumph in the twentieth century. It was

9. P. 17.

shown in the definite incursion of neoromanticism (especially among the women poets, in the stylistic evolution of an Henri de Régnier or a Francis Jammes), and in the logical processes of neoclassicism. Such triumph was only partial. Despite their sociological intent, the Créteil poets generally pursued the way of concision, or absence of poetic adornment. Even if Claudel's odes are long, the autonomy and density of the "versets," the silences between utterances align him to a degree with Jacob's definition of modern poetry. The "poètes fantaisistes" usually made their expression proportionate to the frailty of their theme, and, wit and irony being so hostile to amplification, they did not waste many words in explanation.

"La poésie moderne saute toutes les explications," for all its generality and dogmatism, has meaning for modern taste. The rising fame of Gérard de Nerval, the posthumous discovery of H.-J.-M. Levet (1874–1906) whose complete poems were printed in 1921, our appreciation of the poems of "A. O. Barnabooth," of the *Stèles* (1917) of Victor Segalen, of the contemporary poets whom we generally regard as the greatest are all signs of this characteristic. Reverdy's dictum, "Rien ne vaut d'être dit en poésie que l'indicible, c'est pourquoi l'on compte beaucoup sur ce qui se passe entre les lignes," [10] applies to works of the most admired of present-day poets, those who have rejected description, exposition, and narration as procedures inappropriate to that fusion of idea and emotion which becomes the poem.

For many modern poets, this fusion is a real explosion, a conflagration. It places poetic style at the opposite pole from the studied achievements of a Mallarmé or a Valéry. Paul Eluard, in *Les Sentiers et les Routes de la poésie,* has vigorously expressed this modern tendency: "Rien de plus affreux que le langage poétisé, que des mots trop jolis gracieusement liés à d'autres perles. La poésie véritable s'accommode de nudités crues de planches qui ne sont pas de salut, de larmes qui ne sont pas irisées." [11]

And the same poet repeatedly stated, "la poésie est dans la vie." Here, in the pronouncement of a later voice, we can see the link with the past. The poetry of the group of Créteil, the verse of André Spire, the "poèmes-conversations" of Apollinaire, the realism of the "fantaisistes" were all tending in that direction. Of course, "la vie" for the poet does not signify the merely terrestrial: for many the spiritual side of existence will be the all-important. Claudel, in "La Muse qui est la Grâce," voiced the debate between the two poles, the material and the metaphysical, of human condition. He, like Milosz and Saint-John Perse, could not, in his spiritual flight, eradicate the earthly, human state. The actual present anguish of man, the immanent struggle, has given a dramatic quality even to lyricism which is farthest from the temporal level. Reverdy, though asserting that poetry is

10. *Le Livre de mon bord,* p. 74.   11. P. 6.

neither "dans la vie" nor "dans les choses," yet defined it as "la forme la plus ardente et la plus imprécise de la vie." [12]

Did surrealism, certainly one of the most potent forces in contemporary verse, act in an absolutely contrary direction? Did Breton's "l'existence est ailleurs" mean that lyricism would abandon immediate actuality? In at least one sense, a negative reply is possible. Even if surrealism did preach the discovery of a new world, the exercise of an untried vision, it was always a protest. The movement chose its saints from spirits in revolt: Rimbaud, Lautréamont, Sade. In the "Notes sur la poésie," signed by Breton and Eluard in *La Révolution surréaliste* (December 1929), appeared the sentence "Le lyrisme est le développement d'une protestation," and in Breton's *Les Vases communicants* (1932) the nature of this poetic revolt was expounded. Breton there described the poet as "porté par la vague de son temps" but insurgent against the simple logical explanation of phenomena.

A word made famous by Apollinaire was much used by the surrealists in discussion of poetry. This was "aventure." Adventure and risk have no doubt been present in the minds of poets of all times, whenever innovation has been attempted, but surrealism, in its assault on conventional logic, gave new meaning and depth to the word. From the narrow limits of the poetic image to the broad sweep of cosmic viewpoint, divorce with the past was indicated. The first years of the century seem cautious and fettered when contrasted with this new liberty. Poetry reached a point where it renounced loyalty to its various heritages. And, as subsequent events showed, not even the new guidon of surrealism could long retain the allegiance of its followers.

12. *Le Livre de mon bord,* pp. 74, 72.

A Selective Bibliography of Books concerning
French Poetry, 1900–1920

Note: Place of publication is Paris unless otherwise indicated.

Part I. Anthologies of Poetry

Anthologie des écrivains morts à la guerre, 1914–18. 5 vols. Amiens, Malfère, 1924–26.

Anthologie des poètes de la N.R.F. Préface de Paul Valéry. Gallimard, 1936.

Anthologie des poètes nouveaux (avec une préface de M. Gustave Lanson). Figuière, 1913.

Béalu, Marcel. *Anthologie de la poésie féminine française de 1900 à nos jours.* Stock, 1953.

Bloch, Richard. ed. *Anthologie de l'Effort.* Poitiers, L'Effort, 1912.

Boase, Alan M. *The Poetry of France from André Chénier to Pierre Emmanuel. An Anthology.* London, Methuen, 1952.

Chaigne, Louis. *Anthologie de la Renaissance catholique. Tome I. Les Poètes.* Ed. Alsatia, 1938.

Clancier, Georges Emmanuel. *Panorama critique de Rimbaud au surréalisme.* Pierre Seghers, 1953.

Dumas, André. *Poètes nouveaux.* Delagrave, 1937.

Hackett, C. A. *Anthology of Modern French Poetry.* London, Blackwell, 1952.

La Vaissière, Robert de. *Anthologie poétique du XXᵉ siècle.* 2 vols. G. Crès, 1923.

Montfort, Eugène. ed. *La Poésie d'aujourd'hui. Anthologie nouvelle.* 2 vols. Première série, Les Marges, 1928; deuxième série, Librairie Valois, 1929. (These are special issues of *Les Marges,* comprising Nos. 163–5 and Nos. 182–4 respectively.)

Séché, Alphonse. *Les Muses françaises.* 2 vols. (Vol. 2, twentieth century,) L. Michaud, 1909.

Van Bever, A. et Léautaud, Paul. *Poètes d'aujourd'hui.* 3 vols. Mercure de France, 1945.

Walch, G. *Anthologie des poètes français contemporains.* Vol. 3. Delagrave, 1937.

Walch, G. *Poètes d'hier et d'aujourd'hui.* Delagrave, 1919.

Walch, G. *Poètes nouveaux.* Delagrave, 1925.

Part II. General Reference

Aeschimann, Paul. *Vingt-cinq ans de la littérature française* (article "La Poésie"). Librairie de France, 1926.

BEAUNIER, ANDRÉ. *La Poésie nouvelle*. Mercure de France, 1902.

BOCQUET, LÉON. *Les Destinées mauvaises*. Malfère, 1923.

BOWRA, C. M. *The Heritage of Symbolism*. London, Macmillan, 1943. (Valéry, Rilke, George, Blok, Yeats).

BOSCHOT, A. *Chez nos poètes*. Plon, 1925.

BRAUNSCHVIG, MARCEL. *La Littérature contemporaine*. A. Colin, 1929.

CARCO, FRANCIS. *Les Derniers Etats de la poésie*. Chiberre, 1920.

CASELLA, GEORGES et GAUBERT, ERNEST. *La Nouvelle Littérature, 1895–1905*. Sansot, 1906.

CLOUARD, HENRI. *La Poésie française moderne, des romantiques à nos jours*. Gauthier-Villars, 1924.

DAXHELET, ARTHUR. *Une Crise littéraire*. Brussels, Weissenbruch, 1904.

DÉRIEUX, HENRY. *La Poésie française contemporaine, 1885–1935*. Mercure de France, 1935.

DORNIS, JEAN. *La Sensibilité dans la poésie française, 1885–1912*. Fayard, 1912.

DUHAMEL, GEORGES. *Les Poètes et la poésie, 1912–1913*. Mercure de France, 1914.

DUHAMEL, GEORGES et VILDRAC, CHARLES. *Notes sur la technique poétique*. Figuière, 1910.

FLORIAN-PARMENTIER. *Histoire contemporaine des lettres françaises de 1885 à 1914*. Figuière, 1914.

FONTAINAS, ANDRÉ. *Dans la lignée de Baudelaire*. Nouvelle Revue Critique, 1930.

FONTAINAS, ANDRÉ. *La Poésie française d'aujourd'hui*. Nouvelle Revue Critique, 1931.

FORT, PAUL et MANDIN, LOUIS. *Histoire de la poésie française depuis 1850*. Flammarion, 1926.

GHIL, RENÉ. *Les Dates et les Œuvres*. Crès, 1923.

GOURMONT, JEAN DE. *Muses d'aujourd'hui*. Mercure de France, 1910.

GOURMONT, REMY DE. *Promenades littéraires*. 7 series. Mercure de France, 1905–27.

HENRIOT, ÉMILE. *A quoi rêvent les jeunes gens*. Champion, 1913.

JAMMES, FRANCIS et GIDE, ANDRÉ. *Correspondance, 1893–1938*. Gallimard, 1948.

LARBAUD, VALERY. *Une Campagne littéraire. Jean Royère et la Phalange*. C. Bloch, 1927.

LÉAUTAUD, PAUL. *Journal littéraire*. 4 vols. Mercure de France, 1954–57. *Henri de Régnier*. Sansot, 1904.

LEBESGUE, PHILÉAS; GOSSEZ, A.-M.; STRENTZ, HENRI. *Essai d'expansion d'une esthétique*. (Three lectures given in Rouen, January 1910, on the influence of Whitman, on dynamism in poetry, and on the work of P.-N. Roinard.) Le Havre, Ed. de la Province, 1911.

LE CARDONNEL, GEORGES et VELLAY, CHARLES. *La Littérature contemporaine*. Mercure de France, 1905.

LEMAÎTRE, GEORGES ÉDOUARD. *From Cubism to Surrealism in French Literature*. Harvard University Press, 1941.

MAURRAS, CHARLES. *L'Avenir de l'intelligence*. Fontemoing, 1905.

MICHAUD, GUY. *Message poétique du symbolisme*. 3 vols. Nizet, 1947.

MORNET, DANIEL. *Histoire de la littérature et de la pensée françaises contemporaines.* Larousse, 1935.

NANTEUIL, JACQUES. *L'Inquiétude religieuse et les poètes d'aujourd'hui. Jules Laforgue, Albert Samain, Charles Guérin, Francis Jammes.* Bloud et Gay, 1925.

RAYMOND, MARCEL. *De Baudelaire au surréalisme.* Corréa, 1933.

RICHARD, NOEL. *Louis le Cardonnel.* Marcel Didier, 1946.

RIVIÈRE, JACQUES et ALAIN-FOURNIER. *Correspondance.* 4 vols. N.R.F., 1926–28.

RIVIÈRE, JACQUES. *Etudes.* N.R.F., 1913.

ROINARD, P. N.; MICHELET, V. E.; APOLLINAIRE, GUILLAUME. *La Poésie symboliste.* L'Edition, 1909.

ROUSSELLE, JACQUES. *Au commencement était le rythme. Essai sur l'intégralisme.* Ed. des Poèmes, 1900.

ROUVEYRE, ANDRÉ. *Souvenirs de mon commerce.* Crès, 1921.

SALMON, ANDRÉ. *Souvenirs sans fin.* Gallimard, 1955.

SÉCHÉ, ALPHONSE. *Les Caractères de la poésie contemporaine.* Sansot, 1913.

SCHLUMBERGER, JEAN. *Eveils.* Gallimard, 1950.

SÉNÉCHAL, CHRISTIAN. *Les Grands Courants de la littérature française contemporaine.* Malfère, 1941.

VARILLON, PIERRE et RAMBAUD, HENRI. *Enquête sur les maîtres de la jeune littérature.* Bloud et Gay, 1923.

VISAN, TANCRÈDE DE. *L'Attitude du lyrisme contemporain.* Mercure de France, 1911.

VISAN, TANCRÈDE DE. *Paysages introspectifs* ("Essai sur le symbolisme" printed as a preface to the volume). Jouve, 1904.

Part III. Contemporary Monographs on Poets

AMIEL, DENYS. *Henry Bataille.* (Célébrités d'aujourd'hui.) Sansot, 1912.

BAZALGETTE, LÉON. *Emile Verhaeren.* (Célébrités d'aujourd'hui.) Sansot, 1907.

BERRICHON, PATERNE. *Jean-Arthur Rimbaud, le poète.* Mercure de France, 1912.

BERSAUCOURT, A. DE. *Charles Guérin.* Ed. du Temps présent, 1912.

BERSAUCOURT, A. DE. *Francis Jammes, poète chrétien.* Ed. du Temps présent, 1910.

BERSAUCOURT, A. DE. *Louis le Cardonnel.* Falque, 1909.

BERSAUCOURT, A. DE. *Paul Verlaine, poète catholique.* Falque, 1909.

BERTON, HENRI. *H. de Régnier, le poète et le romancier.* Grasset, 1910.

BILLY, ANDRÉ. *Apollinaire vivant.* La Sirène, 1923.

BOCQUET, LÉON. *Albert Samain, sa vie, son œuvre.* Mercure de France, 1905.

BUISSERET, GEORGES. *L'Evolution idéologique d'Emile Verhaeren.* Les Hommes et les Idées, 1910.

CLAUDEL, PAUL. *Verlaine.* N.R.F., 1923.

COULON, MARCEL. *Témoignages.* 3 vols. Mercure de France, 1910–11.

DURTAIN, LUC. *Georges Duhamel.* Cahiers des Amis des livres, 1920.

FERREZ, PIERRE. *Le Poète Louis le Cardonnel* (extract from *l'Université Catholique*). Lyon, Imprim. Vitte, 1905.

GAUBERT, ERNEST. *Jean Lorrain*. (Célébrités d'aujourd'hui.) Sansot, 1905.

GAUCHEZ, MAURICE. *Emile Verhaeren*. Brussels, Ed. du Thyrse, 1908.

GILLOUIN, RENÉ. *La Comtesse de Noailles*. (Célébrités d'aujourd'hui.) Sansot, 1908.

GOURMONT, JEAN DE. *Jean Moréas*. (Célébrités d'aujourd'hui.) Sansot, 1905.

GOURMONT, JEAN DE. *H. de Régnier et son Œuvre*. Les Hommes et les Idées, 1908.

LÉAUTAUD, PAUL. *Henri de Régnier* (Célébrités d'aujourd'hui.) Sansot, 1904.

LEPELLETIER, EDMOND. *Paul Verlaine, sa vie, son œuvre*. Mercure de France, 1907.

MANDIN, LOUIS. *Etude sur les Ballades françaises de Paul Fort*. Figuière, 1909.

MOCKEL, ALBERT. *Charles Van Lerberghe*. Mercure de France, 1904.

MOCKEL, ALBERT. *Emile Verhaeren, un poète de l'énergie*. La Renaissance du livre, 1917.

PILON, EDMOND. *Francis Jammes et le sentiment de la nature*. Les Hommes et les Idées, 1908.

RAYNAUD, ERNEST. *Apothéose de Jean Moréas, poète français*. Mercure de France, 1910.

ROYÈRE, JEAN. *La Poésie de Mallarmé.* (Conférence prononcée le 14 nov. au Théâtre de la Renaissance.) Emile-Paul, 1919.

THIBAUDET, ALBERT. *La Poésie de Stéphane Mallarmé*. N.R.F., 1912.

VAN BEVER, ADOLPHE. *Maurice Maeterlinck*. (Célébrités d'aujourd'hui.) Sansot, 1904.

VIOLLIS, JACQUES. *Charles Guérin*. Mercure de France, 1909.

ZWEIG, STEFAN. *Emile Verhaeren* (translated into French by P. Morisse and H. Chervet). Mercure de France, 1910.

INDEX OF NAMES

YALE ROMANIC STUDIES: *Second Series*